INTERSECTIONAL SOCIALISM

A Utopia for Radical Interdependence

Charles Masquelier

BRISTOL
UNIVERSITY
PRESS

First published in Great Britain in 2025 by

Bristol University Press
University of Bristol
1–9 Old Park Hill
Bristol
BS2 8BB
UK
t: +44 (0)117 374 6645
e: bup-info@bristol.ac.uk

Details of international sales and distribution partners are available at bristoluniversitypress.co.uk

British Library Cataloguing in Publication Data
A catalogue record for this book is available from the British Library

ISBN 978-1-5292-1258-7 hardcover
ISBN 978-1-5292-1259-4 paperback
ISBN 978-1-5292-1260-0 ePub
ISBN 978-1-5292-1261-7 ePdf

Cover design: Hayes Design and Advertising
Front cover image: iStock/daz2d

Bristol University Press uses environmentally responsible print partners.
Printed in Great Britain by CPI Group (UK) Ltd, Croydon, CR0 4YY

FSC
www.fsc.org
MIX
Paper | Supporting
responsible forestry
FSC® C013604

To Sam, with all my radically
interdependent love

Contents

Acknowledgements

Writing this book took several years. Over that time much in my life has changed. Meeting Sam and moving in with him in a Cornish town called Lostwithiel (UK) were unequivocally the key highlights. They gave me a strength I had never previously had the chance to encounter on a personal level: the strength afforded by the everyday experience of radical interdependence. I therefore wish to dedicate this book to Sam.

I would also like to thank my ex-colleagues and friends Matt Dawson and Luke Martell for the precious comments they provided on a draft of this book. Their insights have, as always, been immensely valuable and appreciated. Many thanks also go to Shannon Kneis, for her support at the proposal stage of the book, and to Victoria Pittman for her support in the latest stages of publication.

Warmest thanks also go to my colleagues Harry West, Jane Elliott, and Katharine Tyler in the Sociology, Philosophy and Anthropology Department (Exeter), whose moral support over the last stages of completion of the book was invaluable. I do not think I can overstate how grateful I am for what you have done.

Many others have brought much virtual or real-life joy and support over the years. I would particularly like to thank Adrian, Anna-Mari, Amanda, Blaire, Carlie, Chris, Darren, David, Izzy, Graham, Geoff, Jo, Joel, Kirsten, Lisa, Lucy, Neil, Sally, Suzie, and Tom for being such awesome people. They have all contributed, in their own way, to the creation of this book.

Introduction

It is the summer of 2022. British Prime Minister Boris Johnson has resigned and two members of the British Conservative Party, Liz Truss and Rishi Sunak, are competing to replace him. Several short debates have been taking place, during which the two candidates presented their solutions to problems such as the 'cost of living crisis', the war in Ukraine and, on some rare occasions, climate change. Both have been working hard to differentiate their vision from one another. What seems to separate them is the fact that while Truss thinks lowering taxes ought to be a priority, Sunak wants to tackle inflation before tackling taxes. Meanwhile, the leader of the opposition, Keir Starmer, has been seen attempting to pitch the Labour Party's own ideas for addressing those problems. Central to his vision is what the Party sees as its, admittedly vague and familiar, 'mission for economic growth'.

Ostensibly, then, all seem to favour different measures. One Conservative candidate wants to tackle inflation, the other one wants to lower taxes and the Labour Party leader wants to prioritize economic growth. But, in reality, there is very little that differentiates them. Truss and Sunak simply disagree about when to lower taxes, and I doubt they would disagree with Starmer on the idea that growth should be strong. Starmer himself has been warning against raising taxes at a time when many are struggling to pay their household bills. He has also been trying very hard to show that his party no longer subscribes to the more left-wing ideas of his predecessor Jeremy Corbyn. None of them seems to question the fundamentals of the existing political-economic architecture. Yet, never had the need for a radical change of system been so pressing. Inequalities are sharpening and while many cannot afford to heat their homes, supercar sales are accelerating (Neate, 2022). Climate change has become a reality, causing unprecedented numbers of floods, fires, and record temperatures. Major transformations are required. Bold ideas are needed. For, those crises cannot be solved by tinkering around the edges. They require us to think the world anew.

Such a task has become particularly difficult in an era marked by what German philosopher Jürgen Habermas (1986) called the 'exhaustion of utopian energies'. Capitalism, it seems, is the 'end of history' (Fukuyama, 1989). Socialism, capitalism's historical counter-culture, appears to have lost its status as 'active utopia', that is, as a vision that lays bare capitalism's limitations and proves that 'tomorrow should and can indeed be different' (Bauman, 1976: 109). Nowhere is such an apparent demise of the socialist utopia more visible than in the evolution of left-wing parties across the advanced capitalist world. Take the example of France, where the *Parti Socialiste* won the presidential election of 1981 on the basis of one of the most radical left-wing manifestos ever to be voted into power by the French electorate. Known as the *Programme Commun*, the manifesto was formulated around a core principle known as *autogestion* in French and often translated into English as self-management. But soon after his victory, Francois Mitterand abandoned many of his radical promises to favour a kind of economic austerity and fiscal stability that would enable France to stay in the European Monetary System. He chose monetary credibility over a range of measures that could have radically transformed France's political economy and society. This decision, known as Miterrand's U-turn, marked a move of the party towards the right, which it has not corrected since 1983. But what it also marked is the party's own role in causing the demise of socialism as 'active utopia'.

The French left is however not alone in having exhibited such tendencies. The British Labour Party under Tony Blair's leadership, the American Democratic Party under Bill Clinton, and the Social Democratic Party of Germany under Gerard Schröder, have all marked a turn towards the right for mainstream socialist parties and, with it, a recognition that socialism is not so much an alternative to, or counter-culture of, capitalism as a set of diluted principles broadly compatible with it. As a result, traditional left-wing voters have turned to right-wing parties who have appeared to offer ostensibly more radical proposals than mainstream left-wing parties (Piketty, 2020). Socialism, it seems, has been abandoned by both the political class and traditional electorate.

Why, then, bother with socialism? Why continue to believe in its desirability and possibility amid such a remarkable lack of support for the counter-cultural vision it offers? First, it is important to note that socialism is not reducible to the heavily centralized form of state control observable in the likes of the USSR. Equality cannot genuinely exist or be tolerated without freedom (Bauman, 1976). I follow Horvat (1980) in his depiction of socialism as underpinned by three core values: equality, freedom, and solidarity. Second, it is by drawing on those values that socialism cultivates the 'desire for a just society, coupled with the renunciation of the present one as unjust' (Bauman, 1976). It opposes calls for individual empowerment marking capitalism with demands for 'social empowerment' (Wright, 2010). As such, socialism continues to offer the most radical alternative to the competitive pursuit of self-interest around which the capitalist political-economic vision is articulated. Finally, while many prefer to use terms like 'post-capitalism' over socialism, the alternative they offer tends to reflect many of socialism's core values and principles. Take, for example, Paul Mason's *Postcapitalism* (2015). Here the British journalist defends 'post-capitalist' measures like collaborative business models and a basic income that echo many of the cooperative and redistributive goals of socialist André Gorz (2012).[1] Mason, it seems, defends a socialist alternative without wishing to name it so.

The word 'socialism' may have become electorally toxic, but it is my view that it best captures what stands in opposition to capitalism. As such, it continues to be the best term to imagine the world anew. A key aim of this book therefore consists in breathing new life into socialist thought and, ultimately, helping restore socialism's status as active utopia. This is not to say that socialist thought is unproblematic; quite the contrary. Many socialist visions have, I wish to argue, failed to capture the complexity of capitalist domination's operations and consequently fallen short of offering visions of emancipation capable of providing the kind of counter-cultural insights that can inspire diverse struggles for justice to act collectively for radical social change. Axel Honneth (2017), for example, condemned the economic monism of early socialist thinkers like the Owenites and Fourierists, who tended to reduce socialism to a mere re-organization of economic life. An identical charge was also levelled at socialist thought by socialist feminists, who sought to overcome this economic monism by rethinking socialism as an alternative economic and cultural system (Gibson-Graham, 2006).

For decolonial scholars, however, the problem with socialism runs deeper than the one identified by the likes of socialist feminists. Since it is an inherently modernist invention seeking to offer an alternative to the 'bourgeois way of dealing with the issues of modernity' (Bauman, 1976: 48), it is shot through with modernism's 'assumptions, principles, regulations' (Mignolo, 2018: 222) about being in the world and apprehending it. This is why, for those scholars, Marxism (whether conventional or feminist) has failed to provide a genuine alternative to capitalism:

> The defeat of capitalism was intended several times in the name of Marxism. And several times it failed because Marxism remained within the frame of CMP [colonial matrix of power]: it opposed the content but did not question the terms ... of the type of knowledge within which capitalism would not exist. (Mignolo, 2018: 222)

Decolonial scholars insist on the fact that domination ought to be construed as something even deeper than the material domination of groups over others. What domination serves to repress, they argue, is also particular modes of knowledge, schemes of perception, or worldviews (Mignolo, 2018). They are critical of Marxism and, more broadly, socialism, for not paying sufficient attention to such operations of power and domination and, as a result, either propose an outright rejection of socialism or a significant reworking of its content. I would argue that the task of liberating humanity from the perils of capitalism is better served by rethinking socialism than by abandoning it. In my view, there is no reason why socialism could not accommodate the concerns and demands of decolonial scholars. In fact, I contend that the values and principles of socialism are inherently compatible with decolonial thought's own postulates. Take, for example, decolonial scholarship's insistence on the 'radical interdependence of all living things' (Escobar, 2020: 40). Socialism, as a vision, sets out to affirm such a 'relational way of being, knowing, and doing' (Escobar, 2020: 40) by postulating a conception of freedom that is inherently social or, as Honneth (2017: 66) put it, a freedom exercised 'in solidarity'. The kind of freedom socialists tend to envision is not of an individualist nature, whereby freedom is reducible to a minimization of constraints on individual flourishing. It is, instead, a freedom that confidently asserts mutual reciprocity. It is therefore a kind of freedom entirely compatible with the counter-cultural vision offered by decolonial thought. But while they are compatible, they are not identical. The notion of 'radical interdependence' entails something deeper than mere solidarity. It entails something more than relations of mutual support or, for that matter, relations of dependence emanating from, say, a well-defined division of labour. First, it defines a vision of society in which humans are conscious of their dependence on one another and the non-human world for the realization of the common good. Second, it presupposes a form of mutual dependence whereby the free realization of one's ends depends on the free realization of others'; whereby caring for the self is, at once, caring for others because 'nothing preexists the relationships that constitute it' (Escobar, 2020: 40). Radical interdependence is adopted here as a core guiding principle for a society comprised of institutions affirming the necessary complementarity between individuals, as well as between the human and non-human world. This, as I will show in Chapter 2, is what unites the approach to intersectionality deployed in this work to decolonial thought and partly why the book could be regarded as an attempt to decolonize socialism too.

What is also missing from socialist thought, however, is not, as Honneth (2017) understood it, its incapacity to envision the operations of 'social freedom' in the sphere of 'family, love and marriage'. For, this is precisely what many socialist feminists like Maria Mies (2014a) and Silvia Federici (2019) have sought to do. Rather, it lacks an explicit and extensive attempt to rethink emancipation and conceptualize alternative institutions on the basis of a dialogue between diverse knowledge projects, both within and outside of the Global North, and emanating from struggles for justice external to the labour movement. In this work I fill those gaps and propose to do so through the prism of intersectionality theory, which will be treated here as both a tool for analysing power and domination under capitalism, and on the basis of which socialism comes to be reimagined.

This book should therefore be regarded as an invitation to think the socialist future at the intersection of diverse struggles for justice both within and outside of the Global North. In doing so, it offers the kind of bold and holistic thinking the present situation calls for. Before explaining how I intend to deploy intersectionality for those ends, let me clarify the conception of utopia adopted in this work.

Utopia, intersectionality, and socialism

Utopia is colloquially used as a term intended to criticize ideas or goals deemed unfeasible or unrealizable. For example, the idea that we could live in a world stripped of conflict is often considered utopian. For many, like Theodor Adorno (1991), utopia is even dangerous. For example, they tell us that the postulation of an image of how things could become could lead, for example, to a tacit acceptance of the status quo by providing individuals with a way to escape it in thought. A degree of utopianism is here accepted as long as it cultivates a critical attitude towards existing reality, or as long as it helps individuals discriminate the 'badly existing' from the 'Not-Yet-Become' (Bloch, 1986: 148). It is the latter kind of utopian thinking that is adopted in this work.

Some of the origins of this utopian stance can be traced back to William Morris' (1995) own idea that '[d]esire must be taught to desire, to desire better, to desire more, and above all to desire otherwise' (Abensour, 1999: 145–6). Here utopia is not a goal to achieve or the perfect image of an alternative world to turn into a reality. It is instead a tool or, as Ruth Levitas (2013) put it, a 'method' for social change. Rather than providing a blueprint, utopia provides us all with the imaginative energies to think the world anew. It provides hope and evidence for another, better, world. It serves to 'reactivate beyond historical sedimentation a new being-in the-world grounded in the play of multiple energetic and violent passions' (Abensour, 1999: 134). After all, how can change be desired without hope for another world and how can such a hope exist without the knowledge that things could be otherwise? This book, then, shares the following diagnosis and implications drawn from it:

> in recent decades, much of critical thinking and left politics, particularly in the global North, seems to have lost the capacity to formulate the idea of a credible postcapitalist future … The

problem is that without a conception of an alternative society, the current state of affairs, however violent and morally repugnant, will not generate any impulse for strong or radical opposition and rebellion. (de Sousa Santos, 2014: 24)

To treat utopia as a method rather than a blueprint means to cultivate the desire for change. It does not mean constructing an image of a perfect world to be turned into a reality. This book was written in that vein, that is, in an effort to remind those who choose to read it that the reality we are confronted with on a daily basis is not inevitable. Things could have been and could become otherwise, and utopia acts as a reminder of this. As such it 'becomes an extreme disruption of everyday life, a new way of living, a presentation of new surroundings at once the product and the instrument of new modes of behaviour – a poetry of the future' (Abensour, 1999: 137). But since 'what is analysed today may no longer exist tomorrow' (de Sousa Santos, 2014: 33), the insights utopia offers – those images of another world – are necessarily flawed and fallible (Levitas, 2013). This is why they are also 'necessarily provisional, reflexive and dialogic' (Levitas, 2013: 149). This book, then, is an invitation to think the world anew on the basis of provisional propositions regarding the kind of socialist alternative intersectionality theory can help us imagine. It is an invitation to engage in a dialogue about the future diverse struggles for justice could help build through their joint action.

What precise role, then, is intersectionality expected to play in all of this? What affinities are there between utopia, socialism, and intersectionality? First, let me explain what I understand intersectionality to mean and do. There are many definitions and uses of intersectionality. In Chapter 2 I specify what characterizes the approach to intersectionality I chose to adopt in this work. Here I shall limit myself to explaining what, generally speaking, intersectionality is and how it has been deployed in the relevant scholarship. Intersectionality could be viewed as a 'tradition' (Bohrer, 2019) or 'field' (Cho et al, 2013) comprising:

> three loosely defined sets of engagements: the first consisting of applications of an intersectional framework or investigations of intersectional dynamics, the second consisting of discursive debates about the scope and content of intersectionality as a theoretical and methodological paradigm, and the third consisting of political interventions employing an intersectional lens. (Cho et al, 2013: 785)

What unites those different approaches is the deployment of intersectionality for understanding the operations of power and domination in society. This 'tradition' is concerned with making explicit how diverse structures of power shape individuals' experiences of oppression. But for some, like Patricia Hill Collins (2019), intersectionality is also orientated towards social justice. As such it is to be regarded as a critical theory, that is, a theory that both seeks to examine structures of power and domination and overcome them. It involves 'interpretations for how and why things are the way they are as well as what they might or might not become' (Collins, 2019: 4). It is as a critical theory, I contend, that intersectionality shares the closest affinity with utopian thinking.

What I also want to clarify here is that intersectionality can also be deployed as a method with which to rethink socialism. For, while there is something inherently counter-cultural about some understandings of intersectionality (see Chapter 2), it also provides a fruitful method for broadening the scope of socialism and overcoming the problem of economic monism discussed earlier. I call this method the *intersectional lens*, which consists in tackling particular issues – say, work – from a diverse range of standpoints and conceptualizing an alternative (to capitalist work) based on the intersection of those different standpoints. More concretely, it entails conceptualizing alternative economic and socio-political institutions on the basis of a dialogue between knowledge projects emanating from different struggles for justice. The knowledge projects I explore in this book have emerged from the labour movement, anti-racism, feminism, anti-colonialism, environmentalism, and critical disability studies. I therefore formulate a socialist utopia through the prism of the intersection of those struggles and associated knowledge projects; through the deployment of an intersectional lens.

But in addition to deploying it across different human-to-human struggles, such a lens is deployed in an analysis of power and domination between humans and non-humans. Just like first generation critical theorists of the Frankfurt School (Masquelier, 2014), ecofeminists like Val Plumwood (2002) or Maria Mies (2014a) and decolonial scholars like Arturo Escobar (2018), Walter Mignolo and Catherine Walsh (2018), and Malcolm Ferdinand (2022), this work treats relations of domination in society as inextricable from relations of domination between society and nature. In the intersectional socialist utopia offered here, humanity is decentred to the extent that it 'is concerned with overthrowing the economic ideology that turns human and non-human living environments into resources serving an unequal capitalist enrichment' (Ferdinand, 2022: 177).

But the intersectional lens is also deployed to decentre the Global North in the formulation of a socialist alternative to capitalism. This may sound surprising given the decision to rethink what is a distinctively modern and Global North alternative like socialism. However, as alluded to earlier, socialism is in my view potentially compatible with knowledge projects emanating from the Global South in the form of subaltern epistemologies

(Spivak, 2010; de Sousa Santos, 2014; Go, 2016). What form this socialism could take is a key concern of this book. Its aims are therefore not limited to achieving social, economic, and environmental justice but also to tackling the Eurocentric character of critical theorizing and socialist thought. Thus, it is consistent with the goals set out by the likes of Raewyn Connell (2007), Julian Go (2016), and Boaventura de Sousa Santos (2014), which consist in 'tak[ing] what we find from the rest of the world and then assess[ing] Eurocentric theories against them' (Go, 2016: 175). It is about ensuring that the (socialist) 'future [is] found at the crossroads of different knowledges' (de Sousa Santos, 2014: 200).

The deployment of an intersectional lens for the formulation of a socialist utopia that decentres both humanity and the Global North is, I would contend, something many recent contributions to the literature on alternatives to capitalism tend to overlook. Take, for example, the approaches to post-capitalism that treat technology, more specifically automation, as the driving emancipatory force (see for example Mason, 2015; Bastani, 2019; Benanav, 2020). Here much is said about the liberating potential of technology and the need for accompanying it with an 'appropriate politics' (Bastani, 2019: 62). In short, if *used* differently, technology could lead to the creation of a society articulated around the values of freedom, equality, and solidarity. But little is said about the epistemological foundation of this technology. Little, if anything, is said about Global South critiques of technology and the science that underpins it (see for example Bon et al [2022]). No genuine attempt to engage in a dialogue with different knowledge projects is made here. The automation literature, in fact, has a distinctively Eurocentric character.

Proponents of the degrowth approach to post-capitalism do nevertheless draw to a larger degree on Global South modes of knowledge. Central to this approach is the notion that individuals across the globe need to live differently and abandon the consumerist, individualist and materialist culture marked by the growth paradigm. Living differently here entails articulating economic and society around different modes of knowledge. It means changing how we relate to the self, others, and nature. To formulate their approaches, degrowth scholars partly draw on the Global South. In fact, key degrowth proponent Serge Latouche (2009: 59) claims the idea of degrowth itself was 'born in the South and, more specifically, in Africa'. Decolonial scholar Escobar (2020: 78) even characterized degrowth as an 'important area of research, theorization, and activism for both Epistemologies of the South and political ontology'. This literature could therefore be said to share a much closer affinity with the present work than its automation counterpart or other recent contributions such as Sunkara's *The Socialist Manifesto* (2019), which falls short of engaging seriously with struggles beyond the labour and environmentalist movements. But while degrowth alternatives are conceptualized at the intersection of critiques of social and environmental domination and do draw on Global South epistemologies, they, too, tend to lack the scope of the intersectional lens deployed in the formulation of a socialist utopia offered in this book. Indeed, while a text like Giorgos Kallis et al.'s *The Case for Degrowth* calls for challenging 'inherited gender and racial hierarchies' (2020: 22), little is done to engage explicitly with the relevant knowledge projects and understand how they might inform the degrowth alternative in question. For example, it tells us little about the way a Black feminist critique and activist practices within the anti-racist movement could help shape the post-capitalist future. It is one thing to recognize the importance of diverse structures of domination and another to inform the conceptualization of a socialist utopia on the basis of knowledge projects devoted to the critique of those structures. This book undertakes both tasks.

Finally, I would expect informed readers to draw close parallels between the utopia formulated here and the project known as 'convivialism', which many scholars across the Global North and Global South have subscribed to (Convivialist International, 2020). I would not blame them for doing so, for the adoption of concepts like 'pluriversality' and the strong emphasis placed on the 'shared concern for the care of the world' (Convivialist International, 2020: 7) found in *Intersectional Socialism* suggest a close affinity with convivialist principles. In fact, one could certainly regard this book as a project significantly informed by convivialist principles. What differentiates the manifesto from my work, however, are both the depth of engagement with different knowledge projects and detailed insights into alternative institutions offered here. The convivialist manifesto provides a broad diagnosis of the present global situation and some general principles for thinking the world anew. *Intersectional socialism*, on the other hand, envisions alternative economic and socio-political institutions that could bring those principles to life.

Structure of the book

The formulation of an intersectional socialist utopia this book offers is preceded by both a detailed discussion of the approach to intersectionality adopted in this work and a critique of capitalist domination informed by that approach. In Chapter 2, I explain that *Intersectional Socialism* heavily draws on the 'co-formation' approach to intersectionality identified by Patricia Hill Collins (2019) and make explicit parallels with the concept of pluriversality found within Latin American decolonial scholarship. The relationality presupposed by such a pluriversal approach to intersectionality, I further argue, distinguishes itself from other relational approaches like actor-network theory in its attempt to analyse power by exposing the radical interdependence of diverse structures of domination. The chapter ends with a discussion of the affinity between pluriversal intersectionality and the libertarian strand of socialist thought and shows how, broadly speaking, the latter can provide a fruitful basis upon which to institutionalize radical interdependence.

In Chapter 3, I deploy the intersectional lens offered by pluriversal intersectionality to probe the operations of capitalist domination. I begin this task by engaging with the distinction Nancy Fraser (1995) makes between struggles for redistribution and those for recognition. Such a framework, I claim, serves as a useful starting point for thinking about pluriversal intersectionality. More specifically, contrasting it with Fraser's conceptual distinction helps clarifying what pluriversality sets out to achieve in terms of analysis of power and domination. Then I proceed with highlighting the importance of recognizing that the society/nature binary is not simply an outcome of capitalist social domination but predicates it. It marks an attempt to clarify the relationship between social and environmental domination analysed through the prism of pluriversal intersectionality. Finally, I present the story of capitalist domination as a story of dispossession by exposing the different dispossessional practices capitalism has paved the way for.

The intersectional socialist utopia whose contours I begin to draw from Chapter 3 aims to offer an alternative to such dispossessional practices. To this end, it is grounded in a conception of emancipation which is directed at large-scale structural change and articulates self-actualization with radical interdependence. In Chapter 4, then, I justify the decision to choose the term emancipation and clarify its use in the book. A particular emphasis is placed on the relationship between difference/individuality and commonality/collectivity entailed by pluriversal emancipation. It is shown that pluriversal emancipation presupposes a distinctive form of identity thinking whereby difference is treated as a bond. I end the chapter with a discussion of the subject of pluriversal emancipation, whose mobilization emerges from the diverse struggles' recognition of their radical interdependence. The key contribution of this chapter, then, lies in laying the conceptual groundwork for envisioning radical interdependence in an intersectional socialist utopia. The following three chapters clarify the institutional framework that could bring this radical interdependence to life.

In Chapter 5, I tackle the re-organization of economic life. I begin with reimagining work by grappling with the debate between the emancipation *from* work and emancipation *through* work thesis marking socialist thought. I argue that instead of attempting to leave work behind, it must be collectivized and affirm radical interdependence by being re-orientated towards social value creation. It is also argued that such a conception of work presupposes a re-organization of the system of allocation of resources. An alternative to the market, which brings democratically organized associations of producers, consumers, and user groups into dialogue with one another is offered. Finally, I tackle the issue of property, making explicit the reasons why a relationalized form is most suitable for affirming radical interdependence.

The task of Chapter 6 consists in both further clarifying what such a model entails and providing utopian insights beyond those making up economic life. I start by exposing the central role played by the sexual division of labour between production and reproduction in capitalist domination. More specifically, I show that the separation of society into a private sphere of domesticity and public sphere of work is itself underpinned by divisive and hierarchizing binaries around which capitalist domination operates. Then, I turn to the task of envisioning an alternative to this division of labour. I draw on Maria Mies' (2014a) notion of 'production of immediate life' to affirm the radical interdependence between production and reproduction in the dialogically coordinated allocation of resources. The chapter ends with insights into alternative kin relations that such a new relationship between production and reproduction paves the way for. Overall, this chapter aims to show that in order to move beyond the production/reproduction split marking capitalist domination, one must not only institutionalize caring practices within material production, but also treat reproductive life as a form of labour akin to the labour of care imagined in productive life.

In Chapter 7, I tackle utopian insights into political life. I begin my line of reasoning with the deployment of an intersectional lens for the critique of the state. Domination, I argue, is integral to the modern liberal-capitalist state. For this reason, it must be replaced by an alternative socio-political institution. As an alternative I propose to envision what anarchists and libertarian socialists called the 'commune'. I complement this insight with a system of representation articulated around the notion of function – functional representation – on the basis of which representatives at local, regional societal, and governmental levels are periodically elected. This system, I contend, is not only a more democratic and effective mode of representation, it is also particularly well-suited for bringing radical interdependence to life. This is why, finally, I propose to re-organize international relations away from the state and towards need/function by drawing on the work of international functionalists.

What this book offers, then, is a socialist utopia whose counter-cultural force is drawn from both its intersectional outlook and the principle of radical interdependence. It opposes capitalism's divisions, hierarchies, and individualist outlook with the vision of a society organized around relations of mutual reciprocity and complementarity. But consistent with the approach to utopia as method adopted here, the vision in question is not to be regarded as a blueprint. Rather, it is an invitation for dialogue around what a world affirming the radical interdependence of all living things could look like. Intersectional socialism is not expected to be accepted as it currently stands. It would need to pass the test of dialogue and be modified by it. But in doing so I hope its underlying principles and some of its key orientations will be valuable for thinking the world anew and imagining a post-capitalist future.

2

Intersectionality, Pluriversality, and Libertarian Socialism

Introduction

After discrediting the Left's redistributive outlook by dismissing it – often very successfully – as economically irresponsible, the right turned to populism and devoted its attention to the culturally progressive aspect of left-wing thinking. Terms like 'wokeness' and 'culture wars' are symptomatic of the right's attempts to discredit what remains of progressive thinking in advanced capitalist societies. To understand what led to this state of affairs and where intersectionality stands in it, one must turn to neoliberalism. The latter established itself as a political-economic vision ostensibly compatible with cultural struggles for justice. For example, some neoliberal governments gave same-sex couples the right to marry.[1] Neoliberalism, it seems, tolerates and sometimes even backs cultural struggles for justice, while contesting the value of their economic counterpart. Having successfully discredited redistributive struggles, such a 'progressive neoliberalism' (Fraser, 2019) eventually paved the way for a reactionary politics that set out to redress socio-economic injustices by wrapping them up in issues of identity. In a context of acute economic precarity and sharp socio-economic inequalities, for example, migrant others are blamed for the economic deprivation of autochthons. What is more, the latter do not just expect to hold exclusive rights as autochthons. They are also highly critical of any attempts to question their position of privilege, often dismissed as unreasonable, unproductive, and unacceptable instances of 'wokeism'. Since the establishment of neoliberalism, then, one can observe 'unproductive battles over economic versus cultural politics' (Duggan, 2003: xix) which laid the groundwork for a right-wing populism that seeks to resolve this tension by turning cultural struggles into a reactionary form of identity politics.

Contrary to interpretations that equate it with a culture war, I would argue that intersectionality provides an immensely fruitful alternative to the kind of identity politics that have made their way into the political mainstream in many advanced capitalist societies. Intersectionality, it will be shown, does not divide but provides a framework for thinking oppression and emancipation across economic and cultural politics. To be sure, the field of intersectionality studies counts a very broad range of theoretical, methodological, and empirical scholarship. There have also been and continue to be disagreements on what exactly qualifies as intersectionality, what it aims to achieve and how it should be deployed in social research and beyond. For example, some treat it as a framework of analysis or lens for making sense of power and oppression (Crenshaw, 1989; Collins and Bilge, 2020). Others view it as a theory of political representation (Severs, Celis, and Erzeel, 2016) or 'critical theory' (Collins, 2019). It is also possible to find approaches highlighting the role intersectionality can play in developing new ways of thinking and being in the world (May, 2015; Hancock, 2016) and informing 'resistance strategies' (Cho, Crenshaw, and McCall, 2013: 798). While notable and non-negligible differences exist between those approaches, they can conceivably complement one another. For example, it is perfectly conceivable to find an approach that treats intersectionality as an analytical tool and critical theory. The latter, in fact, presupposes the deployment of an intersectional lens – intersectionality as a tool – for the analysis of power and domination. It is not inconceivable either to find an application of intersectionality devoted to probing experiences of oppression along with their intersection, while seeking to forge political coalitions. Different forms and uses of intersectionality can therefore co-exist in one particular approach.

It is nevertheless helpful, and indeed important, to begin the argumentation for the intersectional socialist utopia developed in this book by specifying the approach to intersectionality that will be adopted. This discussion will be followed by making explicit the contrast of what I chose to call *pluriversal intersectionality* with other relational approaches, and the nature of its relation and affinity with socialism. In so doing, I aim to highlight the distinctive form of relationality entailed by the intersectional approach deployed in this work for rethinking socialism, while showing that pluriversal intersectionality itself can offer counter-cultural tendencies consistent with socialist values and principles.

Choosing a distinctively counter-cultural approach

While the rich variety of intersectional approaches does make it challenging to find a definition all intersectionality scholars agree upon, it is possible to identify a range of elements that more or less unite them. Such elements are included in the following definition provided by Patricia Hill Collins and Silma Bilge in the second edition of *Intersectionality*:

> Intersectionality investigates how intersecting power relations influence social relations across diverse societies as well as individual experiences in everyday life. As an analytic tool, intersectionality views categories of race, class, gender, sexuality, class, nation, ability, ethnicity, and age – among others – as interrelated and mutually shaping one another. Intersectionality is a way of understanding and explaining complexity in the world, in people, and in human experiences. (Collins and Bilge, 2020: 2)

To deploy an intersectional lens, therefore, means to probe the complex operations of power and domination, along with concomitant experiences of oppression. What is meant by 'complex' here is the fact that power structures are understood as interacting and even intertwining with one another in the production of inequalities. Such an approach to power distinguishes itself from the more simplistic additive or multiplicative models, whose 'mechanistic understandings of relationality' (Collins, 2019: 230) fall short of grasping how, for example, capitalism and patriarchy become mutually constitutive. Also, to envision experiences oppression as the effect of independent and multiplying structures of power, such as the independent effects of class, gender and race in the case of the 'triple jeopardy' approaches, does not tell us enough about the creative ways oppressed groups come to make sense of their oppression (King, 1988). Instead, intersectionality emphasizes the 'inseparability of oppressions' (Bohrer, 2019: 91) and recognizes the 'complexities and ambiguities that merge a consciousness of race, class, and gender' (King, 1988: 72). After all, each of us, as individuals with intersecting identities, such as a white middle-class homosexual man, accumulates experiences (of privilege and/or marginalization) resulting from combined operation of diverse structures of power, whose effects cannot be discriminated in practice.

But intersectionality can, and often does, set out to achieve more than simply shed light on the operations of power and domination. As a critical theory, it is also 'rooted in efforts to change societal conditions that create and maintain oppressive power hierarchies' (Smooth, 2013: 24). As such, it assumes an emancipatory outlook. It offers a basis upon which to grasp complex operations of power with 'an eye toward creating possibilities for change' (Collins, 2019: 4–5). Thus, for many (see for example Smooth, 2013, May, 2015, and Collins, 2019), the critique of power and domination it offers is not regarded as an end in itself but, rather, a means to transform society. Also, since the kind of social transformation a theory with an emancipatory intent aspires to is necessarily informed, if not decisively shaped, by the nature of the critique it formulates, intersectionality could be said to offer something distinctive both in terms of critique and 'possibilities for change'. Such a distinctiveness lies, I would argue, in its relational character.

Not all approaches to intersectionality nevertheless share the same understanding of relationality. Patricia Hill Collins, for example, distinguished between 'relationality through articulation' and 'relationality through co-formation' (2019: 241).[2] To speak of articulated structures of power means to acknowledge the significance of ideas in domination, highlighting how they relate to social forces and structure individuals' experiences (Collins, 2019). It entails accepting that different structures of power interact and mutually support one another in domination, while recognizing the contingency of such conjunctures and the 'distinctiveness of various parts' (Collins, 2019: 241). Such intersectional work echoes the articulation of class, race, identity, oppression, and resistance found in cultural studies such as Stuart Hall's own *oeuvre* (see for example Hall, 2018). Since it presupposes categories and recognizes both the complexity of their interaction and difficulty in distinguishing their respective effects on individuals, it could be said to deploy categories while remaining critical of them. In this sense it is akin to what Leslie McCall (2005) identified as the 'intracategorical' version of complexity.

Co-formation approaches to relationality are somewhat more radical. Often found in the work of Global South feminists like Gloria Anzaldúa (1983; 1987) or Cherrie Moraga (Moraga and Anzaldúa, 1983), this way of doing intersectionality disintegrates the very categories whose distinctiveness articulation seeks to preserve (Collins, 2019). Under its guise, power is analysed holistically, as a 'seamless process of mutual construction of race, class, and gender' (Collins, 2019: 241). Rather than a conjuncture of, say, ideas and social forces, co-formation constructs 'in-between spaces', blends, margins, or, to use Anzaldúa's (1987) own terminology, 'borderlands'. In such spaces, which are constructed through dialogical engagement, individuals develop knowledge that they are 'in symbiotic relationship to all that exists and co-creators of ideologies – attitudes, beliefs, and cultural values' (Anzaldúa, 2002: 2). But in addition to being 'unstable, unpredictable, precarious, always-in-transition [and] lacking clear boundaries' (Anzaldúa, 2002: 1), those spaces are transgressive and transformative. They open up an horizon of possibilities for collaboration and change that would not have otherwise been possible without the kind of relational thinking afforded by co-formation. For this reason, this understanding of relationality and way of doing intersectionality is particularly suitable for engaging in critical theorizing (Collins, 2019). It is closest to what McCall (2005) chose to name 'anticategorical complexity' insofar as an analysis of power and domination through co-formation necessarily leads to the dissolution of categories. It entails both asserting the inseparability of those categories and the structures upholding them as well as questioning the categories themselves, in a manner echoing, for example, queer theorists' own critique of the categories used to define sexual and gender identity.

Since co-formation could be said to offer, more fully and explicitly than its articulatory counterpart, not just a critique of power but also a basis on which to imagine how different things could become, it is particularly suitable for the task set out in this work. The in-between spaces or borderlands this approach paves the way for hold the potential to confront capitalism as its counter-culture or, as Vivian May (2015) put it, a 'resistant imaginary'. Because it entails a particularly advanced mode of relational thinking (Collins, 2019: 250), it could help step outside of the capitalist, patriarchal, and colonial logic, and oppose the divisions, binaries, and hierarchies marking those systems of domination by reimagining 'a holistic world of connectedness and interdependence for the future' (Collins, 2019: 248). It could help develop new ways of thinking and being in the world opposed to those emanating from the image of a bounded and adversarial individual. Relationality through co-formation could in this sense shed light on a new epistemology and ontology around which to articulate an alternative to capitalism. It is thus both an *epistemological practice* that contests dominant imaginaries' and an *ontological project* that accounts for multiplicity and complex subjectivity' (May, 2015: 34, emphasis in original).

For these reasons, intersectionality as co-formation also provides a basis on which to develop forms of identity and subjectivity in opposition to those underpinned by capitalist relations. Its profoundly relational character fosters 'alternate ways of perceiving each other and ourselves' (Keating, 2002: 8). This is because by understanding power as diffuse and operating through diverse intersecting structures, it opens up the scope for the 'creation and deployment of overlapping identity categories' (Cho, Crenshaw, and McCall, 2013: 797). Not only does co-formation offer a prism through which to grasp the existence of various grounds of identity, it also helps develop an understanding of 'the other [as] posited within the self' (Morris, 2002: 140). Subjectivity and, more specifically, the experience of oppression, is here understood as 'coalitional' (May, 2015) to the extent that the categories responsible for the physical and structural violence inflicted on, for example, Black women cannot be clearly delineated. While it is possible to recognize the respective role patriarchy and racism play in engendering experiences of oppression, intersectionality as co-formation does not so much seek to disentangle them to assess their relative force, as highlight what Ashley Bohrer (2019) called their 'equiprimordiality', that is, their equally fundamental importance as entwined structures of power and domination. With such a profoundly relational view of power one can therefore anticipate the development of an understanding of identity that breaks away from the 'atomized logics of liberal individualism' (May, 2015: 52). More concretely, it offers, at once, a critique of power and a basis on which to recognize that '[w]e are interrelated and interdependent – on multiple levels and in multiple ways: economically, socially, ecologically, emotionally, linguistically, physically, and spiritually' (Keating, 2009: 88).

Implied by such a coalitional understanding of identity and subjectivity is the view that they are not given to individuals but collectively arrived at. They do not make up an essence but change depending on the context and relations individuals cultivate (Bilge and Collins, 2020). It presupposes a self inseparable from community and a conception of '[s]elf-determination [that] is both individual and collective' (Johnson, 2002: 99). This is why, under the guise of intersectionality as co-formation, it is more appropriate to speak of identities deriving from individuals' politics rather than politics deriving from their identities (Cho, Crenshaw, and McCall, 2013: 803). It follows that the term identity politics, as depicted in mainstream politics, fails to capture what is going on here. For, identity politics tend to exhibit the kind of essentialist tendencies that practitioners of intersectionality as co-formation find highly problematic. The term is more appropriate for making sense of politics emanating from additive analyses of power of the kind briefly discussed earlier and according to which structures and experiences of oppression can be clearly delineated (Yuval-Davis, 2009). This is not to say that co-formation collapses differences between individual experiences but, rather, that it recognizes 'commonality within the context of difference' (Anzaldúa, 2002: 2). As such, it does not 'discard differences for some underlying essence' (May, 2015: 42). Difference and commonality are not here pitted against one another. They are instead understood as mutually necessary. Otherness is treated as 'a bond rather than a division' (Walker, 2020: 148), thereby echoing the relational ontology found within many Indigenous communities in America.

In turn, intersectionality as co-formation could be said to rest on a dialogue for making explicit experiences of oppression and the complex entwinement of structures of domination, as well as for facilitating the development of collective identities. Dialogue both plays an emancipatory and identificatory role. The former position reflects Paolo Freire's (2005) own work on the importance of dialogic action for emancipation. It is observable in the intersectional work of Audre Lorde, for whom dialogue facilitates the 'transformation of silence into language and action' (1984: 42). For bell hooks, it is a 'liberatory expression' (hooks, 2015: 53); 'it challenges and resists domination' (hooks, 2015: 221). Dialogue is emancipatory because '[i]n hearing responses, we come to understand whether our words act to resist, to transform, to move' (hooks, 2015: 40). It is essential for making explicit silent or hidden forms of oppression, for exposing structures of power shaping our experiences and forging solidarities. But the move to action it serves need not entail sacrificing difference for sameness. As Judith Butler herself put it, 'dialogic understanding entails … the acceptance of divergence, breakage, splinter, and fragmentation' (1990: 20) and, in this sense, thrives on difference.

But, even more fundamentally, dialogue is expected to facilitate identity formation. In fact, I view intersectionality as co-formation as an approach presupposing a conception of self-hood akin to Charles Taylor's idea of 'webs of interlocution', whereby the self is said to exist only in relation to 'partners in conversation', who are 'essential to my achieving self-definition' (1989: 36). Expressing ourselves in the presence of others and listening to others' perspectives are both essential steps for learning about oneself, others and the world around us and, consequently, developing a self-hood. Dialogue is 'an act of self-revelation' (Lorde, 1984: 42), both individual and collective, which opens up 'the possibility of articulating the variety of ways we experience and negotiate our identities' (Alsultany, 2002: 110). In this sense, dialogue is a practice through which we make explicit our relational self-hood and the complex systems of power structuring our experiences of privilege and marginalization.

The co-formation approach to intersectionality, then, offers a profoundly relational approach to power and domination, while providing a basis for resisting the dominant (capitalist) imaginary. It presupposes a relational conception of self-hood and coalitional subjectivity. But what distinguishes it from other relational approaches? Why choose this particular relational understanding of power and domination over others? It is to those questions that I now turn.

From intersectionality as co-formation to pluriversal intersectionality

Over the last two decades, relational social theories have proliferated in Western academia. Actor-network theory (ANT), which has been gaining prominence for some time now, is one such theory. Decolonial thought represents another which, at the time of writing this chapter, is beginning to gain traction across the Global North. Much separates the two theoretical frameworks. While decolonial thought locates the operations of power at the centre of its analysis, ANT aims to describe or, to use one of its main proponents' phrase, to 'reassemble the social' in an effort to provide a 'narrative ... where all the actors [human and non-human] do something and don't just sit there' (Latour, 2005: 128). Decolonial thought is a critical theory and is consequently informed by a social justice imperative; ANT treats critical theory with contempt (Latour, 2004) and claims to offer new – better – conceptual tools for understanding the social. However, ANT has, too, been deployed to make sense of the operations of power, as illustrated by Bruno Latour's (1990) own work, Julian Go's (2016) attempt to draw on its relational outlook for postcolonial theorizing, or Kemple and Mawani's

(2009) ANT-informed 'sociology of empire'. What, then, differentiates those frameworks with the approach to intersectionality discussed earlier? What can intersectionality bring to our understanding of power and domination that those paradigms cannot offer?

Let me start answering those questions by addressing ANT's relationality, along with that of its slightly younger sibling known as new materialism. The reason for tackling those two perspectives together is due to the post-humanist stance they share, along with the view that matter matters in social analysis. But it is also due to the fact that the theoretical developments they embody originate, contrary to decolonial thought, from the Global North. This origin is rather important, for both ANT and new materialism scholars have defined their perspective in opposition to the onto-epistemic regime dominating that region of the world: modernity or, as Latour (1993) put it, the 'modern Constitution'. They are critics of modernism's separation of nature and society which, they argue, makes theory, and more generally knowledge, unable to appreciate the role non-humans (ANT) or matter (new materialism) plays in social action. Consequently, a better form of knowledge is one that recognizes that action is not something exclusive to the world of humans or, put differently, something that cannot be adequately understood without grasping the way the human and non-human world relate to one another. Actor-networks (ANT) and *assemblages* (new materialism) are therefore favoured over 'structures' or 'social forces', which rest on modernist dualisms, such as structure vs. action, and tend to overstate the regular and stable character of the social (Latour, 2005; Fox and Alldred, 2018).

Such concepts or (relational) lenses can, we are told, offer powerful new insights into the operations of power and domination in society and across the globe. Here, though, power is not a given force in the form of a person/ group or structure causing a particular effect, such as domination. Rather, power is itself an effect, or something that has to be 'produced, made up, composed' (Latour, 2005: 64). Power has no centre. It is the result of a particular configuration of elements within an actor-network and without which none of the individual elements would hold power. In principle, then, one key advantage of such a relational lens is that it widens the scope of analysis to include 'actants' that would otherwise be excluded in our understandings of power and domination. Take, for example, Julian Go's (2016) application of ANT to postcolonial theory. Here, ANT is praised for going further than the likes of dependency theory by defining 'actor-networks as consisting of people, things, and concepts' and, consequently, opening up the scope for analysing colonialism through networks that are at once 'material and semiotic, human and nonhuman' (Go, 2016: 132). In short, it provides a basis upon which to circumvent the problem of economic reductionism in the study of imperialism. But as Go further put it, ANT also offers a way out of a 'Eurocentric narrative that locates modern capitalism, democracy, or civilization in a core that spreads outward' (2016: 133). Instead, it 'invites us', we are told, 'to consider how preexisting chains of relations ("heterogeneous networks") are "consolidated" from their diverse points into an overarching whole' (Go, 2016: 133). In short, it opens up the scope for recognizing that agency and change do not flow in one direction (from Global North to Global South or from humans to non-humans) or are limited to the actions of particular actants (within the Global North or among humans).

Such a relational lens is also visible within the new materialism scholarship[3] which, like ANT, seeks to 'explain how a range of heterogeneous elements from the physical, biological, economic, semiotic and other "realms" may be assembled to produce this or that social aggregation' (Fox and Alldred, 2018: 19). New materialists, too, think that powerful insights can be gained from deploying such a lens in the study of power. Like ANT scholars, new materialists are critical of conventional analyses of power and domination which, in their view, overstate the stability of the social or patterns within the social. But their critique of essentialism tends to be somewhat more radical than ANT's own. In fact, some proponents of new materialism charge ANT for displaying a 'residual essentialism' (Fox and Alldred, 2018: 326) particularly manifest in the way it partitions the world into humans and non-humans or, more specifically, between 'hotel managers and guests (people), weighty fobs and keys (material artefacts) and signs (texts)' (Whittle and Spicer, 2008: 615). In short, the problem with ANT consists in its incapacity to overcome the very divisions it claims to do away with and, in turn, move beyond the notion that actants have both fixed attributes and their own agency. New materialism is resolutely anti-dualist (Dolphijn and van der Tuin, 2012) and anti-essentialist.

Thus, in their analysis of power and domination, new materialists prefer to speak of 'relational capacities of assembled bodies' (Fox and Alldred, 2018: 323) or '*agencements* of desire' (Dolphijn and van der Tuin, 2012) and to treat 'power [as something that is] revealed and deployed at the very local level of actions and events' (Fox and Alldred, 2018: 323, emphasis in original). They insist on the 'agential or *noninnocent* nature of all matter' (Dolphijn and van der Tuin, 2012: 101), including the flesh. The level of analysis is the everyday life of matter in all its forms and relations. Rather than speaking of intricately imbricated structures or systems of power and domination, as in intersectionality scholarship, they tend to speak of 'micropolitical patternings in time and space [that] may lead to continuities of hierarchic relations' whose 'regularity is illusory' (Fox and Alldred, 2018: 323). The social, and more specifically power, continuously flows and all we can expect to achieve as researchers is to follow those flows or, put more concretely, describe how 'affects between both human and non-human relational materialities' assemble in daily events (Fox and Alldred, 2018: 323).

What, then, can new materialism tell us about specific forms of power and domination like patriarchy? In their work, Nick Fox and Pam Alldred provide elements of an answer:

> the gendered expressions of power and oppression between young people in school settings are not products of abstracted structural forces such as 'patriarchy' or 'hegemonic masculinity'. Instead, they are the outcomes of micropolitical material forces and intensities operating within the daily round of events in and out of the classroom. (Fox and Alldred, 2018: 323)

According to this analysis, gendered power relations are best researched and understood not by seeking to expose or even speak of structures regulating individuals' behaviour but by seeing 'affective flows' producing assemblages of bodies, ideas, things, social institutions and the gendered expressions of power and oppression resulting from them. The individual is decentred and structures are abandoned in favour of matter affecting and being affected relationally. What we appear to end up with, then, is a detailed description of daily events that sets out to show how matter in all its forms responds to a particular arrangement of material relationalities within a particular daily event. This is why new materialists often speak of 'micropolitical power'. Whether this micropolitical *assemblage* produces a gendered expression or not does not depend so much on the existence of a structuring force as on the flows marking a particular event. New materialists, then, mainly aim to interpret the flows marking daily existence. They do not want to 'critique collective (molar) inscription, but rather ask ... how, in life, the creation of the woman (and the man) comes about in the (mute, fleshy, molecular) affects to which these collective inscriptions *respond*' (Dolphijn and van der Tuin, 2012: 153). It seeks to capture gender as it emerges from the affective flows.

Both ANT and new materialism, then, set out to 'rewrite' (Dolphijn and van der Tuin, 2012) the way we analyse power and domination. They do so by alerting us to the importance of relationality in social analysis, by bringing our attention to matter, contingency and heterogeneous chains of relations. But their theoretical approach, which relies on what I shall name a *relationality of aggregation*, contrasts sharply with the relationality of intersectionality. What is more, I would also argue that intersectionality offers much more powerful relational insights than those ANT and new materialism could ever offer. In what follows I set out to demonstrate how and why this is the case by reviewing some of ANT and new materialism's key limitations and exposing how an intersectional lens of the form discussed in the previous section can help overcome them.

A fruitful and particularly appropriate issue to start this discussion with is the claim that ANT and new materialism scholars provide a new basis for analysing the social and, more specifically, power and domination. For ANT scholars, conventional scholarship of the form of, for example, critical sociology is not only misled in attempting to engage critically with the world, it is also thought to rely on an unacceptable onto-epistemic dualism between humanity and nature (Latour, 1993, 2005). A similar set of claims is made by new materialists who set out to '"travers[e]" the dualisms that form the backbone of modernist thought' (Dolphijn van der Tuin, 2012: 86). Relationality is thus thought to be predicated upon a critique of modernism, particularly its body/mind and nature/society dualisms, and its resulting anthropocentrism. ANT and new materialism, however, are not the first set of approaches to offer a critical assessment of modernist binaries and the human-centredness they entail. As Sherilyn MacGregor (2021) brilliantly demonstrates in her critical assessment of new materialist green political theory, such an anti-dualist stance can be traced back to the (far too often overlooked) work of ecofeminists. Take, for example, the following passage by Val Plumwood:

> Human/nature dualism … is a system of ideas that takes a radically separated reason to be the essential characteristic of humans and situates human life outside and above an inferiorised and manipulable nature. Rationalism and human/nature dualism are linked through the narrative which maps the supremacy of reason onto human supremacy via the identification of humanity with active mind and reason and of non-humans with passive, tradeable bodies. We should not mistake rationalism for reason – rather it is a cult of reason that elevates to extreme supremacy a particular narrow form of reason and correspondingly devalues the contrasted and reduced sphere of nature and embodiment. (Plumwood, 2002: 4)

Like its post-humanist counterparts, ecofeminism is critical of modernism's anthropocentrism. For ecofeminists, the dualisms upon which it rests do not just engender divisions, but also underpin hierarchies that are not limited to the supremacy of nature by humanity. In fact, central to Plumwood's (2002) critique of Global North (modernist) reason is its tendency to drive a 'human-centredness' that does not only result in environmental domination but also produces human-to-human hierarchies such as patriarchy, white supremacy, and class oppression. In the work of ecofeminists, different structures of social domination are said to intersect with one another and with environmental domination. What we find here, therefore, is the foundation for an intersectional critique of modernist dualisms.

Herein lies one of ecofeminism's key strengths. For, unlike ANT and new materialism, ecofeminists are able to turn their critique of modernist dualisms into a basis for understanding power and domination in modern-capitalist societies. This step is one that their post-humanist counterparts are both unwilling and unable to take. For this would contradict their descriptive stance and self-proclaimed value-neutrality. It would, too, force them to pose questions they are unwilling to ask. Indeed, their insistence on shifting our attention towards matter and to analyse the social through the prism of actor-networks or *assemblages* tends to divert attention away from relations of power between actants. The fact that the action of an actant might depend on another actant to be able to take place should not divert our attention away from the fact that an actant can have more power than another or simply ask for whom those hybrids, actor-networks or *assemblages* work (Haraway, 2018: footnote 1 pp 294–5; MacGregor, 2021: 52). It should not distract us from the task of recognizing how the power in question could acquire a structural form either. By devoting their attention to the description of flows and contingent aggregations making up the everyday dimension of social life, ANT and new materialism do indeed fail to equip us with the requisite conceptual tools for recognizing the structural and systematic character of an actant's power. Consequently, we are not in a position to ask whose interests particular actions and practices are structured by, which, in turn, means adopting a position on, say, 'environmentalism[,] that erases, like an astronaut, the socio-economic, political, and imaginary continuities between humans and non-humans constitutive of the Earth' (Ferdinand, 2022: 182). An intersectional lens of the form offered by ecofeminism does nevertheless allow us to do all of this by presupposing the existence of agents more powerful than others precisely because of the structural advantages afforded by their position in society, such as the power of men over women. Their relational stance does not only lead one to ask whether a particular association of actants is stronger than another or whether an actant is able to act as a result of another but, rather, to place 'gender in relation to, and often in tension with, other axes of difference as a necessary component of a comprehensive analysis' (MacGregor, 2021: 56). Unlike the kind of analyses offered by ANT and new materialist scholars, the relationality of an ecofeminist intersectional approach tackles social justice issues head on.

But an intersectional lens also allows us to circumvent an equally fundamental and problematic issue emanating from ANT and new materialism's overt tendency to avoid treating humans as ontologically distinct: the failure to provide 'conceptual tools to understand how systems of domination might be resisted' (Whittle and Spicer, 2008: 621). According to ANT scholarship, for example, both humans and non-humans have the power to make one another part of a network. One can in fact, and indeed must, be 'enrolled' by the other to participate in a network (Amsterdamska, 1990: 499). By insisting on the equal capacity for action of all matter or nodes within a network, those two theoretical paradigms refuse to recognize that since humans 'generate and interpret meaning' (Whittle and Spicer,

2008: 621), they are in a rather unique position within the social or have a unique capacity to enrol other actants. The '*meaningful* character of human action' (Whittle and Spicer, 2008: 621, emphasis in original) therefore seems to play little, if any, part in their understanding of agency and, consequently, power. As a result, they fall short of equipping us with the conceptual tools needed for understanding the process through which meanings are made, interpreted and legitimated or even for assessing the symbolic power of one or more actants to enrol others in a network (Whittle and Spicer, 2008: 621). Agency is here so radicalized that an analysis of power is condemned to missing the meaningful character of human action and failing to recognize the important relations of power at play within it.

Ecofeminists, however, adopt a relational ontology that does not collapse the two realms of action, while recognizing their respective agentic capacities. Many ecofeminists do indeed recognize that 'humans as a species ... emerged from and is embedded in organic, material nature' (MacGregor, 2021: 50) while insisting that 'women and nature ... shar[e] ... a common oppression' (Mellor, 1992: 236). Humans are here understood as belonging to nature while not being reducible to it – and they are not reducible to it precisely because they are capable of recognizing 'the sufferings of the natural world' (Mellor, 1992: 236) they have caused. Like ANT and new materialist scholars, ecofeminists eschew human-centredness by stressing the 'agentic ... potentialities' (Plumwood, 2002: 177) of non-humans, but insist on recognizing difference and multiplicity, particularly in the structural distribution of power. For, building a 'multiparty, mutualistic ethical relationships ... requires not just the affirmation of difference, but also sensitivity to the difference between positioning oneself with the other and positioning oneself as the other' (Plumwood, 2002: 202).

In short, instead of collapsing human and non-human action, ecofeminists stress the need for an ethical project where humans have a particularly important and timely role to play in moving away from the material and symbolic human-centredness responsible for both social and environmental domination. In addition to making explicit the complex intersections of social structures of domination, ecofeminism opens up the scope for making explicit the intersectional of social and environmental domination. But under its guise, humans retain the capacity to distinguish good/legitimate from bad/illegitimate practices in accounting for power. Humanity might be decentred but not to the point of being completely stripped of its humanism.

What we have learned so far, then, is that to adopt a relational stance setting out to probe power and domination and overcome modernist dualisms need not entail abandoning the goal of social justice in favour of a detailed description of everyday flows and the associations they give rise to, or to overlook the distinctive capacity for meaningful and ethical action humans possess. Such conclusions were drawn by pitting the relational stance of

ANT and new materialist scholars against the relationality of ecofeminist intersectionality. But more is needed here to refine our understanding of intersectional relationality, especially given the rather singular character of intersectionality as co-formation. To do so, I propose to venture onto the terrain of decolonial thought, where much of the relational content of intersectionality as co-formation derives from.

Within that body of work, which heavily draws on Amerindian Indigenous cosmologies, one finds an understanding of relationality that does not only distinguish itself from ANT and new materialism's own in terms of the way they construe power and domination, but also in terms of its *modus operandi*. Instead of a network with different nodes or an assemblage of different components, decolonial scholars prefer to speak of a 'colonial power matrix', 'entanglement' of (material and symbolic) power structures or even 'intersectionality of multiple and heterogenous global hierarchies' (Grosfoguel, 2007: 217). Understanding social life is not so much a matter of aggregating its different components into a network or *assemblage* as it is of capturing its complex entanglements. Furthermore, in attempting to expose the intricately imbricated structures of power and domination, decolonial relationality does not limit itself to making a claim about the way power operates but also tells us something about the nature of being; it makes an ontological claim. Like ANT and new materialism, the ontology in question is of a relational form. But rather than speaking of hybrids or material relationalities, decolonial scholars prefer to insist on the fact that 'all existence is radically interdependent' and that '[e]verything exists in relation, arising and developing in meshworks of relations' (Escobar, 2020: 4). The modernist dualism of nature/society is rejected in favour of an analysis that recognizes the social in nature and the natural in the social. So while it echoes, for example, ANT's own call for moving beyond the modernist ontological distinction between nature and society, decolonial relationality does more than simply alerting us to the fact that the distinction is a modernist illusion or that anthropocentrist accounts of the social are problematic. Like ecofeminism, it also insists on the inscription of human-centredness in intersecting power structures like patriarchy and colonialism. This is why James Lovelock's Gaia hypothesis, which has significantly informed the work of ANT scholar Bruno Latour and presupposes a mutually constitutive relationship between the human and non-human that excludes an account of the way power structures have historically underpinned this relationship, tends to be rejected in favour of other models like Ayiti (Ferdinand, 2022). The latter is indeed thought to be more capable of grasping 'the ecologico-political imbrication of modernity's colonial constitution within the ways of inhabiting the Earth, which is the cause of today's ecological crisis' (Ferdinand, 2022: 182).

Furthermore, and in contrast with ANT and new materialism, decolonial relationality lays the groundwork for what AnaLouise Keating called an 'ethics of radical interrelatedness' (2009: 84) that is, one through which humans can begin to care for both non-humans and other humans by asserting their radical interdependence with them. It is therefore an approach to relationality through which one is encouraged to think along the following lines:

> When I see something that looks racist, I ask, 'Where is the patriarchy in this?'
> When I see something that looks sexist, I ask, 'Where is the heterosexism in this?'
> When I see something that looks homophobic, I ask, 'Where are the class interests in this?' (Matsuda, 1991: 1189)

Such an approach effectively draws an Amerindian Indigenous cosmologies to envision a person construed as the 'locus of multiple other selves with whom he or she is joined in mutual relations of being' (Salhins, 2008: 48). As such, it shares with the relationality of intersectionality as co-formation the position that 'life [and this includes identity and self-hood] is interrelation and interdependence through and through' (Escobar, 2018: 101). It also directly draws on Anzaldúa's (1987) own concept of 'borderlands' and what decolonial scholar Walter Mignolo (2000) called 'border thinking', which sets out to bring different decolonial projects together in the constitution of a new ways of thinking and being in the world that thrive on diversity and interdependence. Another concept used in that literature to capture the essence of this co-existence between difference and interrelatedness is the 'pluriverse' (Mignolo, 2000; Escobar, 2018, 2020). It originates in the Zapatista movement whose slogan '*a world where many worlds fit*' (Escobar, 2018: xvi, emphasis in original) emphasizes the value of difference while recognizing that the different worlds in question 'are completely interlinked, though under unequal conditions of power' (Escobar, 2020: 27). It celebrates difference while asserting radical interdependence and dissolving categories, which modernity had created to divide the world and hierarchize it. Like intersectionality as co-formation, then, it recognizes difference while making explicit the complex relationality of our existence, including the complex relationality of intersecting structures of power and domination. For this reason, I shall from now on refer to the version of intersectionality adopted in this work as *pluriversal intersectionality*. I shall also name the relationality it deploys *relationality of radical interdependence*, which contrasts with the relationality of aggregation in virtue of making explicit altogether different forms of connections. While the latter searches for hybrids, the former searches for reciprocity.

What we have here, then, is a form of relationality that, in addition to exposing the intricate imbrication of structures of power and domination, offers an ontology and ethics of radical interdependence on the basis of which to imagine a world beyond modernist dualisms and the structural oppressions resulting therefrom. It is therefore capable of achieving the kind of goal post-humanist approaches like ANT and new materialism sought to achieve while remaining to some degree compatible with the humanist project. It can also perform the kind of analysis that led postcolonial theorists like Go (2016) to draw on ANT, that is, to bring together the 'material and semiotic, human and nonhuman' of social life. The decolonial concept of 'coloniality of power' coined by Aníbal Quijano (2007), for example, reflects perfectly the kind of relationality Go seeks out. For, here repression is not only said to operate across intersecting and mutually constitutive systems of domination – colonial, patriarchal, capitalist, environmental and so on – but also 'over the modes of knowing, of producing knowledge' (Quijano, 2007: 169) of colonized peoples. It understands power and domination as 'material and semiotic, human and nonhuman'. Why Go and several other postcolonial scholars did not choose to draw on the relationality embodied in decolonial scholarship is a mystery to me. Its overtly critical outlook on power and domination, along with its counter-cultural potential, make it a particularly suitable candidate for postcolonial theorizing. However, as I wish to show now, pluriversal intersectionality does not only distinguish itself in those terms, but also in virtue of sharing a close affinity with the libertarian strand of socialist thought; an affinity which is the object of the next and final section of this chapter.

Pluriversal intersectionality and libertarian socialism

In 1977, a group of women of colour activists known as the Combahee River Collective (CRC) wrote a statement that would become highly influential among intersectionality scholars. In it, one finds one of the very first explicit references to the notion of 'interlocking' systems of oppression (CRC, 2017: 15). The aim of the statement was to provide a 'road map for liberation' (Ransby, 2017: 180), summarized as follows:

> We realize that the liberation of all oppressed peoples necessitates the destruction of the political-economic systems of capitalism and imperialism as well as patriarchy. *We are socialists* because we believe that work must be organized for the collective benefit of those who do the work and create the products, and not for the profit of the bosses. Material resources must be equally distributed among those who create these resources. We are not convinced, however, that a socialist revolution that is not also a feminist and antiracist revolution will guarantee our liberation. We have arrived at the necessity for developing an understanding of class relationships that takes into account the specific class position of

Black women who are generally marginal in the labor force ...
Although we are in essential agreement with Marx's theory as it
applied to the very specific economic relationships he analysed,
we know that this analysis must be extended further in order
for us to understand our specific economic situation as Black
women. (CRC, 2017: 19–20, my emphasis)

Members of the CRC, then, explicitly self-identified as socialist. The form
of socialism they had in mind, though, includes, but is certainly not limited
to, the task overcoming socio-economic inequalities. In the statement
CRC members take great care of emphasizing the necessity to grapple with
the complex imbrication of issues of race and gender with issues of class.
A diverse range of struggles must therefore feed into socialist thinking and
work 'together across differences' (Smith, 2017: 64). Driven by the belief in
'a nonhierarchical distribution of power within our own group and in our
vision of a revolutionary society' (CRC, 2017: 27), CRC members hoped
that their activist work would 'add to the synthesis and creation of a new
hybrid like socialism' (Frazier, 2017: 140). Intersectionality, then, made one
of its first appearances as an analytical tool with the explicit goal of breathing
new life into socialist thought.

But even older precursors to intersectionality theory 'were committed
Marxists and/or socialists' (Bohrer, 2019: 31). Take, for example, Black
feminists such as Esther Jackson and Bonita Williams. Not only was their
political action directed against the eradication of sexism and racism, it also
'unequivocally opposed capitalism and imperialism' (McDuffie, 2011: 6). For
Bonita Williams, for example, the Communist Party in the US represented
the best way for Black women to oppose those systems of domination and
address the problems the Great Depression had inflicted on Black Americans
(McDuffie, 2011: 2). Black left feminism was therefore a vibrant movement
in early twentieth-century America, which saw 'massive upsurge in black
participation in socialist, communist, and Marxist organizations', especially
among Black women (Bohrer, 2019: 42). That period could in fact be said
to have prepared the ground for the 'socialist feminist manifesto' (McDuffie,
2011: 4) of the CRC and, more broadly, to have initiated what would become
a significant and sustained inter-penetration of ideas between intersectionality
and Marxism until the 1980s.

Such an overlap is also visible in the work of another famous precursor
to intersectionality theory: W.E.B. Du Bois. While he is best known for his
work on race and concepts like 'double consciousness' (Du Bois, 2008) or
his views on the 'negro problems' (Du Bois, 1898) and the reconstruction
period following the American Civil War (Du Bois, 1998), he could also be
regarded as a figure within the intersectional tradition (Rabaka, 2009; Clark
et al. 2018) and committed socialist. His intersectional outlook stems from

his concern with the complex imbrication of issues of race, colonialism, class, and even gender (Rabaka, 2009). For, in his work he explicitly refused to 'isolate economic exploitation from racial domination and gender discrimination' (Rabaka, 2009). It is his critique of economic exploitation that led him to engage with Marxism, albeit critically, mainly condemning the lack of attention paid to issues of race, racism, and colonialism (Rabaka, 2009). This did not, however, deter him from becoming a member of the Socialist Party of America in 1911 and vacillating between a socialist alternative articulated around associationalism and cooperativism, such as the one depicted in *Dusk of Dawn* (2007), and one postulating a strong welfare state as promoted in his 1960 speech *Socialism and the American Negro*.[4] Thus, whether one turns to Black radicalism tradition or Black left feminism, one is in a position to observe a rather sustained overlap between socialism and intersectionality theory.

But in this section, I am particularly interested in making explicit the main features of pluriversal intersectionality's 'silent utopia', drawing on Ruth Levitas' (2013) works. In addition to treating utopia as a 'method', Levitas (2013) argued that sociological perspectives, particularly critical theories, tend to embody an implicit image of a good society. This is because by problematizing 'what is', critical forms of sociological thinking entail an overt evaluative relation to the world and are, in turn, marked by a more or less explicit normative outlook (Levitas, 2013). According to Levitas (2013), we must make explicit such implicit utopias so that they can help cultivate the desire for change. What I therefore wish to do here is to reveal the 'silent utopia' of pluriversal intersectionality. More specifically I show that the associationalist and cooperativist model briefly mentioned earlier shares the closest affinities with this approach to intersectionality.

Let me explain why. First, it is important to note that intersectionality theory itself has not only shared a history with Marxism, it has also comprised a non-negligible tradition of associationalism and cooperativism. Take, for example, the activist practices of Black women. Phenomena like 'othermothers', involving 'women who assist bloodmothers by sharing mothering responsibilities' (Collins, 2000: 178), are practices informed by a spirit of mutuality, community, support, and peace. They have, as Collins took great care of highlighting, served to challenge 'prevailing capitalist property relations' (Collins, 2000: 182) and facilitated the development of 'interpretive frameworks' that are essential for 'constructing new knowledge' (Collins, 2000: 286). More broadly, Black feminist activist practices have taken the form of what Zenzele Isoke (2013) called a 'politics of homemaking', through which Black women seek to create spaces for associationalist practices aimed at supporting Black communities, while fostering a 'radical black subjectivity' (Isoke, 2013: 95) affirming individual empowerment through cooperation.

Furthermore, the relational ontology of pluriversal intersectionality exhibits counter-cultural characteristics that broadly reflect the associationalism and cooperativism at the heart of libertarian socialism. But what exactly characterizes libertarian socialism and what differentiates it from its statist counterpart? The answer lies in the form of socialization each entails. The latter involves a socialization from above, that is, one in which the state administers the satisfaction of needs. Here enterprises of various forms are nationalized. The state controls production and consumption. Libertarian socialism, on the other hand, warns of the risk of sacrificing 'the autonomy of the individual to the all-pervading interference of the State' (Kropotkin, 2002: 52). Instead, it argues in favour of a socialization from below, that is, one in which workers and consumers collectively manage the economy. But while the term 'libertarian' might, because of its more frequent use within the right of the political spectrum, appear to lead to a defence of rugged individualism, the freedom advocated by libertarian socialists is inherently social. It does not pit the individual against the community or collective but, instead, seeks to align the latter with the former. Libertarian socialism marks a 'synthesis of the ideas of equality and liberty' (Guérin, 2017: 82) made possible by a central organizing principle known as self-management. Defined by Henri Lefèbvre as 'the theoretical essence of liberty' (1975: 18), and Mihailo Markovic (1975: 345) as a 'necessary condition of a new, genuinely socialist society', this principle is crucial for the operationalization of libertarian socialism's 'social freedom' (Honneth, 2017). Under the guise of self-management, each enterprise is collectively owned and democratically organized, like in worker cooperatives. Consumers are collectively organized to be able to communicate effectively their needs. This creates conditions favourable for mutual reciprocity, cooperation, and solidarity and, ultimately, for an experience of freedom that is not self-directed and self-interested but social or collective. Here an individual is thought to be 'really free to the extent that his [sic] freedom, fully acknowledged and mirrored by the free consent of his fellowmen, finds confirmation and expansion in their liberty' (Bakunin, 2002: 76). Libertarian socialists[5] resist favouring equality at the expense of liberty, they also refuse to sacrifice equality in the name of liberty. They are therefore acutely critical of both the various hindrances an interventionist (socialist) state imposes on freedom and the rampant individualism and sharp inequalities unleashed by capitalist economic relations.

Associationalism and cooperativism are also central to the libertarian socialist vision in virtue of providing the organizational principles needed for the realization of social freedom. They offer democratic structural arrangements on the basis of which an individual's freedom is realized through another individual's. In fact, like pluriversal intersectionality theorists, libertarian socialists treat the self and freedom as social.

Associational life is here expected to foster what Cole (1980: 46) described as a 'communal spirit', upon which the realization of one's desires relies. For, '[t]he consciousness of a want requiring co-operative action for its satisfaction is the basis of *association*' (Cole, 1920: 34, emphasis in original). The mutualist and cooperativist attitudes an association fosters are in this sense central to the development of self-hood in a libertarian socialist vision. In turn, self-hood could be said to develop a dialogical form and reflect the characteristics of pluriversal intersectionality's very own vision of self-hood. For, like proponents of the latter, libertarian socialists recognize that an individual 'is born a sociable being' (Proudhon, 1993: 192). Like them, they 'grapple with the interconnectivity of our *mutual* living' (Violet, 2002: 488, emphasis in original). Both, then, share a conception of the self and freedom that is social and dialogically realized. For this reason, it could be argued that libertarian socialists seek to give radical interdependence its institutional form.

Furthermore, libertarian socialists seem, like pluriversal intersectionality theorists, inclined to 'run against conventional ideas of identity' (May, 2015: 41). The kind of 'associationalist society' they have in mind is one of 'varied and overlapping planes of social identity and cleavage' (Hirst, 1994: 67).[6] Because, in this alternative vision, individuals are expected to join associations based on their desires, each association is expected to realize one facet of their identity or, put more boldly, one of their identities. It is almost as if they had listened carefully to Gloria Anzaldúa's demand:

> Think of me as Shiva, a many-armed and legged body with one foot on brown soil, one on white, one in straight society, one in the gay world, the man's world, the women's, one limb in the literary world, another in the working class, the socialist, and the occult worlds. A sort of spider woman hanging by one thin strand of web. (Anzaldúa, 1983: 228)

Thus, libertarian socialists do not only conceptualize institutions that are expected to give form to ontological relationality. They, along with pluriversal intersectionality theorists, also recognize that individuals are ontologically plural and identity is coalitional.

How then, do libertarian socialists expect difference, which they are keen to assert, to be negotiated with commonality, which they also highly value? The answer lies in the dialogical character of associations. G.D.H. Cole's libertarian socialist vision is particularly instructive in this regard and is worth exploring in some detail here. In a praise of Jean-Jacques Rousseau's work, which significantly influenced the guild socialist's ideas,[7] Cole interpreted the relationship between particularism/difference and universalism/commonality in associational life, as follows:

> whenever [individuals] form or connect themselves with any form
> of association for any active purpose, [they] develop in relation
> to the association an attitude which looks to the general benefit
> of the association rather than their own individual benefit. This
> is not to say that they cease to think of their own individual
> advantage – only that there is, in their associative actions, an
> element, which may be stronger or weaker, of seeking the
> advantage of the whole association, or of all its members, as
> distinct from the element which seeks only personal advantage.
> (Cole, 1950: 114)

Under a libertarian socialist system, associations become spaces for self-expression and sites of social freedom *par excellence*. While the individual is 'the source and sustaining spirit of every association' (Cole, 1920: 191), personal freedom is not pitted against the interest of other members or the association as a whole. This is because in virtue of being formed in order to satisfy a want that requires cooperative action, democratically organized associations are extensions of their individual members' interest or, as Rousseau would put it, of their will. Indeed, through dialogical engagement, individuals negotiate their desires with other members of the group and are in turn able to align collective conceptions of the good life – the common good – with individual ones. For example, each member has an equal vote (individual) to choose the decisions (collective) they will eventually have to conform to. They are in a position to recognize that while the 'self is radically other from the other' this other is also 'posited within the self', whether this other is another member, the interest of the association as a whole or the rules members have to conform to. Associational life, therefore, 'organizes convergences without denying differences' (Guérin, 2017: 142), while securing 'obedience to the law which we prescribe to ourselves' (Rousseau, 1993: 196). In sum, libertarian socialists share with pluriversal intersectionality yet another characteristic, namely the concern for co-existence of interdependence and difference.

But in virtue of fostering spontaneous self-determination through dialogical engagement, associations also develop a dynamic character, thereby echoing pluriversal intersectionality's own emphasis on the continuous re-fashioning of identity. Indeed, while associations are not leaderless, leaders and representatives are democratically elected '*ad hoc* authorities' (Cole, 1980) who can be recalled by members (Cole, 1920). As such, 'there is no fixed and constant authority, but a continual exchange of mutual, temporary, and, above all, voluntary authority and subordination' (Bakunin, 1970: 33). Associational life in the libertarian socialist utopia is therefore expected to be far from static. By securing 'open communication, free expression of critical opinions, and dialogue' (Markovic, 1975: 331), associations provide a space for 'provisional analyses that can be perpetually recast' (Collins, 2019: 234). They perform an essential emancipatory function by facilitating an 'on-going reconstruction of the way you view your world' (Anzaldúa, 2002: 560). In short, associations provide a space for the 'creative re-working, rather than stabilising of identity' (Taylor, Hines, and Casey, 2010: 5).

Finally, in the libertarian socialist utopia, self-managed associational life is expected to guide the re-organization of the political sphere, in the form of what is known as political pluralism. Political pluralism is 'strongly anti-statist' and highlights the 'vitality and the legitimacy of self-governing associations as a means of organizing social life' (Hirst, 1989: 2). It rejects all forms of 'politically organized power above society' (Super, 1975: 6) and the tendency to 'sacrifice 'the autonomy of the individual to the all-pervading interference of the State' (Kropotkin, 2002: 52). Parliamentary forms of representation are therefore severely criticized by libertarian socialists. Instead, they favour a functional form of representation (Horvat et al, 1975; Hirst, 1989) over what they regard as an 'omnicompetent State' and 'omnicompetent Parliament' deemed 'utterly unsuitable to any really democratic community' (Cole, 1980: 32). For, as G.D.H. Cole himself put it, what 'is represented is never man [sic], the individual, but always certain purposes common to groups of individuals' or, in the case or Harold Laski, 'territories and industrial interests' (Hirst, 1989: 35). In turn, '[t]rue representation … is always specific and functional, and never general and inclusive' (1920: 106). Thus, functional representation could be regarded as a necessary (political) corollary of self-managed organizations and a principle of political life essential for giving political expression to the ontological relationality and plurality embodied in pluriversal intersectionality.

However, it is worth reminding ourselves here that the socialist vision just drawn has a distinctively male and Western favour. For, despite finding some references to issues like gender and race in the work of a prominent libertarian socialist figures like Kropotkin (2002), the kind of emancipation these socialists had in mind was first and foremost the emancipation of labour. Proudhon's (1993) own record on the matter is even more problematic, with an economic reductionism accompanied by overtly sexist and anti-Semitic remarks. To make matters worse, the record of the labour movement in advanced capitalist countries like the UK and US is far from impressive with regards to race issues, at times even tolerating openly racist members (Marable, 2001; Shawki, 2006; Dawson, 2013; Virdee, 2014). But when issues other than class are addressed, they always seem to lead to the issue of labour emancipation. Take, for example, the work of 'libertarian communist' Daniel Guérin, who despite explicitly and consistently advocating for the emancipation of all groups subjected to domination (Guérin, 2018: 37), said little about the way self-management, for example, could lead to the emancipation of different oppressed groups at once. Similar limitations are visible in the work of Piotr Kropotkin (2012). For example, he recognizes that women 'no longer want … to be the beast of burden of the house' (2012: 11) and calls for an 'emancipation from domestic toil' (2012: 12). He envisages this emancipation to be driven by the application of 'machinery' to 'household cares' (2012: 12). Here, then, women's oppression is predominantly construed as a problem of economic exploitation to be overcome by replacing their labour with the labour of machines. A range of highly significant issues affecting women that cannot be adequately captured by the focus on economic oppression are being overlooked here and which, whenever they are mentioned, tend to be treated as mere after-thoughts. Domestic violence, sexual oppression, reproductive rights, and so on, cannot be accounted for by narrowing the scope of analysis to what Nancy Fraser (1995) called the struggle for redistribution. There is, as Honneth (2017) himself noted, an unacceptable economic reductionism in the work of these socialists. This is why in order to satisfy the demands of pluriversal intersectionality and particularly its demand for grasping interlocking systems of oppression, it is imperative to broaden the scope of the critique of capitalism upon which the socialist vision rests. This task will be the object of the next chapter.

Conclusion

With its relationality of radical interdependence, pluriversal intersectionality does not limit itself to a detailed descriptive account of diverse actants' capacity to act, their inter-relations, and the flows resulting from them. Nor does it merely aim to take a snapshot of material relationalities in movement. What it does seek to do, however, is offer a basis upon which to achieve social justice through an overt critique of intricately imbricated structures of power and domination, expected to inform resistance against both oppressive dualisms and the image of the bounded individual, as well as underpin the formulation of an ethics of radical interdependence. It does not therefore simply describe how the world is. It negates it while offering a basis upon which to imagine another way of thinking and being in the world. What will be imagined in this book is akin to Anzaldúa's (1987) 'in-between spaces' or 'borderlands', to the extent that what is envisioned results from a dialogue between different struggles for justice, whose intersection opens up new ways of thinking about socialism.

In the process of making the relationality of intersectionality as co-formation explicit, I took the reader through a range of knowledge projects. I showed that the former shares much closer affinities with decolonial thought and ecofeminism than with ANT and new materialism. On the one hand, this is because intersectionality as co-formation effectively originates from decolonial critiques of power and, as such, is able to make explicit the complex relationality of existence while recognizing the divisive, yet intricately imbricated, structures of power and domination affecting that existence. On the other, it shares with ecofeminism the view that patriarchy, class oppression, racial and colonial domination all intersect in complex and even mutually constitutive ways. But what it also does is, like many decolonial critiques of capitalism and modernism also do (see for example Ferdinand, 2022), expand the scope of intersectionality to the study of the intersection of social and environmental domination. In this sense the concept of pluriversal intersectionality I adopt here does not only share affinities with decolonial thought and ecofeminism, it is also influenced by them.

Finally, in this chapter I limited my analysis of pluriversal intersectionality's counter-cultural potential to the task of making explicit its silent utopia and, more specifically, revealing its affinities with the libertarian strand of socialism. It was shown how the associational and cooperative institutions at the heart of this socialist strand do not just reflect some key features of the approach to intersectionality formulated in this chapter, but also provide an institutional basis for radical interdependence. It therefore holds the potential for providing an alternative to capitalism that eschews its distinctively modernist human-centredness. From Chapter 3 onwards I turn to the task of realizing the counter-cultural potential in question. The aim will be to show how pluriversal intersectionality itself can help breathe new life into socialist thought and formulate a (provisional) intersectional socialist utopia. Before exploring it, however, I devote my attention to the formulation of a critique of power and domination under capitalism, analysed through an intersectional lens, and informing the conceptualization of an intersectional project of emancipation.

3

Pluriversal Intersectionality and Capitalist Domination

Introduction

The lasting influence of Marxism on the critique of power and domination under capitalism has meant that it has been a lot easier to equate capitalist oppression with class oppression than with any other forms of domination. However analysing domination through the lens of pluriversal intersectionality holds the potential for significantly broadening our understanding of capitalism and, in turn, overcoming the limitations of male- and Eurocentric libertarian socialism. First, though, let me clarify what I intend to mean by the term 'capitalism'.

While capitalism 'is and always was about capital accumulation, or … economic growth' (Streeck, 2016: 201), it ought to be studied as more than an economy or economic system. Wolfgang Streeck (2016) insists on treating it as a 'society', that is, 'as a system of social action and a set of social institutions falling in the domain of sociological rather than today's standard economic theory' (2016: 201). Under such a reading, the term capitalism is not so much a system of satisfaction of needs driven by the profit motive as a system with its own economic, political, and cultural spheres of action that are fundamental for its survival. Understanding capitalism in this way allows us to grasp the range of 'extra-economic arrangements that enable the endless expansion and private appropriation of surplus value' (Fraser, 2016: 173). Capitalism, it could be argued, has given rise to historically distinctive institutions, norms of behaviour, and ways of life that are 'deeply interwoven with how people organize even their most personal and intimate social life' (Streeck, 2016: 216).

What is also useful about adopting this understanding of capitalism shared by the likes of Michael Dawson (2016) and Nancy Fraser (2016), is that it allows one to bring a range of practices, institutions, and discourses within the scope of analysis that would otherwise be neglected under a predominantly economic treatment of capitalism. In turn, it ensures that the critique of power and domination is extended beyond the economic sphere. The various discussions included in this chapter will therefore be informed by the view that capitalist mechanisms of power and domination permeate forms of social action across the economic, political, and cultural spheres. But since capitalism also affects the way humanity relates to nature, it is also essential to account for those actions and practices within the humanity/ nature nexus itself.

In this chapter I aim to show what a pluriversal intersectional analysis of power and domination – one that presupposes the intricate imbrication of diverse systems of oppression – drawn from a broad range of standpoints and struggles for emancipation entails. In short, I develop a critique of diverse intersecting structures of capitalist domination. This is executed in three steps: first, I reflect on the implications of the Fraser (1995, 1998) and Butler (1998) debate on the relationship between the struggle for redistribution and the struggle for recognition for the critique of capitalism. This discussion will help further illuminate what a pluriversal intersectional critique of capitalism does and does not entail and what effectively distinguishes it from other forms of critical theorizing. Then I turn to what I chose to call the struggle for nature, all in an effort to grapple with its intersectional with human-to-human forms of domination. Finally, I contend that the overarching story of pluriversal intersectional capitalist domination is best told through the prism of the concept of dispossession.

Beyond the redistribution/recognition debate

In the second half of the 1990s, the *New Left Review* featured articles by Nancy Fraser and Judith Butler aimed at engaging critically with the increasingly widespread view that social movements have turned away from economic or redistributive concerns, and towards lifestyle issues or issues of recognition (Fraser, 1995). Such a development, they thought, was highly problematic for the Left as it marked a failure to appreciate the complex entanglement of the struggle for redistribution with the struggle for recognition. But, while both agreed on rejecting the aforementioned view and insisted on the intricate entwinement of the two struggles for justice, they offered contrasting ways of making sense of their imbrication. For this reason, the debate between those two prominent feminist figures provides a rather convenient starting point for addressing some of the complex conceptual questions involved in developing a pluriversal intersectional critique of capitalism, that is, for probing the radical interdependence of structures of capitalist domination.

Let me begin the analysis with a review of some key features of Fraser's own approach, as the debate published in *New Left Review* effectively starts with her position. The struggle for redistribution, exemplified by the struggle against economic exploitation, is defined by Fraser as a struggle against 'socioeconomic injustice ... rooted in the political-economic structure of society' (1995: 70–1). 'Cultural or symbolic' injustice, on the other hand, is 'rooted in social patterns of representation, interpretation, and communication' (Fraser, 1995: 71). It manifests itself in the form of, for example, cultural disrespect such as xenophobia or racism. But Fraser does insist that those distinctions are mainly analytical and that 'in the real world, of course, culture and political economy are always imbricated with one another' (1995: 70). The same goes for the 'remedies' to those 'injustices'. Redistributive remedies involve a 'political-economic restructuring of some sort' in the form of, for example, the creation of a welfare state (Fraser, 1995: 73). Remedies for 'cultural injustice', on the other hand, tend to involve 'some sort of cultural of symbolic change', such as 'recognizing and positively valorizing cultural diversity' (Fraser, 1995: 73). But, like the injustices themselves, the remedies are intricately imbricated in practice. For example, 'redistributive remedies generally presuppose an underlying conception of recognition' (Fraser, 1995: 73).

Fraser, then, is keen to emphasize that despite establishing an analytical distinction between cultural and economic struggles for 'heuristic purposes' (Fraser, 1995: 70), both are inseparable in practice. Had Fraser ended the discussion here, little could have been done to contest her line of argumentation. However, things begin to fall apart when she provides examples aimed at illustrating her claims. I shall concentrate on her discussion of sexuality, on which Butler (1998) herself chose to focus in in her critique of Fraser's stance:

> Sexuality in this conception is a mode of social differentiation whose roots do not lie in the political economy, as homosexuals are distributed throughout the entire class structure of capitalist society, occupy no distinctive position in the division of labour, and do not constitute an exploited class. Rather, their mode of collectivity is that of a despised sexuality, rooted in the cultural-valuational structure of society. From this perspective, the injustice they suffer is quintessentially a matter of recognition. (Fraser, 1995: 77)

Sexuality is, in Fraser's perspective, at one extreme end of the spectrum of injustices: the end of recognition. Issues regarding sexuality are, under her reading, inherently cultural. They relate to matters of disrespect and cultural devaluation in the form of discrimination or intolerance of homosexuals' ways of life. No issue other than sexuality, it seems, can better illustrate the struggle for recognition.

This claim is astonishing for two main reasons. First, it seems to contradict what Fraser herself claimed in an earlier part of the essay, namely that the distinction between economic and cultural injustices is analytical. If this is so, why insist on stripping, as she does in the earlier passage, sexuality from all its possible economic manifestations? Why claim that it is a 'mode of differentiation whose roots do not lie in the political economy'? Second, as Butler herself noted, Fraser appears to ignore the work of socialist feminists who, in the 1970s, took great care of exposing the ways in which 'the regulation of sexuality was systematically tied to *the mode of production* proper to the functioning of political economy' (1998: 40). Consequently, while Fraser appears to insist on both the desirability and possibility for diverse struggles to work together towards a socialist transformation, her conceptual framework inadequately accounts for the complex ways they intersect, even at what she regards as the extreme ends of the injustices spectrum. In turn, her approach runs the risk of reproducing the kind of divisions between economic and cultural struggles upon which capitalism, and more specifically its neoliberal form, thrives (Duggan, 2003).

But in her reply to Butler's critique, Fraser (1998) makes an important point about the need to develop a historicized account of capitalism and charges the former for failing to do so. She takes issue with the socialist feminist critiques of the 1970s, which in her view provided a totalizing and ahistorical account of capitalism. This is because 'many of the feminist arguments during that time sought … to identify the family as part of the mode of production' (Butler, 1998: 39–40). Here, Fraser contends, the claim seems to consist in showing how the family relates to any mode of production, rather than how it relates to capitalism itself. The claim in question, therefore, appears to universalize a phenomenon Fraser insists was specific to capitalism. Thus, while Fraser contradicts herself by establishing more than a mere analytical distinction between economic and cultural injustices, Butler weakens her attempt to expose their intricate imbrication by falling short of making sufficiently explicit the historically distinctive character the relationship between gender/sexuality with political economy.

To overcome those different limitations, more needs to be done to understand how different structures of domination intersect under capitalism. What I propose to do is turn to the relationality of pluriversal intersectionality and make explicit the radical interdependence between economic and cultural structures of domination. Such a relational understanding is, for example, observable in the work of ecofeminists and queer scholars. For ecofeminist figures like Silvia Federici (2004) and Maria Mies (2014a), capitalist domination is best understood by grasping the complex operations of power involved in the witch hunt that took place across Europe. For them, the hunt was marked by a process of mutually constitutive processes of material and cultural/symbolic subjugation. Here is how Federici herself depicted it:

The expropriation of European workers from their means of subsistence, and the enslavement of Native Americans and Africans to the mines and plantations of the 'New World', were not the only means by which a world proletariat was formed and 'accumulated'. This process required the transformation of the body into a workmachine, and the subjugation of women to the reproduction of the workforce. Most of all, it required the destruction of the power of women which, in Europe as in America, was achieved through the extermination of the 'witches'. Primitive accumulation, then, was not simply an accumulation and concentration of exploitable workers and capital. It was *also an accumulation of differences and divisions within the working class,* whereby hierarchies built upon gender, as well as 'race' and age, became constitutive of class rule and the formation of the modern proletariat. We cannot, therefore, identify capitalist accumulation with the liberation of the worker, female or male, as many Marxists (among others) have done, or see the advent of capitalism as a moment of historical progress. On the contrary, capitalism has created more brutal and insidious forms of enslavement, as it has planted into the body of the proletariat deep divisions that have served to intensify and conceal exploitation. It is in great part because of these imposed divisions – especially those between women and men – that capitalist accumulation continues to devastate life in every corner of the planet. (2004: 63–4, emphasis in original)

Under such a reading it is not possible to separate the material subjugation entailed by economic exploitation from the symbolic construction of the exploited as exploitable, and the 'differences and divisions' this entails. Nor is it possible to separate class domination from patriarchal domination or colonial/racial rule. Each is constitutive of the other and 'capitalism, as a social-economic system, is necessarily committed to racism and sexism' (Federici, 2004: 17).

Such a radical interdependence of structures of power and domination in the analysis of capitalism is echoed in the work of queer scholars. John D'Emilio (1993), for example, demonstrated in rather compelling ways how the capitalist separation between the private and public sphere effectively led to the creation of a heterosexual identity, idealized, and celebrated through its othering from a despised homosexual identity. Thus, because the capitalist re-organization of social life entailed the construction of new economic relations through the construction of sexual *identities*, the task of finding remedies for the problems of heterosexism and homophobia requires one to recognize that, in the 'most profound sense, capitalism is the problem'

(D'Emilio, 1993: 474). What we find here, then, is an historicized account of the complex imbrication of sexuality and political economy.

Federici and D'Emilio, therefore, offer a way out of the limitations found in both Fraser's and Butler's account of the relationship between economic and cultural struggles. They are also able to achieve something that lies at the core of pluriversal intersectionality, that is, to go beyond the oppressive dualisms engendered by, and sustaining, the capitalist order. By identifying binaries where they do not exist, Fraser 'entrench[es] the split she describes in ways that implicitly recreate the hierarchy she eschews' (Duggan, 2003: 82). Her approach, in turn, fails to grapple adequately with the kind of imbrications that mark capitalist systems of oppression. As Federici, D'Emilio and others – not to mention Michel Foucault (1990; 1992; 1998) – showed, the regulation of sexuality did have and continues to have an important and direct role in capital accumulation. Not being in a position to grasp this role paves the way for the sort of conceptual blind spot responsible for succumbing to what Duggan called the 'ruse' of neoliberal capitalism, that is, to obscure the 'intricate imbrications of relations of race, gender, sexuality, and class in the institutions of capitalist modernity' (2003: 83). What Fraser therefore risks achieving with her binaries is to present 'a historical effect' – such as the class vs. homosexuality binary – 'as an ontological given' (Hennessy, 2000: 221). For, as queer scholar Rosemary Hennessy put it, 'there are and historically have always been uneven, complex material connections between the unequal relations of production … and the production of identities, knowledges, and culture' (2000: 221).

It must be noted here, however, that Fraser (1995) did not limit the scope of her analysis to the study of what she regarded as an extreme end of the injustices spectrum like the issue of sexuality. In her work, she also engages with the categories of race and gender in quite some depth. Unlike sexuality, though, race and gender are understood as 'bivalent collectivities' insofar as women or racial minorities 'suffer injustices that are traceable to both political economy and culture simultaneously' (Fraser, 1995: 78). They are not, to borrow Butler's (1998) terminology, 'merely cultural' or merely economic collectivities. They are 'hybrid modes that combine features of the exploited class with features of the despised sexuality' (Fraser, 1995: 78). Finding remedies for the injustices articulated around the categories of race and gender, therefore, implicate both political-economic restructuring and 'upwardly revaluing disrespected identities' (Fraser, 1995: 73). In the case of bivalent collectivities there is no redistribution without recognition and no recognition without redistribution. Unlike her account of sexuality, Fraser's conceptualization of struggles for justice articulated around race and gender issues seems, at first glance, capable of grasping some of the complex ways in which capitalist oppression operates. But upon closer inspection her 'bivalent collectivities' exhibit identical problems to those found in her conceptualization of sexuality.

A first problem is the relationality entailed by construing a category like gender or race as a 'bivalent collectivity'. What Fraser intends to mean here is that race and gender are two-dimensional. They are both an economic and cultural phenomenon. The domination they entail is both a matter of maldistribution and disrespect. But while this two-dimensional view does suggest that material and symbolic issues 'impinge on one another in ways that can give rise to unintended effects' (Fraser and Honneth, 2003: 64), it falls short of providing much-needed insights into the way the two dimensions effectively constitute one another. Put differently, in Fraser's critique of capitalism structures of domination are not radically interdependent or mutually constitutive but are instead treated as ontologically separate structures that, at times, confront and even affect one another. Her understanding of relationality is more 'additive' (Yuval-Davis, 2011) than intersectional and appears to overlook the existence of 'multiple grounds of identity' (Crenshaw, 1991: 1245).

More, albeit similar, problems are visible in her exchange with political scientist Michael Dawson on the issue of race. Explicitly drawing on Fraser's 'expanded understanding of the contours of the modern capitalist order' (Dawson, 2016: 146), that is, on her conceptualization of capitalism as a 'social order', Dawson sets out to analyse the intersection(s) of race and capitalism. He observes:

> the process of expropriation marked by colonial logics is different from that described in traditional Marxist analyses due to its racialization. The colonial logic of superior/inferior human includes not only ongoing expropriation and exploitation, but disposability, and an attenuated extension of citizenship or subject 'rights', if they are extended at all. Racially expropriated labor never becomes 'free labor' in the classic Marxist sense that Fraser argues is a central feature of capitalism. (Dawson, 2016: 151)

It follows that in order to understand racial domination, it is essential that we expand our analysis of domination beyond class exploitation to include the phenomenon of expropriation. For, the colonial logic of othering that hierarchizes humans along a racial axis means that some are afforded rights that others are denied.

Dawson's article, particularly the earlier passage, prompted Fraser to formulate a response in which she sought to clarify her stance. Written in ostensible agreement with Dawson, I would argue the response implicitly contributed to creating a chasm between her stance and Dawson's own. Indeed, while Fraser agrees on the importance of accounting for capitalism's colonial logic, she takes the distinction identified by Dawson much further than he himself wished to. Under her reading, one finds 'free exploitable citizen-worker, on the one hand, and the dependent expropriable subject, on the other' (2016: 171–2). Such a separation was not, however, found in Dawson's work. For, rather than postulating two separate groups, Dawson wanted to highlight within-group differences. While some workers' experiences are best captured by the term exploitation, others do not even hold the means for selling their labour freely and are effectively expropriated. In short, some workers might be more exposed to expropriation than others. So, the aim here was not to create an artificial division between two different 'statuses' but simply to highlight that different axes of hierarchization – race and class – intersect to produce diverse experiences of oppression. He aimed to study intersections rather than explain how ontologically separate categories interact.

What, then, can be concluded from this discussion regarding the logic(s) of capitalist oppression? While Fraser did consistently remind her readers that the distinction between struggles of justice is mainly an analytical one, she fell short of preventing her conceptual framework from severing inherent ties between what are intricately imbricated struggles for justice. Issues of sexuality, for example, appear construed as extrinsic to capitalist political economy. Economic and cultural struggles for justice, such as those articulated around race and gender, might 'impinge on one another', but little is said about the multiple ways in which identity is constituted. The problem with this approach is twofold. On the one hand, the problem of oppression is here framed in dualist terms and, consequently, Fraser does not do enough to transcend the potentially oppressive binaries upon which modern-capitalist hierarchies have been constructed. On the other hand, one's understanding of the way different structures of domination relate to one another under capitalism risks being limited to a simplistic additive model, through which *separate structures combine* to produce particular experiences of oppression (Yuval-Davis, 2011). More concretely, it means closing off critique from the kind of approach that is able to 'transcend … the logic of segregation' (Collins, 2019: 228) underpinning capitalist domination. It follows that while Fraser's approach can explain how, for example, domination articulated around race and gender is both economic and cultural, it is unable to equip critique with the requisite conceptual tools for thinking emancipation in non-dualist terms. For, there is a crucial difference in claiming, on the one hand, that heterosexist and racial domination interact, and, on the other, that they mutually constitute one another, or that 'racism has played a central role in creating the prevailing repressive sexual environment', as the likes of Angela Davis sought to show in great detail (James, 1998: 16). This difference, then, reflects the difference between a relationality of aggregation and one of radical interdependence.

But I wish to conclude this section by looking at one key reason Fraser provides for not construing capitalist domination in the latter terms.

This reason was made explicit in her reply to Butler's critique, in which Fraser equates her feminist peer's analysis with the 'over-totalising' view of functionalist sociology and socialist feminism:

> With her functionalist argument, Butler has resurrected what is in my view one of the worst aspects of 1970s Marxism and socialist feminism: the over-totalized view of capitalist society as a monolithic 'system' of interlocking structures of oppression that seamlessly reinforce one another. This view misses the 'gaps'. It has been resoundingly and persuasively subjected to critique from many directions, including the poststructuralist paradigm that Butler endorses and the Weberian one adapted by me. Functionalist systems theory is one strand of 1970s thought that is better forgotten. (Fraser, 1998: 147)

What is rather surprising for a scholar who devoted her career to the critique of capitalist domination with an emancipatory intent like Fraser, is her lack of recognition of the work of ecofeminists or Black feminists like Kimberlé Crenshaw, bell hooks, or Patricia Hill Collins, who have succeeded in identifying 'interlocking structures of oppression' without replicating the pitfalls of, say, functionalist sociology. To recognize that structures of domination are mutually constitutive need not entail overlooking gaps or cracks within a totalized capitalist system, but to provide a much-needed analysis of the complex ways in which capitalism reproduces itself through a 'tendency ... to differentiate' (Robinson, 1983: 26). While such an approach has entailed deploying the logic of intersectionality to reveal the *breadth and depth* of capitalist domination, it has also involved a pronounced and consistent focus on mutualist and cooperative practices that reveal the *limits* of domination and sheds light on life *beyond* its confines. Presupposing the existence of interlocking structures of (capitalist) domination, therefore, need not entail treating capitalism as a monolith. To suggest that capitalist political economy has relied on a colonial logic of 'othering' and domination is not to fall necessarily into an over-totalizing functionalist view of capitalism, but simply to contend that adequate remedies for socio-economic injustice cannot be found until one grasps the role played by, say, the 'repression ... over the modes of knowing, of producing knowledge, of producing perspectives, images and systems of images' (Quijano, 2007: 169) in engendering maldistribution. It means ensuring that experiences of privilege, such as those associated with white supremacy, do not obscure those of marginalization. It means recognizing that 'while people can identify with one identity category ... their social location is concretely located along multiple, if mutually constitutive, intersected categories of social power' (Yuval-Davis, 2011: 161). In short, it means deploying a relationality of radical interdependence. Finally, focusing on interlocking systems of oppression does not entail de-historicizing capitalism either. As was observed in the discussion of D'Emilio's work, there is something rather distinctive about the way sexual identities are inscribed in capitalist relations and *vice versa*. The fact of highlighting such a historically distinctive mutual constitution between sexuality and political economy allows one to go beyond simply claiming that both cultural and economic remedies are necessary for emancipation. It warns us about the necessity to adopt a pluriversal intersectional lens in an effort to grasp the *mutual constitution* of our multiple grounds of identity, of cultural and economic remedies, and of different categories of oppression.

Something is nevertheless missing from this discussion, namely an engagement with a defining struggle of our times I shall refer to here as the struggle for nature. Since nature is not a social group or category, the choice to include it in a discussion on intersectionality might seem rather strange, if not misguided. However, capitalism also structures the way humanity relates to nature – a relationship marked, too, by a logic of domination. In what follows I make a case for including nature within a pluriversal intersectional analysis of domination and show how its relationship to other structures of domination can be conceptualized.

Intersectionality and the struggle for nature

In the Costa Rican city of Curridabat, now known as Ciudad Dulce (Sweet City), urban planners chose to alter the relationship between the urban environment and its natural counterpart. They did so by creating green spaces and, more remarkably, giving citizen status to bees, plants, trees, butterflies and other non-humans. As the city mayor Edgar Mora put it 'Pollinators are the consultants of the natural world, supreme reproducers and they don't charge for it. The plan to convert every street into a biocorridor and every neighbourhood into an ecosystem required a relationship with them' (Edgar Mora cited in Greenfield, 2020, online resource).

Urban planners of Curridabat effectively chose to alter the relationship between humans and non-humans by recognizing the agency of the latter and, in the process, moving beyond othering practices of the kind that support humanity's domination of nature. What urban planners of this Costa Rican city therefore did is to institutionalize new ways of thinking about and relating to nature. What they did is to affirm the radical interdependence of the human and non-human world, which, I would argue, must be central to any utopia taking seriously the challenges posed by the likes of climate change and biodiversity loss.

I would further argue that this form of thinking, which echoes the calls for rights of nature embodied in the Latin American social philosophy known as *Buen Vivir*, can best develop on the basis of a critique of domination that not only recognizes the domination of humanity over nature but also the ways in which this form of domination intersects with human-to-human domination. Pluriversal intersectionality will therefore be deployed here in an attempt to recognize such a complex intersection and counter human-centredness that informs anthropocentric accounts of power and domination. I do so by bringing into dialogue the work of ecological Marxists and ecofeminists, as well as Indigenous and decolonial thought,[1] for it is in those contributions that one finds the most developed attempts to deploy the logic of pluriversal intersectionality for the study of power and domination *across* human-to-human and human-to-non-human relations.

Before I engage with that literature, though, let me proceed with the clarification of a term I shall use both within and beyond this chapter, namely the term 'nature', as I intend to minimize, as much as it is possible, any ambiguity regarding its meaning. Since I wish to emphasize that, as humans, we are part of nature, the latter shall be used to refer to nature in both the human, that is people, and non-human sense, such as animals, land, sea, and so on. It follows that, to speak of a 'struggle for nature' entails recognizing that the environmentalist struggle is a struggle for both human and non-human nature and, while inextricably linked to other systems of domination, humanity's domination of nature exhibits features that are not reducible to other forms of domination and constitutes a site of struggle *sui generis*. For example, the struggle against climate change and biodiversity loss cannot, despite their complex imbrication, be reduced to the struggle against racism. In what follows I nevertheless differentiate human nature from non-human nature, all in an effort to make explicit at once their difference and radical interdependence.

How, then, could a pluriversal intersectional critique of capitalist domination be formulated on that basis? Nancy Fraser's work is, once again, a convenient starting point for thinking of an answer. In the article on which Michael Dawson based his critique of racialized capitalism, the feminist philosopher devoted some of her attention to the relationship between capitalism and nature overlooked in her piece on the 'expanded conception of capitalism':

> society, polity and nature arose concurrently with economy and developed in symbiosis with it. They are effectively the latter's 'others' and only acquire their specific character in contrast to it. Thus, reproduction and production make a pair, with each term co-defined by way of the other. Neither makes any sense apart from the other. The same is true of polity/economy and nature/human. Part and parcel of the capitalist order, none of the 'non-economic' realms affords a wholly external standpoint that could underwrite an absolutely pure and fully radical form of critique. (2014: 70)

Two correlated claims about the way capitalism and nature relate are observable in this passage. First, Fraser seems rather unequivocal about the intricate imbrication of economic and extra-economic spheres under capitalism. By asserting that 'nature arose concurrently with the economy' she, on the one hand, wishes to highlight both nature and the capitalist economy's historical character. For, it entails recognizing that there is something historically distinctive about the way we relate to, and treat, nature. Capitalism, to borrow J.W. Moore's (2015) terminology, marks a specific 'way of organizing nature'. On the other hand, and consequently, it is not possible to address environmental problems adequately without formulating a critique of capitalist political economy or by studying the domination of nature as something separate from the logic of, say, class and patriarchal oppression. Capitalism, she argued, turns nature 'into a resource for capital' (Fraser, 2014: 63), creates an apparent structural division between the natural and economic realms, and causes the kind of 'metabolic rift' Marx and ecological Marxists after him (see for example Foster, Clark, and York, 2010) regarded as a key feature of the capitalist domination of nature. Capitalism, she further noted, 'brutally separated human beings from natural, seasonal rhythms, conscripting them into industrial manufacturing, powered by fossil fuels, and profit-driven agriculture' (Fraser, 2014: 63). For Fraser and ecological Marxists, then, the 'ecological rift is, at bottom, the product of a social rift: the domination of human being by human being' (Foster, Clark, and York, 2010: 47).

But despite all the talk about the role of capitalism in creating rifts, divisions, and boundaries with devastating effects on nature and society, their critique falls short of moving beyond the kind of dualisms they condemn. For example, while a notion capable of grasping a close, dialectical, and dynamic interaction between human and non-human nature, metabolic rift is regarded as a 'product' of human-to-human domination. Referring to the tradition of ecological dialectics, which they claim to belong to, Foster, Clark, and York even spoke of the 'production of society' involving 'a constant interaction with the natural world' (2010: 262). In a similar vein, Fraser described capitalism as responsible for a 'hardening of a pre-existing distinction between the human ... and non-human nature' (2014: 63). Capitalism, here, is not said to cause the distinction in question, but simply to 'harden' it. While the former claim tends to externalize non-human nature, the latter underplays capitalism's role in externalizing it. Furthermore, under both readings, non-human nature is affected by capitalism but little is said about how it affects humanity. Because the domination of non-human nature is the result of the domination of humans by other humans, little is said about non-human nature's role in shaping 'structures of power and production' (Moore, 2015: 38). For example, they can tell us little about the way climate is 'present at, and implicated in, the birth of these structures' (Moore, 2015: 38). It follows that the nature/society binary is treated as a mere consequence of human-to-human domination, thereby denying it a causal role 'in the colossal violence, inequality, and oppression of the modern world' (Moore, 2015: 2). Fraser and ecological Marxists are not, therefore, in a position to appreciate fully how '[m]odern class relations emerge through ... an audacious movement of environment-making' like 'capitalism's primitive accumulation', or how '[m]odern gender relations were forced through this same process of capitalist agrarian transformation' (Moore, 2015: 9). While they might see capitalism in nature, they cannot see nature in capitalism (Moore, 2015). Thus, by retaining an anthropocentric character those analyses of domination fall short of adequately grasping the complex ways human-to-human and human-to-non-human domination intersects under capitalism.

In order to overcome those limitations, I propose to turn to the work of ecofeminists and Indigenous worldviews, where one finds critiques of capitalism that are, at once, critiques of anthropocentrism. Take, for example, the work of ecofeminist Val Plumwood, who sought to explain the logic of domination inherent in capitalism in the following terms:

> The sharing of this logic of Othering between different kinds of centric oppression helps to explain the ready transfer of metaphors between them, and the reinforcement of the ideologies of 'nature' which support one kind of centric oppression by drawing on the Othering logic for another. Thus racial and ethnic inferiorisation drew strongly on assimilating racially subordinated groups to women, or to animals and children. The rationalist ideology of reason as an elite characteristic in opposition to Otherised characteristics such as emotion, animality and the body played a major role too in replicating the logic of Othering through different spheres of oppression. Conversely, the sharing of the basic logic of Othering helps explain the way liberation perspectives and insights have historically supported one another and transferred from one area of oppression to another, for example in the nineteenth century between women's oppression and slavery, and in the mid-twentieth century from movements against racism to feminist movements. And as we shall see, the historical development in our time of a critical environmental approach to the human-nature relationship has exhibited this pattern of political transfer of insights from other liberation perspectives in an especially striking way. (2002: 106)

According to Plumwood, capitalism is best understood in relation to the broader (rationalist) project of modernity. Under the guise of a Cartesian dualism that underpins much of Enlightenment thinking, reason is harnessed for the purpose of dividing and conquering through the deployment of a logic of othering. The reason/nature dualism, for example, serves to justify humanity's mastery of nature. The white/black racial dualism serves to justify the colonizer's rule over, if not extermination of, Indigenous populations. The treatment of women as 'the Others of reason, which is treated as the province of elite men' (Plumwood, 2002: 19) serves to justify patriarchy. Capitalism is thus understood as a project that shapes both how we relate to the world around us (ontological) and what we know about this world (epistemological) through a logic of othering. Each of the dualisms this logic gives rise to engenders and naturalizes forms of domination that are not reducible to one another but are coded through a binary lying at the centre of the capitalist order: the society/nature binary. For, by famously claiming 'I think, therefore, I am', René Descartes did not only externalize the body but equated what it means to be human with the capacity to think or reason. The typically Cartesian dualism of humanity and nature corresponds to a 'system of ideas that takes a radically separated reason to be the essential characteristic of humans and situates human life outside and above an inferiorised and manipulable nature' (Plumwood, 2002: 4). As a society, 'institutionalised social order' or 'way of organising nature and society', capitalism brings this system of ideas to life by setting in motion processes of exploitation and expropriation justified and resting on this particular binary. Under capitalism, for example, unpaid reproductive labour, colonization, and slave labour are justified by casting women as emotional, irrational and, generally, 'closer to nature', and people of colour as 'inferior or "barbarian" others who are [also] closer to nature' (Plumwood, 2002: 21). In sum, the metabolic rift capitalism engenders is just as much the 'product' of class oppression, colonialism, and patriarchy as it is the product of the 'view of Nature as external' (Moore, 2015: 2). The latter is in fact 'a fundamental condition of capital accumulation' (Moore, 2015: 2).

By providing a way out of the binary thinking that underpins capitalist forms of oppression, Plumwood is not only in a position to shed light onto the mutually constitutive character of capitalist structures of domination. She also engages with the kind of relational thinking that lies at the core of pluriversal intersectionality and has informed 'all Indigenous philosophies around the world … for centuries' (Mignolo, 2000: xvii). In fact, Plumwood (2002) herself, along with several other ecofeminists like Maria Mies and Vandana Shiva (2014), claim to have drawn inspiration from Indigenous worldviews. To be sure, given the multiplicity of Indigenous worldviews (Engel-Di Mauro, 2013) it would be unreasonable and problematic to portray Indigenous thought as homogenous. However, some common traits can be identified amid this diversity (Blanco, 2013). One of those traits that is particularly relevant to the present discussion is the notion of the earth as mother (Simpson, 2011; Blanco, 2013; Mies and Shiva, 2014). Under this reading, the earth is not treated as an object to be mastered or resource to be manipulated, for nature is not externalized. If nature is our mother then we are necessarily part of nature. But if nature is our mother we are also expected to respect and care for nature. To harm nature is to harm a 'subject, animated matter, materializing spirit' (Mies, 2014b: 161). This is why ecofeminists inspired by Indigenous worldviews 'have repeatedly stressed that the rape of the Earth and rape of women are intimately linked' (Shiva, 2014: xvi). This is also why, when asked about his view on 'sustainable development', a member of the Nishnaabeg people responded by insisting that no such concept can be found in Nishnaabeg thought (Simpson, 2011). For, it contradicts the idea that 'we should be as gentle as possible with our mother, and that we should be taking the bare minimum to ensure our survival' (Simpson, 2011: 141).

Deploying pluriversal intersectionality in the analysis of capitalist domination opens up the scope for moving beyond binary thinking and re-assessing the way domination itself is conceptualized. Under its guise, the domination of non-human nature is, at once, the domination of humans by humans. Correspondingly, non-human nature is not external to the project of human emancipation but integral to it. Its domination by humanity is not the mere product of social domination; both forms of domination depend on and mutually constitutive one another. The ecofeminist and Amerindian Indigenous standpoint allows one to move from a Global North position where treating nature as another subject is regarded as inconceivable and absurd to a position from which externalizing nature and seeking to master it for economic ends are themselves unimaginable and dangerous. At this stage, it is worth reminding ourselves of the critique of Global North philosopher Jürgen Habermas directed at his fellow Frankfurt School member Herbert Marcuse, who envisioned a reconciliation of humanity and nature in emancipation. What Habermas emphatically – and rather sarcastically – dismissed was the idea that one could 'impute subjectivity to animals and plants' and treat non-human nature as a 'partner' in emancipation (Habermas, 1971: 88). His work, therefore, reminds us of the externalization of nature characteristic of this anthropocentric and dualist thinking – a thinking that leads to a conceptualization of emancipation and communication that is strictly incapable of positing the kind of 'fraternal' relation to nature that is at the core of Indigenous worldviews. To do so is, for the modernity/ Habermasian standpoint, to romanticize non-human nature and to adopt the unrealistic position that one could achieve solidarity with it. But, drawing on Indigenous worldviews, Plumwood reminds us that 'it is not the primitiveness and unworthiness of the Other but our own species' arrogance that is the main barrier to forming ethical and responsive relationship with earth others' (2002: 167). She reminds us that dualist thinking of the kind that informs 'rationalist models' of communication, 'which delegitimate the more emotional and bodily forms and aspects of communication, operate to exclude non-humans from full communicative status' (2002: 191). Treating the earth as mother or non-human nature as an earth other, provides a basis upon which to transcend oppressive dualisms, rethink the role of nature in domination and emancipation and visualize a range of possibilities excluded from the Global North perspective on such matters. As we shall now see, it also opens up the scope for clarifying the story of intersectional capitalist domination.

Sketching the story of intersectional capitalist domination

The previous sections were devoted to a discussion of the way structures of domination intersect but provided limited insights into the experiences engendered by capitalist domination. Indeed, while they tackled the logic of othering underpinning diverse structures of domination and upon which capitalism relies to sustain itself, little was said about the way oppression itself is experienced. To explain why and how dualisms are responsible for a range of hierarchies between humans, as well as between humans and non-humans, is one thing. To explain what consequences those hierarchies bear on the human and non-human world is another. Because a sufficiently detailed and robust intersectional analysis of capitalist domination must involve undertaking both tasks, I now turn to the latter.

First, let me reiterate a point central to the analysis developed in earlier parts of this chapter: capitalist structures of domination are mutually constitutive but not reducible to one another. This, in turn, means that while class entails its own logic of domination and engenders experiences that contrast with those marked by patriarchal and environmental domination, the subjugation of nature, women, and colonized peoples made important contributions to the bourgeoisie's supremacy. But how exactly has this mutual constitution manifested itself under capitalism? What kind of story of intersectional capitalist domination could be formulated based on the presuppositions made in the earlier parts of this chapter? Elements of an answer can be found in the work of Anne McClintock (1995), who devoted particular attention to the imperialist tendencies of the Global North and formulated a rather compelling critique of intersectional capitalist domination. Modern colonial power, she argued, justified their imperialist actions on the basis of a myth, which she described as follows:

> The myth of the virgin land is also the myth of the empty land, involving both a gender and a racial dispossession. Within patriarchal narratives, to be virgin is to be empty of desire and void of sexual agency, passively awaiting the thrusting, male insemination of history, language and reason. Within colonial narratives, the eroticizing of 'virgin' space also effects a territorial appropriation,

for if the land is virgin, colonized peoples cannot claim aboriginal territorial rights, and white male patrimony is violently assured as the sexual and military insemination of an interior void. (1995: 30)

Under her reading, the colonial appropriation of land across the globe was made possible by setting in motion a logic of othering whereby both the violently appropriated land and dispossessed Indigenous peoples were gendered, sexualized, and racialized. Both the metropolis and colonies making up the capitalist order, she further noted, came to be subjected to a 'triangulated' system of 'degeneration', in which:

[t]he 'natural' male control of reproduction in heterosexual marriage and the 'unnatural' bourgeois control of capital in the commodity market were legitimized by reference to a third term: the 'abnormal' zone of racial degeneration. Illicit money and illicit sexuality were seen to relate to each other by negative analogy to race. In the symbolic triangle of deviant money – the order of class; deviant sexuality – the order of gender; and deviant race – the order of empire, the degenerate classes were metaphorically bound by a regime of surveillance and were collectively figured as transgressing the proper distributions of money, sexuality and property. (1995: 44)

In order to operate the colonial, patriarchal, heterosexist, and ableist capitalist order must rely on a range of symbolic and material resources. For example, the (material) dispossession of Indigenous peoples rested on their (symbolic) construction, as well as the symbolic construction of women and the land, as 'degenerate classes' (1995: 44). To be exploited, individuals and natural resources must first be deemed exploitable. To be expropriated, they must first be regarded as expropriable. Such a position, that is, the focus on symbolic and material resources for the analysis of intersectional capitalist domination, is aligned with the kind of analysis found within Indigenous worldviews, whereby experiences of violent dispossession make the colonizers' reliance on the construction of those Indigenous peoples as inferior plain to see. But it is also observable in the work of ecofeminists like Plumwood, whose work was discussed earlier, and Dawson, whose critique of 'racialized capitalism' recognizes the importance of 'ideological apparatuses' that 'demonized "inferior humans"' and led to the 'expropriation, exploitation, demonization, and oppression' of people of colour in the USA and elsewhere (2016: 152).

In her response to Dawson's article, however, an ostensibly approving Fraser elaborates on her article devoted to an 'expanded conception of capitalism' and Dawson's own claims, to end up with an approach that falls victim to binary thinking. Such a shortcoming is once more instructive for the task at hand in this section, namely for formulating a story of intersectional capitalist domination. For this reason, it is worth addressing the exchange between Fraser and Dawson again here. In his article Dawson noted that capitalism is racialized to the extent that race has created a within-group differentiation between 'full humans who possess the right to sell their labor and compete within markets, and those that are disposable, discriminated against, and ultimately eliminated or superexploited' (2016: 147–8). Although '[i]nspired by Dawson's discussion', Fraser (2016: 169) took the distinction a step further. She chose to distinguish two logics: one of expropriation and one of exploitation. This distinction, she claims, 'correlates roughly but unmistakably with the "color line"' (2016: 168). Thus, as already noted in earlier parts of this work, Fraser turns a within-group differentiation into a separation between two groups: one of expropriated people of colour and one of exploited white workers. While capitalism relies on both these 'drivers of capital expansion' (Fraser, 2016: 176), one – expropriation – has, under capitalism, historically correlated with racial oppression and the other – exploitation – with class oppression. In so doing, however, Fraser departs from the position of McClintock and, to a certain extent, that of Dawson too. For, to suggest that each logic applies to a different group risks implying that the oppressive mechanisms each entails only applies to one particular group when in fact it can apply to both. What Dawson mainly wanted to highlight is simply that there is something distinctive about the colonial logic of expropriation and exploitation. In addition to this, Fraser's depiction of the latter two mechanisms of oppression as 'drivers of capital accumulation' could mean missing the symbolic processes at work in constructing exploitable and expropriable groups. To be sure, Fraser acknowledges some of those limitations, recognizing, for example, the fact that 'the historically specific cultural logics that promote and authorize' exploitation and expropriation are 'missing' from her account (2016: 176).

Why, then, bring Fraser's work back into a discussion on the story of intersectional domination? Because like many of her articles, her response to Dawson raises a range of crucial issues for conceptualizing domination, while addressing them in problematic terms. Here Fraser does not tell one story but two. Capitalist oppression is the story of exploitation for some and expropriation for others. What this risks achieving is, as already indicated in earlier parts of this work, not only to erect barriers where they do not exist, but also misunderstand the operations of capitalist domination. For, despite recognizing that the two logics 'work together' (2016: 171) and even regularly 'mutually constituted one another' (Fraser, 2016: 172), she reduced this mutual constitution to a mere juxtaposition. As she put it, in the 'United States … the status of the citizen worker acquired much of the aura of freedom that legitimates exploitation by contrast to the dependent, degraded condition of chattel slavery and Indigenous peoples' (2016: 172).

So, rather than showing how, for example, the construction of individuals as not fully humans could, as noted by McClintock, directly contribute to both expropriation and exploitation, she devoted her attention to what separates the two groups. Difference is therefore being established without radical interdependence.

How, then, should one be expected to tell the story in question? I propose to review some of the key and broad ways in which a range of structures of domination have shaped experiences of oppression materially and symbolically. Let's start with class oppression. While it manifests itself materially in the form of, for example, economic exploitation or precarity, dominant economic groups have also been in a position to subjugate lower classes culturally and impose their own 'symbolic forms of thought' on them (Bourdieu, 2000: 175). The dominant classes have economic and cultural/symbolic power. Such a twofold domination is also visible in relation to patriarchal domination. Here, men do not only exert their power economically by confining women to unpaid (reproductive) or precarious forms of labour, but also by celebrating socially constructed masculine norms of behaviour, such as emotional detachment and adversarialism, and denigrating socially constructed feminine norms, such as emotional attachment and altruism (Benería, 1999; Acker, 2004). But race, too, has been deployed as a materially and symbolically structuring principle. Not only has racialization served the purpose of depriving colonized peoples of their land and securing the 'superexploitation' of racialized others, it has also led to their 'demonization' and treatment as 'disposable' individuals (Dawson, 2016). In the metropolis, racial minorities are not only over-represented in the informal economy, prisons, or more likely to perform precarious jobs than white workers, they are also 'locked into the infernal circle' (Fanon, 2000: 261) of racialization, which denies them the capacity for self-definition. Similar oppressive traits can be found in relation to sexual minorities. As D'Emilio (1993) compellingly demonstrated, the emergence of the bourgeois family and corresponding distinction between an idealized sexual identity (heterosexuality) and a despised one (homosexuality), framed the development of capitalist economic relations. In fact, as a 'heterosexist institution that is primarily about the accumulation and distribution of property' (Davis, 2012: 161), the family was instrumental in facilitating, at once, class and sexual oppression. More recently, the legal access to marriage granted to homosexuals led to their assimilation within 'dominant heteronormative assumptions and institutions' (Duggan, 2003: 50), thereby paving the way for a 'demobilized gay constituency and a privatized, depoliticized gay culture anchored in domesticity and consumption' (Duggan, 2003: 50). Their symbolic domination evolved from an attempt to assert their difference – as a pathology or crime – before setting out to eliminate it, to a direct neutralization through assimilation. Finally, the domination of nature, in the form of, for example, intense resource extraction, has relied upon the typically Western and gendered (Merchant, 1990) construction of nature as an object to be mastered and manipulated. Thus, it has also entailed both a material and symbolic domination.

I wish to argue that, uniting the experiences of oppression engendered by different, yet intersecting, structures of domination, is the practice of dispossession. The latter term was defined by Butler and Athanasiou as 'a way of separating people from means of survival [that] is not only a problem of land deprivation but also a problem of subjective and epistemic violence; or, put another way, a problem of discursive and affective appropriation, with crucially gendered and sexualized implications' (2013: 26).

Dispossession not only shapes the experiences of oppression across different structures of capitalist domination, it does so by enforcing the deprivation of material resources like land and symbolic resources like belief systems. In so doing, it inscribes itself on humans and non-humans, bodies and subjectivities. The practice constitutes the central operational logic of what Quijano (2000) called the 'colonial matrix of power', which involves 'exploitation and domination exercised in multiple dimensions of social life, from economy, sexual, or gender relations, to political organizations, structures of knowledge, state institutions, and households' (Grosfoguel, 2007: 218). Because, as I use it here, dispossession refers to the broad but highly oppressive process whereby individuals are denied access to resources, be they material, legal, symbolic, or epistemic, its meaning expands beyond the narrow economic/material version offered by David Harvey (2003) and Robert Nichols (2020), to include the deprivation of extra-economic resources. Take, for example the experiences of dispossession of many asylum seekers who, after enduring dispossession through persecution and violence in their home country, are far too often denied asylum by judges effectively refusing to accept 'their story' and 'their very place in the world' (Washington, 2020: 50). Such an understanding of dispossession is not only shared by Butler and Anathasiou (2013), but also draws on the likes of Simone de Beauvoir (1997), Frantz Fanon (2000), and Gayatri Spivak (2010), who compellingly demonstrated that oppressed individuals are not only denied access to material resources like land but also tend to be denied the capacity to define themselves or 'speak'. For example, Fanon (2000: 260) emphasized how the painful daily experience of racialization involved the deployment of race as a symbolic straight-jacket is. In a similar vein, Spivak, who construed the oppressed as the 'subaltern', insisted on the fact that, 'in the contest of colonial production', these people are denied a 'history and cannot speak' (2010: 41). Such states of affairs are thus marked by a symbolic and epistemic violence paving the way for what de Sousa Santos chose to call 'epistemicide', that is, the 'murder of knowledge' (2014: 92) emanating from dominated groups, that also 'involves the destruction of the social practices and the disqualification of the social agents that operate according to such knowledges' (2014: 153).

But such notable overlaps across different structures of domination should not distract us from grasping the equally important fact that each of them engenders a unique set of experiences of oppression. In short, what they share should not prevent us from seeing differences. For, each set of experiences is not reducible to the other. For example, the experiences of racialization and racism depicted in detail by Frantz Fanon and Achille Mbembe, such as being the 'slave ... of [one's] own appearance' (Fanon, 2000: 260) or the 'falsification of oneself by the other' (Mbembe, 2017: 78), distinguish racial domination from, say, the economic exploitation of white workers or the criminalization of homosexuality. A practice of dispossession may be responsible for engendering those experiences, but its manifestation, effects, and implications differ. This is why in addition to recognizing overlaps and radical interdependence between capitalist structures of domination, it is essential to insist on recognizing their differences. But here difference should not be equated with separation and lead to an aggregative or additive understanding of domination. It should instead be understood as a difference that presupposes the mutual constitution of those structures. This is also why a pluriversal intersectional critique of capitalist domination ought to capture the singularity of each site of struggle and learn from the experiences located in them. Finally, this is why before completing my sketch of capitalist domination's brutal story of dispossession, I wish to turn to an often overlooked site of struggle in sociology (Oliver, 1990) and intersectionality studies (Lutz, Vivar, and Supik, 2011: introduction): disability.

It is indeed shocking and surprising that, despite affecting large sections of the population, 'no group on the "revolutionary Left" ... takes disablement seriously' (Sutherland cited in Abberley, 1987: 13). Some have even actively rejected the possibility of including disability within the scope of intersectionality, noting that the 'corporeal reality of disability imposes daily lived constraints and obstacles on persons with disabilities' that are far too distinctive to be qualified as forms of oppression in the same terms as, say, race and gender (Sommo and Chaskes, 2013: 50). Such a position has nevertheless been severely criticized by critical disability scholars like Mike Oliver (1990) and Paul Abberley (1996), who insist on regarding disability as a full-blown form of site oppression, on a par with class, racial, and gender oppression. To them, one ought to regard disability as a social construct: as a socially conditioned set of meanings attributed to an impairment. For example, Oliver (1990: 4) contends that capitalism has contributed to the medicalization of disability and its treatment as a 'handicap', 'abnormality', and personal inadequacy. He traces the origins of this construction to the 'construction of the individual' (Oliver, 1990: 44) that capitalism brought about and served as a basis for the material deprivation and stigmatization of impaired individuals. Capitalism, in short, created economic (wage-breadwinner system and productivism) and cultural (self-reliance, personal responsibility etc.) conditions that played a major role in constructing impairment as a disability and, by the same token, turning it into an oppressive structuring principle in social life. Like class, race, gender, and sexuality, then, disability served to deny groups the capacity to flourish materially and symbolically.

But one also learns something new and important by deploying an intersectional lens and turning to this particular site of struggle. First, doing so reinforces the view that the symbolic logic of othering and material deprivation are mutually constitutive and reiterates the necessity to move beyond oppressive binaries, like the disabled and non-disabled binary. Second, it further entrenches the bourgeois family and the separation between work and home within the capitalist logic of oppression, that is, as an institution not only serving the interests of white heterosexual men, but also those of non-disabled people (Oliver, 1990: 35). Third, it sheds new light onto the conception of the subject inscribed in capitalist relations, exposing how capitalism codes the incapacity to achieve self-reliance and economic productivity not merely as an inferiority but also as a deficiency. Under such a reading, capitalism comes to be seen as a 'social system organised around the taken-for-granted desirability for independence, work and physical normality [that] cannot admit of exceptions to this world-view' (Abberley, 1996: 64). In turn, and as will be further discussed in the next chapter, it encourages one to depart from the 'work-based model of social citizenship and identity' (Abberley, 1996: 74) around which capitalism, as well as dominant socialist perspectives, have been articulated. As such, the site of struggle marked by the category of disability adds its own range of plots and twists to the story of intersectional capitalist domination. Like class, gender, race, sexuality, and nature, it structures experiences of oppression based on a distinct set of features. For this very simple reason, the turn to disability executed earlier could be said to reinforce the view that each of the categories of oppression are not reducible to each other. But of course, one learns more from this exercise. The experiences of oppression structured by disability provide an additional standpoint from which to understand the oppressive character of capitalism and, without which, the full reach, effects, and limits of capitalist dispossessional practices could not be grasped.

So, to understand how intersectional capitalist domination unfolds and operates, a core emphasis must be placed on dispossessional practices, the structures giving rise to them and agencies facilitating their intervention in social life. I would argue that in addition to the *logic of othering*, which an inherently unequal system like capitalism turns into an instrument for justifying oppression, intersectional capitalist domination rests on an *ecology of dispossession* sustained through *agencies of dispossession*. The term ecology is being used here to draw attention the diversity of dispossessional *practices* and *agencies* marking capitalist domination, as well as to the complex and relational character of their interactions. What we learn by bringing different struggles against domination into dialogue with one another is that exploitation and expropriation make up the core of such practices. They are dispossessional to the extent that, on the one hand, exploitation denies humans and non-humans their dignity and access to material resources through taking an unfair advantage of them. This is reflected in, for example, the bourgeois' appropriation of the surplus value created by the worker, or men's treatment of women in, say, prostitution or pornography. On the other, expropriation involves a process through which material and symbolic resources are effectively arrogated. While the former affects action by hindering it, the latter affects it by removing something that is pre-existing. Although they support capital accumulation, exploitation and expropriation are more than merely economic practices with material implications; more than a mere 'accumulation by other means' (Fraser, 2016: 166). They are also the non-coercive but violent confiscation of the power to control the means of representation or, in the case of nature, the denial by human nature of non-human nature's 'materialising spirit'. As a member of the working class, woman, person of colour, homosexual, earth other or disabled person, one is subjected to practices of exploitation and expropriation. Some groups, like Black Americans or Indigenous peoples in the case of expropriation (Dawson, 2016), might be more exposed to one set of practices than others, but all tend to experience oppression in the form of dispossession, often constituted and reinforced by the exploitation and expropriation affecting individuals in other social locations (McClintock, 1995; Plumwood, 2002).

Those practices are upheld by agencies of dispossession: capital, the state, colonialism, (instrumental) reason, and the family. For example, the drive towards capital accumulation leads to the exploitation of workers and expropriation of Indigenous peoples. The state mobilizes the resources and creates the legal system, such as private property rights, that make those practices possible. Furthermore, while the colony administers those practices outside the metropolis, the metropolitan bourgeois family ensures that the wage-earner is freed from the 'burden' of 'private' matters to attain the highest degree of efficiency and productivism. Reason is harnessed for the purpose of extracting resources and value. Each agency, then, facilitates the smooth functioning and/or expansion of the capitalist order. But, in order to do so, they must also play an ideological function. The state, for example, diffuses schemes of perception serving to naturalize particular ways of thinking and behaving, like personal responsibility, individualism, or consumerism (Bourdieu, 2000). The family has served the celebration of heterosexual relations and demonization of homosexuality. Finally, each of those agencies constitute one another. For example, the colony is 'capital in action' (Cabral,

2016: 161). It not only serves capital expansion but is also driven by it. The state enshrines the family in the law. The family secures the reproduction of an efficient and productive workforce, that is, a workforce best suited for accumulating capital. Reason divides, separates, and segregates in the service of capital. To be sure, additional relations of mutual constitution between dispossessional agencies could be reviewed here but they are sufficient to show how and why capitalist domination rests on a complex configuration of practices and agencies, which bears several implications for thinking emancipation and renewing socialist thought – implications that will be discussed at length in the next chapter.

One of the key lessons one can draw from telling the story of capitalist domination as one of dispossession is that in addition to making explicit the relationality of different systems of oppression, it opens up the scope for a form of resistance disposed to assert 'the interdependency of lives that are mutually implicated in one another' (Butler and Athanasiou, 2013: 107). While dispossession can, as shown so far, mark a condition of acute oppression, it is a term that can also become

> an occasion for thinking through the issue of responsiveness and responsibility: taking responsibility for one's own position in the world and relationality to others. We might consider what kinds of enabling spaces of politics open up on occasions where we find ourselves affected, undone, and bound by others' calls to respond and assume responsibility. In a world of differentially shared sociality, if we are already 'outside ourselves', beyond ourselves, given over, bound to others, and bound by claims that emerge from outside or from deep inside ourselves, our very notion of responsibility requires this sense of dispossession as disposition, exposure, and self-othering. (Butler and Athanasiou, 2013: 105–6)

A 'dispossessed subjectivity' is cultivated by the condition of 'non-being and non-having' (Butler and Athanasiou, 2013: 19) and consequently forces individuals to recognize their radical interdependence. The acute vulnerability dispossession engenders compels us to acknowledge our exposure and relationality to others and, in the process, adopt a disposition that recognizes that one's freedom 'can only come into being … on the occasion of relations with others' (Butler and Athanasiou, 2013: 122). Dispossession, therefore, oppresses, but 'dispossessed subjectivities' holds 'subversive potentialities' (Butler and Athanasiou, 2013: 140).

To sum up, then, the story of intersectional capitalist domination offered here shows that the 'domination of nature by man has involved also … the domination of human being by human being' (Davis, 1998: 163), and reveals how the latter is both a contributing factor to, and product of, the former.

It sets out to grasp how, for example, the repression of homosexuality is inscribed in capitalist economic relations (of domination) or how 'the class hierarchies that produce [the] differentiation between the super-rich and the rest of us are already shot through with gender and race and sexual hierarchies' (Davis, 2013: 436). The story of intersectional capitalist domination is, above all, a story of practices of dispossession enacted across a diverse range of mutually constitutive structures of domination and supported by different, but intricately imbricated, agencies. Consequently, the renewal of socialism must be developed on the basis of a careful examination of this ecology and do more than merely limit its scope to the transformation of economic and political structures. It must proceed not only through a re-assessment of the way needs are satisfied and political decision-making is organized, but also through a critique of Cartesian/modernist ontology and epistemology, as well as a critique of institutions often excluded from the scope of the critique of political economy, like the family.

Conclusion

In this chapter I endeavoured to develop an analysis of capitalist domination in pluriversal intersectional terms. I began the discussion with the Fraser/Butler debate, which served to expose the dangers associated with binary thinking. Deploying the relational logic of pluriversal intersectionality in order to transcend this oppressive form of thinking, it was shown, entails more than merely recognizing how a category of oppression compounds another. It entails telling a story of domination very different from the one offered by Fraser. For, there is something qualitatively different about a critique that reveals how the repression of sexuality is shot *through* with class oppression, from a critique that speaks of a despised sexuality in *addition* to class oppression. The implications of this distinction fully unravelled within the discussion of the struggle for nature. Here the mutual constitution of human-to-human and human-to-non-human forms of oppression was highlighted and a non-anthropocentric conception of capitalist domination was proposed. Shifting our attention to the category of nature provided insights into oppression that could not otherwise have been attainable. It turned the critique of (capitalist) binary thinking to a critique of the society/nature binary and revealed its fundamental role in domination. The hierarchizing logic of othering through which capitalism organizes the world, it was shown, creates distinctively favourable conditions for a range of dispossessional practices across diverse but mutually constitutive structures of domination.

   The story of intersectional capitalist domination offered here, therefore, lays the conceptual groundwork for a coalitional understanding of emancipation. This is executed by recognizing the fundamental role of binary thinking, particularly the society/nature binary, plays in upholding the symbolic and material dispossession. Such a story continues to be played out under the neoliberal stage of capitalist development. The privatization of public assets and spaces, withdrawal of social security provisions, the silencing of race through its removal from the 'lexicon of public administrative arrangements' (Goldberg, 2009: 341) and cult of personal responsibility have all, in their own way, served to reproduce, if not exacerbate, the dispossessional character of capitalism across radically interdependent structures of domination (Masquelier, 2017). For example, the decision in the late 1990s by New York Mayor Rudolph Giuliani to privatize several public spaces and close down publicly recognizable sexual outlets like the Times Square sex shops and adult bookstores denied queer people the resources upon which they relied to express their sexuality. Driven by 'real estate interests' and 'petit bourgeois moralism', this form of dispossession is of both a material and symbolic form in virtue of denying queer people both the physical spaces and cultural resources for self-expression (Warner, 1999: 161).

The story of intersectional capitalist domination as depicted in this chapter bears significant implications for the conceptualization of emancipation itself, not least in terms of the symbolic and material practices appropriate for moving beyond oppressive dualisms. It is to those implications which I now turn.

4

Pluriversal Emancipation

Introduction

The project of emancipation has long been central to a wide range of struggles against domination. In the late nineteenth and early twentieth century, for example, feminists drew a lot of their inspiration (Coole, 2015) from the anti-slavery movement's demand for the 'elimination of oppression' (Wright, 1993) as the basis for their emancipation. Inspired by Marx's (2000e) call for 'complete human emancipation', the labour movement also came to adopt it as a core aspiration. Under this guise, it became closely associated with the project of emancipating society from an oppressive capitalist system – from exploitation, alienation, and the oppressive power of the bourgeoise. But from the 1970s onwards, the project fell out of favour among critics of capitalism. With the rise of so-called 'new social movements' and post-structuralist and post-humanist approaches, the possibility and desirability of an emancipatory project came to be questioned. Jean-Francois Lyotard (1984), for example, declared the end of master narratives articulated around a collective vision for emancipation. Similarly, Anthony Giddens (1991) characterized the 'late modern' age partly in terms of a demise of emancipatory politics in favour of 'life politics', thereby marking a turn away from collective and universalizing forms of political demands and action directed at structural change.

But while 'major sectors of the white-dominated left' have been historically unable to articulate their emancipatory politics around a sufficiently robust analysis of interlocking systems of oppression (Dawson, 2013: 15), intersectionality theorists have continued to insist on both the possibility and desirability for such a project, emphasizing the distinctively emancipatory outlook of a theory aimed at developing a nuanced and complex account of capitalist domination (see for example Davis, 2012; Smooth, 2013; Collins, 2019). In this chapter I develop a conceptualization of emancipation based on some of the core elements of the story of intersectional capitalist domination offered in the preceding chapter. The aim consists in drawing the contours of the emancipatory project that will inform the socialist vision formulated in this book. I begin this task by explaining why emancipation is a more appropriate concept than, say, a politics of self-actualization, for capturing the essence of pluriversal intersectionality's critical outlook. I devote the rest of the chapter to exploring what a pluriversal emancipatory vision entails. This is executed by, first, understanding the relationship between particularity and universality. Finally, I turn to a discussion of the agent of change entailed by a pluriversal approach to emancipation.

Why emancipation?

In a footnote devoted to clarifying the origins of the term 'emancipation', Erik Olin Wright (2010: 10) shared an informal conversation he had with the prominent theorist of power, Steven Lukes. The latter, Wright claims, traced the origins of emancipation to the anti-slavery movement. For the movement in question, emancipation came to be associated with 'liberal notions of freedom and achieving full liberal rights' (Wright, 2010: 10). The 'freedom from bondage' or removal of hindrances to self-realization entailed by the term emancipation was thus interpreted as a matter specific to a group denied rights granted to others. As such, it entailed the elimination of slaves' oppression through the equalization of legal rights within the liberal-capitalist order. Emancipation was about giving slaves 'the freedom to determine *what [they] can become*' (Hardt and Negri, 2009: 331–2) within the parameters of the liberal system of rights.[1] This outlook, marked by a drive to liberate a particular group from servitude by campaigning for the introduction of new rights, inspired feminists from the nineteenth century up until the civil rights movements (Coole, 2015). But during the twentieth century the term was 'appropriated' by the Left 'to refer to a broader vision of eliminating all forms of oppression' (Wright, 2010: 10). Emancipation would no longer be confined to a group, for example, slaves or women. It would now consist in universalizing the rights and opportunities for self-realization to all, through the struggle against class oppression. Under this reading, emancipation came to include large-scale social transformation, that is, a complete change of system – socialism – as the goal of collective action. But this approach to emancipation was not confined to the class struggle. Even what came to be known as the LGBT liberation movement demanded radical change, before it shifted its emphasis from a demand for 'universal transformations of social structures' to the much less radical and more assimilationist juridical demand for the recognition of queer identity's legitimacy (Jagose, 1996: 60–1).

What conception, then, best captures the essence of pluriversal intersectionality? Insofar as it is regarded as a critical theory, it embodies 'aspirations for social transformation and social change' (Collins, 2019: 53).

The task of securing emancipation from domination, therefore, presupposes much more than the mere introduction of new rights. This is explained by pluriversal intersectionality's holistic character, that is, its inclination to analyse interlocking and interdependent systems of oppression and postulate an emancipatory project capable to tackling these systems at once. Pluriversal intersectionality paves the way for a holistic conception of emancipation, which could not be realistically given form by merely reforming the established order. The roots of pluriversal intersectional domination are structural. Emancipation construed in pluriversal terms, therefore, entails the removal of those structures of domination. An affinity between the socialist vision of emancipation and pluriversal intersectionality's own can therefore be observed here.

However, it is worth reminding ourselves of the fact that many intersectionality theorists tend to be severely critical of Marxism and, consequently, of the Marxist project of emancipation. They are unsatisfied with it for two main reasons. First, they are uncomfortable with the universalist rhetoric of class politics. Under its reading, the struggle against exploitation and alienation is understood as a struggle for humanity as a whole. The emancipation of the working class is, at once, the emancipation of humanity for, according to Marx (2000b), the working class is the 'universal class'. This vision of emancipation is problematic for intersectionality theorists not only because it appears to exclude a range of oppressive and emancipatory mechanisms within its scope or treats them as 'epiphenomenal to primary class relations' (Bohrer, 2018: 47), but also because it rests on the kind of binary thinking through which capitalist domination operates (Collins, 2000: 270; Bohrer, 2018: 47). Indeed, it entails 'ranking human oppressions' and raising the experiences of oppression of a group of economically exploited and alienated workers, in which white males are over-represented, above all others (Collins, 2000: 270). It mobilizes a universalist rhetoric of class politics that far too closely resembles the kind of logic through which colonial domination operated. As Mbembe noted, colonization was driven by 'universal reason', which 'assumed the existence of subjects of the same name, whose universality was founded on their humanity' and, as such, made possible the 'recognition of a common humanity' (2017: 97). But, at the very same time colonial powers deployed reason to divide and hierarchize. They deployed race as a divisive organizing principle of colonial life so as to justify their violent rule over colonized territories. An abstract universality came to conceal a concrete and very real oppressive process of othering. Reducing the project of emancipation to the struggle against class oppression, therefore, runs the risk of constructing an abstract universality concealing within-group differences and subsuming some struggles under others.

Thus, while the pluriversal project of emancipation is holistic, it cannot aspire to become universalist. Could it therefore be better understood in terms of an altogether different form of political demands, such as those embodied in struggles for self-actualization or what Giddens (1991) called 'life politics'? The answer is, once again, an emphatic 'no'. Like class politics, the term 'life politics' does not adequately capture the essence of demands embodied in the pluriversal emancipatory project. Take, for example, Giddens' definition of the term:

> Life politics does not primarily concern the conditions which liberate us in order to make choices: it is a politics of choice. While emancipatory politics is a politics of life chances, life politics is a politics of life style. Life politics is a politics of a reflexively mobilized order – the system of late modernity. … It is a politics of self-actualization in a reflexively ordered environment, where that reflexivity links self and body to systems of global scope. (Giddens, 1991: 214)

Life politics contrasts sharply with class politics, in as much as it does not predicate self-actualization on the removal of structural hindrances to it. But like class politics, it is an inadequate form of political action for the pluriversal emancipatory project. First, it fails to capture the complex ways in which contemporary political actors articulate their concerns and demands (Pleyers, 2010; Sörbom and Wennerhag, 2011; Flesher-Fominaya, 2014; della Porta, 2015; Masquelier, 2017). Members of the Global Justice and Occupy movements, for example, have combined demands for socio-economic restructuring with demands for self-fulfillment (Sörbom and Wennerhag, 2011; Flesher-Fominaya, 2014; della Porta, 2015). Second, as alluded to earlier, 'life politics' presuppose the possibility for self-actualization without requiring large-scale social transformation. The vast quantity of material goods and information made available by various technological developments supported by the economic and political structures of the late modern world (read: hyper-globalized capitalist world) is thought to have created a 'reflexively ordered environment' in which individuals have become personally responsible for actualizing the self. The 'politics of self-actualization' do, in this sense, lead, at most, to a mere reform of the system, of the kind Giddens (1998) himself contributed to in the form of the New Labour politics in the UK. But it also leads to an individualized form of political action. For the politics of self-actualization are ultimately 'politics of *individual* life style' (Sörbom and Wennerhag, 2011 – emphasis added). Under the 'reflexive environment' marked by late modernity, individuals express political demands that are directed at the realization of 'self-identity' (Giddens, 1991) and not at the collective emancipation of one or more groups. Third, then, the individual outlook of life politics is incompatible with the kind of relational ontology and collective posture marking pluriversal political action.

Many of the features of life politics that are incompatible with the pluriversal emancipatory project can also be found in Foucault's own conceptualization of liberation or self-empowerment. Like the politics of self-actualization, Foucault's approach presupposes an individual form of political action. Whether it is construed as a 'concern for the self' (Foucault, 1997) or 'counter-conduct' (Foucault, 2009), political action aimed at liberating individuals from oppressive structures of power is said to involve an autonomous and independent process of self-transformation (Coole, 2015: 538) that 'tries to avoid the managing of population policies and institutions by acting differently' (Lilia and Vinthagen 2013: 121). Thus, it is at once individualized and transgressive. While the latter feature differentiates it from life politics, Foucault's approach remains a form of micro-politics that tells us little about the way 'counter-conducts' can 'become stabilized into enduring strategic patterns' (Cronin, 1996: 63) and pave the way for new (emancipatory) institutions and practices. For this reason, it is also an inadequate basis upon which to conceptualize the pluriversal emancipatory project.

There is a final set of orientations that intersectionality theory has often been associated with, encompassed by the term 'identity politics'. Both the person who coined the term intersectionality, Kimberlé Crenshaw (1991), and the members of the CRC (Taylor, 2017) used the term in question to describe the form of political action intersectional thinking is expected to lead to. However, the 'academic discourse on identity politics' moved towards a trajectory that would sharply depart from the meaning Crenshaw and others had originally ascribed to the term (Collins, 2019: 138). Despite being originally used to refer to 'inclusionary politics within group-based identity politics' (Collins, 2019: 138), the term came to assume an exclusionary outlook. To speak of a politics of identity came to entail turning one's identity, say a working-class woman of colour, into a basis on which to other and exclude. Identity is here being essentialized and deployed as a means to exclude and hierarchize. Understood in such terms, therefore, identity politics is inherently incompatible with the pluriversal intersectional emancipatory project. Member of the CRC, Barbara Smith, clarified what she and her fellow members intended to mean by the term:

> What we were saying is that we have a right as people who are not just female, who are not solely Black, who are not just lesbians, who are not just working class, or workers – that we are people who embody all of these identities, and we have a right to build and define political theory and practice based upon that reality. That was all we were trying to say. That's what we meant by 'identity politics'. We didn't mean that if you're not the same as us, you're nothing. (Smith, 2017: 61)

Intersectionality theorists condemn the logic of othering upon which capitalist oppression rests. Therefore, they cannot be expected to align themselves with a form of political action that replicates this exclusionary logic. To speak of identity in the terms anticipated by Crenshaw and Smith, among others, means postulating a conception of self-hood that is not essentialized but dialogical and relational. It entails working out a radical interdependence through differences and asserting a conception of identity that is not given or particularistic but results from a dialogical engagement between individuals within diverse social locations. Under this understanding of identity politics, then, people are said to 'derive their identities from their politics rather than their politics from their identities' (Cho, Crenshaw, and McCall, 2013: 803). To become an acceptable basis for a pluriversal intersectional emancipatory project, identity politics must therefore abandon its particularistic aspirations and involve '"negotiated" conceptions' of group-based identities and interests (Bohrer, 2018: 58).

The freedom it seeks to realize is therefore social or collective. The self-actualization of one is thought to be constitutive of the self-actualization of another. Put more concretely, the pluriversal emancipatory project presupposes that no genuine self-actualization for women can be obtained without creating conditions favourable for the self-actualization of, say, people of colour and the working class. This is because, first, a large proportion of women are women of colour and belong to the working class. But it is also because capitalism, patriarchy, racism, and colonialism intersect in ways that make the genuine defeat of one depend on the genuine defeat of the other. Pluriversal emancipation is, in this sense, consistent with Indigenous principles like *Ubuntu* in South Africa or *sumak kawsay* among the Quechua peoples of the Andes. For, under their guise collective well-being, including self-actualization, is understood as a matter of mutual reciprocity. Individual and collective self-actualization are in fact deemed inextricable to the extent that each conditions the other.

But how is such an approach to emancipation expected to counter the dispossessional practices of capitalist domination? As we saw in Chapter 3, to dispossess means to enforce deprivation on humans and non-humans. According to John Washington, to be dispossessed means to be 'denied the right to grow and blossom', to be 'denied freedom and denied life' (2020: 188). It means to deprive non-human nature of its capacity to regenerate itself and of its agential capacities. It means to deprive humans of the symbolic, material and even legal resources required for the full development of their abilities, that is, for their self-actualization. But since, with an emancipatory approach of the kind developed here, self-actualization depends on liberating individuals from structures of domination, countering dispossession effectively entails large-scale structural change. It does not mean opposing dispossession with a 'logic of possession', as feared by Chandler and Reid (2018). The antithesis to dispossession is not the possessive individualism of capitalist relations, but *emancipatory self-actualization*: achieving the kind of structural change necessary for institutionalizing the mechanisms of redistribution and recognition deemed essential for collective self-actualization. It means redistributing resources fairly and equitably, while empowering individuals to shape the political and economic decisions that affect their lives and the norms that govern them. The next chapters shall be devoted to envisioning the institutions and practices such an emancipatory project entails.

In sum, then, a pluriversal intersectional project of emancipation cannot be expected to assume a strictly universalistic or particularistic outlook. While it rejects the logic according to which a particular set of interests is universalized and others are violently repressed, it also condemns the kind of essentializing particularism that does not so much celebrate difference as assert it in order to exclude others. On the one hand, universalist aspirations risk turning into oppressive mechanisms. On the other, particularistic aspirations risk becoming exclusionary. The freedom driving pluriversal emancipation is inherently social, seeking to oppose dispossession with a collective demand for the rights and resources to blossom. In the next section I address the relationship between the particularity/difference and universality/commonality such a conception of emancipation entails.

Conceptualizing pluriversal emancipation

Given the centrality of dualisms in much Global North scholarship, construing emancipation in neither universalist nor particularist terms can prove challenging. This discussion illustrates this well. In an effort to transcend this binary, whose components are construed as antithetical in modernist thinking, attempts to rethink the relationship between particularism and universalism have surfaced. Concepts like 'multitude' (Hardt and Negri, 2004), 'borderlands' (Anzaldúa, 1987), 'pluriversality' (Escobar, 2018), 'commoning' (Federici, 2019) 'dis-identification' (Muñoz, 1999), and 'assemblages' (Puar, 2007) have all, in their own way, represented attempts to remedy the problems associated with the particularity/universality binary. Under a modernist reading, particularism is thought to be incompatible with universalism. While the former highlights the singularity of, say, a group, and proudly asserts its difference often by erecting walls and fences between other groups and itself, the latter cannot tolerate difference and often suppresses it. Both stand in opposition to one another. Thus, under the particularity/universality binary, it has become difficult to envision a situation where the free expression of one's difference does not lead to divisions in the Global North, like the kind of division Donald Trump and Brexit campaigners sought to capitalize on. Conversely, '[m]any fear that universalism implies uniformity and the denial of the extraordinary variety of human life' (Sayer, 2011: 99).

But, as noted, the consequences of this binary do not stop here. The particularity/universality binary, along with its sister binaries nature/culture and body/soul binaries, have also acted as a structuring mechanism within the Global North and in colonies. Under its guise, the 'Western subject is universal, while the racialized subject is particular' (Smith, 2010: 42). Heterosexuality and masculinity are universalized; homosexuality and femininity are particularized. But, as Michael Dawson rightly pointed out, this 'conception of the "universal" is anything but universal' (2013: 149). Instead, 'it is grounded in a European [and heteronormative] historical experience that privileges the experiences of a relatively narrow segment of toilers' (Dawson, 2013: 149). The binary in question upholds a form of thinking that is either exclusionary or repressive and cannot, consequently, be expected to inform a pluriversal conception of emancipation. In what follows I provide an alternative to this binary and do so by drawing inspiration from a range of approaches that have not only condemned it, but also offered different bases upon which to think emancipation, such as Indigenous perspectives and queer scholarship. I will show that moving beyond the tension between particularism and universalism requires us to think differently about identity and difference.

Lessons from queer thought

I begin the discussion with perspectives on the relationship between particularity and universality emanating from studies on gender and sexuality found within the Global North and often referred to as queer studies. This set of approaches is of particular interest here for several reasons. First, like many intersectionality scholars, queer scholars have played a key role in contesting the kind of binary thinking that leads to profoundly oppressive hierarchies like those articulated around sexual identity. Queer thought has in fact emerged in response to the identitarian tendencies found within 'lesbian and gay' studies. Identity is here transgressed for the ends of emancipating the self from the dispossessional tendencies of heteronormative identificatory practice. Second, given queer thought's twofold emphasis on gender and sexuality, it is inherently open to intersectional analysis. Some queer scholars have even gone further, including categories like race within their analysis (Cohen, 1997; Smith, 2010; Puar, 2007).[2] Third, queer thought's celebration of non-essentialist particularity/difference aims to overcome the dangers associated with divisive identity politics (Jagose, 1996). As such, it has contributed to the development of innovative (post-identitarian) conceptions of freedom and equality (Butler, 1990; Muñoz, 2019). Finally, several queer scholars have emphasized, and indeed promoted, queer theory's utopian content

(Halperin, 1995; Muñoz, 2019). Queer scholarship, therefore, provides a rather convenient starting point for beginning to think of liberation beyond binary thinking. But what exactly does queer theory entail? What can one learn from it about the relationship between particularity and universality? What conception(s) of freedom and equality could emanate from this relationship?

The word 'queer' is particularly difficult to define, mainly because definitions tend to entail a kind of structuring and identitarian stability that queer scholars seek to resist (Jagose, 1996). Prominent queer scholar, David Halperin, nevertheless provided a rather detailed and instructive description of the term, which is worth quoting at length:

> queer identity need not be grounded in any positive truth or in any stable reality. As the very word implies, 'queer' does not name some natural kind or refer to some determinate object; it acquires its meaning from its oppositional relation to the norm. Queer is by definition *whatever* is at odds with the normal, the legitimate, the dominant. *There is nothing in particular which it necessarily refers.* It is an identity without an essence. 'Queer', then, demarcates not a positivity but a positionality vis-a-vis the normative – a positionality that is not restricted to lesbians and gay men but is in fact available to anyone who is or who feels marginalized because of her or his sexual practices: it could include some married couples without children, for example, or even (who knows?) some married couples *with* children-with, perhaps, *very naughty* children. 'Queer', in any case, does not designate a class of already objectified pathologies or perversions; rather, it describes a horizon of possibility whose precise extent and heterogeneous scope cannot in principle be delimited in advance. It is from the eccentric positionality occupied by the queer subject that it may become possible to envision a variety of possibilities for reordering the relations among sexual behaviors, erotic identities, constructions of gender, forms of knowledge, regimes of enunciation, logics of representation, modes of self-constitution, and practices of community – for restructuring, that is, the relations among power, truth, and desire. (1995: 62)

Rather than an identity, then, queer could be said to refer to a transgressive attitude. For queer scholars, identity thinking far too easily slips into a reifying and oppressive essentialism. Queer thought is a critique of heteronormativity that, as I will explain shortly, has often developed into a '*critique* of identity' (Jagose, 1996: 131, emphasis in original) *tout court*. Complementing this critique is a 'world-making' (Warner, 1999; Floyd,

2009) function, for queer thought is inherently transformative. Let me start exploring this transformative content by reviewing some of the key features of the queer critique of heteronormativity.

Central to the work of queer scholars is the critique of 'compulsory heterosexuality' (Rich, 1993), that is, the rejection of the running assumption that men and women are innately heterosexual. Their critique consists in both contesting its universalist tendencies by, for example, historicizing sexuality and exposing it as something 'produced' (Foucault, 1978) or 'invented' (Weeks, 2003). Michel Foucault (1978), for example, traced the emergence of an identity constructed around sexual desire to an ostensibly sexually repressive Victorian age that, by the mere fact of having to speak about sex to regulate it 'through useful and public discourses' (Foucault, 1978: 25), led to 'reification of sensory-affect into identities' (Hennessy, 2000: 105). The nineteenth century marked the emergence of the homosexual as 'type of life, a life form, and a morphology' (Foucault, 1978: 43). According to Foucault, the 'sodomite had been a temporary aberration; the homosexual was now a species' (1978: 43). However, while heterosexuality was normalized, homosexuality was pathologized. The regulation of sex and sexuality led to the universalization of heterosexuality and particularization of the homosexual as a 'form of life' to be disciplined. To be queer, then, entails not only recognizing the oppressive character of this universal/particular binary, but also to oppose all attempts at naturalizing sexual identity, whatever its form. For, it is precisely this naturalization that is responsible for the deployment of sex as a regulatory, even repressive, organizing principle of social life.

Inspired by Foucault's work, Butler (1990) condemned just as fervently the 'naturalization' of heterosexuality. She nevertheless insisted that it cannot be understood and explained in isolation from a detailed analysis of the 'sedimentation' and 'reification' of 'gender reality' (1990: xxiii). According to Butler, masculinity and femininity are inextricably tied to sexuality. Under the guise of heteronormativity, to be a man means to be a husband and father; to be a woman entails being a wife and mother. Heteronormativity does not merely assume one's heterosexuality – it discursively constructs this assumption on the basis of a discursively constructed gender reality. Both gender and sexuality are in this sense signified in heteronormative terms. Desire is 'heterosexualised' (Butler, 1990: 23) and gender, like heterosexuality, is a *compulsory* performance' (Butler, 1993: 314–15, emphasis in original). Resisting heteronormativity from a queer perspective, therefore, entails more than merely opposing a hegemonic discourse on sexuality. It also involves deconstructing and transgressing a reified gender reality through the celebration of non-normative performative acts, that is, performances falling outside the discursive scope of hegemonic gender reality. Gender and sexuality would here be re-signified as what has come to be known as 'non-binary' – neither male nor female; neither gay, nor straight. Re-signifying practices of that kind, therefore, could be regarded as performances of resistance against heteronormativity. They constitute what José Esteban Muñoz called a process of 'dis-identification', which entails 'cracking open the code of the majority' and proceeding 'to use this code as raw material for representing a disempowered politics or positionality that has been rendered unthinkable by the dominant culture' (1999: 31).

Because individuals (dis-)identifying as queer not only oppose hegemonic sexual and gender performances, but also resist reifying identificatory practices themselves, they effectively transgress heteronorms by celebrating a non-essentialized and non-particularizable difference. To be queer – or non-binary – means, at least, to resist essentialist and reifying identity thinking (Butler, 1990; Halperin, 1995; Muñoz, 1999) and, at most, resisting identity thinking *tout court* (Jagose, 1996; Puar, 2007; Hardt and Negri, 2009). For, as shown by the likes of Foucault, identity construction is often the first step towards exclusionary and repressive discursive practices. What queer scholarship tends to insist on, in fact, is that it is not only possible to resist existing practices of significatory dispossession (with material implications) associated with compulsory heterosexuality, but also that doing so must involve the transgression of existing identificatory practices. This, as I will show next, need not entail a blanket rejection of identity thinking and, as I will show now, is compatible with holistic thinking.

As Halperin explicitly stated in the passage earlier, queer refers to 'a positionality that is not restricted to lesbians and gay men but is in fact available to anyone'. What queer thinking effectively aims to resist is 'binary and hierarchical reasoning in general' (Marinucci, 2010: 33). For this reason, its critique is particularly well-positioned to expose and oppose the structures of domination marking capitalist modernity. In fact, for many queer scholars, the reach of heteronormativity extends far beyond the realms of sex and gender (see for example Warner, 1999; Hennessy, 2000; Berlant and Warner, 2002; Ferguson, 2004; Floyd, 2009). For example, heteronorms have performed an instrumental function in the reproduction of the capitalist order. As queer Marxist scholar Rosemary Hennessy noted, '[u]nder capitalism the patriarchal heteronorms that the institution of marriage helps secure do not function apart from the relations of production' (2000: 63). 'Marriage', she explains, 'has historically helped provide a system for ensuring women's unpaid household labor' (2000: 63). While she insists that '[c]apitalism does not structurally require patriarchal gender asymmetry' she shows how 'the heteronormative marriage arrangements of private patriarchy secured the bourgeois wife as a domestic worker' (2000: 65). Also, historically, 'marriage has protected property by serving as a dense transfer point for land and inheritance [and] serv[ing] property interests by sanctioning the privatisation of the production of labor power'

(Hennessy, 2000: 64). Those claims, which echo those of several socialist feminists such as those whose work was discussed in Chapter 2, point towards a revolutionary role of queer thinking, where the latter could serve as a means for subverting both capitalism and heteronormativity. For many queer scholars, therefore, resisting heteronormativity entails resisting binary thinking and capitalism at once.

Other queer scholars have identified an even closer, if not inextricable, connection between heteronormativity and capitalism. For example, in texts frequently cited by queer scholars, Samuel Delany (1999) and Michael Warner (1999) analysed the 'zoning laws' introduced in the 1980s by New York mayor Rudolf Giuliani as an instance of class war intertwined with sexual repression. '[D]riven by real estate interests' but introduced in the name of 'safe sex' by the conservative mayor, those laws criminalized a range of sex acts, limited adult establishments of various forms and facilitated the privatization of public spaces (Delany, 1999; Warner, 1999). Their consequences were significant for the queer population in New York:

> Now gay men who want sexual materials, or who want to meet men for sex, will have two choices: they can cathect the privatized virtual public of phone sex and the Internet; or they can travel to small, inaccessible, little-trafficked, badly lit areas, remote from public transportation and from any residences, mostly on the waterfront, where heterosexual porn users will also be relocated and where risk of violence will consequently be higher. In either case, the result will be a sense of isolation and diminished expectations for queer life, as well as an attenuated capacity for political community. (Berlant and Warner, 2002: 191–2)

This passage was written prior to the rapid and widespread use of dating websites and apps among sexually active individuals, but the overall consequences it alludes to remain fully relevant. Indeed, the different apps and websites in question have not reversed the tide of privatization of public spaces and sexual practices. If anything, they have further reinforced it. For what Jasbir Puar (2007: 125) called the 'queer liberal', such a privatization of sex is far from problematic. It is aligned with the 'liberal ideal of home as sanctuary and as property that one owns' (Puar, 2007: 126). But for many others, especially those who relied on 'zones of public space, whether it be cruising areas, sex clubs, restrooms, parks, rest stops, or other spots where queers rendezvous' (Puar, 2007: 125) and could not easily 'traverse across, bounded notions of public and private' (Puar, 2007: 125), the laws came to be experienced as highly repressive. They were responsible for the eradication of a 'complex of social practices … affecting over any year hundreds of thousands of men and women' (Delany, 1999: 144) and through which 'interclass communication takes place' (Delany, 1999: 121). By enforcing a bourgeois conception of sex as a private affair on New Yorkers, the zoning laws have denied many individuals 'repeated, pleasant social interactions with one another' (Delany, 1999: 173), making their life 'more lonely and isolated' (Delany, 1999: 175). As such, they are indicative of the fact that 'heteronormative forms, so central to the accumulation and reproduction of capital, also depend on heavy interventions in the regulation of capital' (Berlant and Warner, 2002: 205). Put differently, the zoning laws illustrate how heteronormativity could be regarded as both an appendage of capitalism and force responsible for structuring 'hierarchies of property and propriety' (Berlant and Warner, 2002: 188). Under this particular reading, it is as important to resist heteronormativity in order to resist capitalism as it is to resist capitalism in order to resist heteronormativity. What we therefore further learn from queer scholarship is the fact that subverting compulsory heterosexuality is not a task confined to the queer community but one intricately imbricated, and indeed central to, the anti-capitalist struggle.

Queer critique, therefore, holds the potential for making explicit the radical interdependence of a range of structures of domination in a manner akin to pluriversal intersectionality. It can treat capitalism holistically, that is, by viewing the sexist and homophobic institutions and practices of heteronormativity and capitalist structures as mutually constitutive components of one and the same system. But while Hennessy construed their relationship in historical terms, Berlant, Warner and Puar seem to suggest that heteronormativity is part and parcel of capitalism's (oppressive) logic. Some non-negligible differences can therefore be found within queer critiques of capitalism seeking to expose the reach of heteronormativity beyond matters of gender and sexuality. They remain nevertheless united in their commitment to condemn the universal/particular binary entrenched in heteronormative institutions and practices, as well as in their proposal to resist the latter through the subversion of essentialist identity thinking. But, while queer thought, along with its Marxist and queer of colour variant (see for example Ferguson, 2004) offer important insights into the oppressive structures of white supremacist heteronormative capitalist oppression, the scope of their intersectional approach tends to be limited. The example of the homonormative queer or, as Puar (2007) put it, the 'queer liberal', discussed earlier should illustrate the critical importance of the holistic approach to critique and emancipation. So should the fact that, as Roderick Ferguson powerfully put it, a 'social order achieves normativity by suppressing intersections of race, class, gender, and sexuality' (2004: 83). A pluriversal project of emancipation can only successfully halt oppressive normativity through a holistic account of domination capable of making explicit the relational character of different structures of domination. As was shown earlier, queer scholarship provides a fruitful basis on which to build such a project.

Furthermore, like many of her fellow queer scholars, Puar is highly critical of identity thinking. Her critique, however, is executed within a discussion aimed at explaining the reasons for favouring the term 'assemblage' over intersectionality (2007: 211–12). Intersectionality is criticized by Puar for its over-reliance on notions of fixed identity and self-hood, and limited capacity to be 'attuned to interwoven forces that merge and dissipate time, space, and body against linearity, coherency, and permanency' (2007: 212). As I have shown in Chapter 1, however, intersectionality is compatible with a version of identity thinking that can circumvent the problems identified by Puar.[3] The pluriversal approach to intersectionality adopted here presupposes a conception of coalitional identity construed dialogically. Crucially, though, for intersectionality scholars identity can, too, be a critical element in liberation, particularly for Indigenous peoples subjected to colonial rule. In fact, by shifting our attention to the work of Global South scholars and Indigenous critiques of (colonial) domination, one can begin to appreciate some important limitations with some of the queer critiques like Puar's.

As shown earlier, queer thought proposes to resist binary thinking through a process of dis-identification (Muñoz, 1999) that, as a 'positionality vis-à-vis the normative', aims to subvert, even transgress, the normative. For proponents of 'borderland' thinking, for which Gloria Anzaldúa is a key figure, this entails developing a '*mestiza* consciousness', that is:

> a tolerance for contradictions, a tolerance for ambiguity. She learns to be an Indian in Mexican culture, to be Mexican from an Anglo point of view. She learns to juggle cultures. She has a plural personality, she operates in a pluralisitic mode – nothing is thrust out, the good the bad and the ugly, nothing rejected, nothing abandoned. Not only does she sustain contradictions, she turns the ambivalence into something else. (1987: 79)

Dualisms and binaries are thus resisted by engaging in a form of thinking that takes one to a 'a vague and undetermined place'; that forces one into a 'constant state of transition' (Anzaldúa, 1987: 3). The goal is to oppose the exclusionary tendencies of dualist thinking with a 'divergent thinking, characterized by movement away from set patterns and goals and toward a more whole perspective' (Anzaldúa, 1987: 79). The latter is thought to be inclusionary in virtue of being constantly on the move and never tying itself to the potentially oppressive logic of stable identity. While this kind of reasoning certainly coincides with elements of Puar's understanding of assemblage it does not necessarily lead to an outright rejection of identity in emancipation. It simply recognizes that identity is a complex affair and warns against conceptions that fail to acknowledge its plural and fluid character. Her approach nevertheless remains intersectional, to the extent that it presupposes a kind of identity that assumes the form of a hybrid or blend resulting from intersecting structures. 'Ambiguity', here, aims to denote an anti-essentialist stance, where identity means openness to difference, change and the possibility for transgression. It entails a form of identity thinking that is inherently dialogical, coalitional, and provisional.

In addition to clarifying that identity thinking need not rest on a fixed notion of self-hood or engender a divisive and oppressive outlook, it is important to remind ourselves of its value in emancipation. Take, for example, transgender communities. Many transgender men and women thrive on asserting a gender identity. For them it is a necessary step towards self-determination and overcoming the dispossessional practices associated with the inability to conform with the officially sanctioned gender. Identificatory practices, therefore, embody an emancipatory potential for many oppressed groups in virtue of equipping them with a range of empowering symbolic resources essential for shaping the self to be (self-)determined.

Such identificatory practices also hold an important place among Indigenous communities, particularly in their attempt to resist colonial oppression. The risk of subverting identity thinking lies in stripping those communities from the symbolic resources to resist the repression of their traditional modes of thought and forms of knowledge. It overlooks the importance of 'Native traditions' in remembering 'their nations not as necessarily structured through hierarchy, oppression, or patriarchy' (Smith, 2010: 50). From the standpoint of Indigenous communities in settler colonies, therefore, liberation does not so much consist in dis-identifying as in re-identifying by taking stock of the past without romanticizing it. It involves not so much a return to the past, as a means for imagining the future by remembering a past identity colonial powers have sought to erase. Both queer and Indigenous forms of resistance could, too, be said to resist the oppressive tendencies of binary thinking. But while, from the standpoint of queer individuals, binary thinking oppresses by *precluding alternative modes of identification*, from the standpoint of colonized Indigenous peoples, it oppresses by *suppressing pre-existing modes of identification*. Both systems of oppression have the effect of dispossessing individuals of a range of resources required for self-actualization, but each operates according to its own logic. A pluriversal conception of emancipation must therefore be conceptualized accordingly, that is, by countering the various ways in which dispossessional practices operate. What we learn from the earlier discussion is that dis-identification should not mean non-identification, for the latter holds the danger of disarming particular communities of essential means for self-determination. A pluriversal emancipatory[4] project must not therefore reject identificatory practice. It must simply postulate forms of identification that are, on the one hand, coalitional and, on the other, asserted beyond the parameters of Global North modernist binaries and normativity.

Lessons from Amerindian Indigenous thought

As this suggests, the identificatory practice entailed by pluriversal emancipation must account for and draw from modes of thinking and relating to others akin to those found among Indigenous Amerindians. Many Amerindian communities have in fact resisted binary thinking by offering an alternative way of understanding identity and self-hood: one presupposing radical interdependence and plurality rather than mere otherness and singularity. Before I explore this approach to identity, however, let me clarify how I intend to address the Indigenous perspectives in question. In their important assessment of the ontological turn, David Chandler and Julian Reid expressed a highly pertinent and urgent concern, namely the fact that Indigenous knowledge has informed the work of (predominantly) white critical theorists, who used them as 'mere props or backstops for the story of how [they] themselves operate to "do difference differently"' (2020: 15). They take issue with the fact that while Global North scholars did seek to challenge epistemic injustice or 'coloniality of knowledge', they often did so for career-related ends and without a concern for the 'coloniality of real inequalities and injustices in the world' (Chandler and Reid, 2020: 11), such as the Amerindian world. The result is an appropriation of Indigenous knowledge by Global North scholars that does very little, if anything, to disrupt the 'coloniality of power'. In fact, this appropriation for self-interested ends tends to 'mimic the most dominant and disempowering cultural and political forms of our times' (Chandler and Reid, 2020: 5). In proposing to develop a critique of capitalist domination and vision of emancipation informed by a dialogue between the latter and its Global North counterpart, I hope to contribute to a reimagining of socialism sensitive to the injustices affecting the Global South. Following Smith (2010) and Chandler and Reid (2020), then, the vision of socialist emancipation proposed in this book draws from experiences of oppression located both within and outside of the Global North, treats the project of liberation as a matter of both epistemic and social justice, and, consistent with pluriversal intersectionality, understands the emancipation of Indigenous peoples as singular yet intricately imbricated with the emancipation of oppressed groups in the Global North.

Shifting our attention towards the experiences shaped by the 'coloniality of power' and modes of anti-colonial struggle provides, as Smith (2010) emphasized, a different perspective on the role of identity in resistance from the one found in many perspectives making up Global North scholarship surfaces. Rather than seeking to dismiss or subvert it, anti-colonial struggles for self-determination tend to regard cultural identity as a core, if not fundamental, component of emancipation. For example, Leanne Betasamosake Simpson's (2011) concept of 'resurgence' aims to make sense of a form of anti-colonial resistance rendered politically active through 'stories of mobilization' drawn from the (Amerindian) people of Nishnaabeg's cultural tradition. She shows how Indigenous thought 'maps a way out of colonial thinking by confirming Indigenous lifeways' (Simpson, 2011: 31–2). Cultural identity is here construed as a tool of resistance. It was, too, a core focus of prominent African anti-colonial leader and black radical, Amilcar Cabral:

> The liberation struggle, which is the most complex expression of the cultural vitality of a people, of its identity, and of its dignity, enriches culture and opens up new perspectives for its development. Cultural manifestations acquire a new content and take on new forms of expression. They also become a powerful instrument of political information and education, not only in the struggle for independence but also in the broader battle for progress. (2016: 179)

From this perspective, identity or self-hood assumes a rather different character from the one found in much of the Global North queer scholarship that rejects identificatory practice. We are in fact reminded here of the important role identity tends to play in liberation struggles, particularly those orientated towards self-determination. Indeed, 'what has been historically sought in struggles for liberation is a realization of a freedom that is inextricably bound to the right to determine one's own life', and thus articulated around a notion of self-hood or identity (Nyman, 2014: 206).

The literary movement known as Negritude echoes such a stance. The movement, which counted the likes Léopold Sédar Senghor and Aimé Césaire among its core proponents, draws on Black colonized Indigenous peoples' experiences of oppression. It articulated a vision of liberation that celebrated identity and difference in opposition to the oppressive assimilationist tendencies of the colonizer's culture. Césaire, for example, has always 'thought the black man [sic] was searching for his identity' (2000: 91). Negritude offers a path for finding it. Called by Senghor 'Africanity' (Rabaka, 2009: 121), Negritude entails opposing the regime of dispossession marking colonial domination by 'affirming … difference' (Césaire, 2003, no page number).[5] It entails developing 'a concrete consciousness of what we are, that is, of the first fact of our lives: that we are black and have a history, a history that contains certain cultural elements of great value' (Césaire, 2000: 91–2). To resist dispossession and the 'atmosphere of rejection' (Césaire, 2000: 91) induced by it means, here, to recognize that 'there have been beautiful and important black civilizations' (Césaire, 2000: 92). It entails overcoming the destruction of those 'civilizations' through a 'return' to Africa, understood as the recognition and assertion of a set of African values that colonization rejected and repressed, but never successfully erased. Negritude is much like Cabral's vision of national liberation, that is, 'an act of culture' (1973: 43), of identity affirmation. For, colonized Indigenous peoples do not have the choice to opt out of identity thinking in their search for self-determination.

But what conception of identity is presupposed here? How different is it from, say, the conception underpinning identity politics or the pluriversal approach to intersectionality developed in this work? While, at first glance, the call for asserting cultural identity might appear to rest on an exclusionary and separatist logic, Césaire had something very different in mind. In a letter to Maurice Thorez published by *Social Text*, Césaire made his position explicit:

> I am not burying myself in a narrow particularism. But neither do I want to lose myself in an emaciated universalism. There are two ways to lose oneself: walled segregation in the particular or dilution in the 'universal'. My conception of the universal is that of a universal enriched by all that is particular, a universal enriched by every particular: the deepening and coexistence of all particulars. (2010: 152)

Conscious of the oppressive logic emanating from both universalist and particularist positions, Césaire encouraged us to rethink difference and otherness in a manner recalling Mbembe's own notion that it is 'our differences that, paradoxically, we must share' (2017: 178). Otherness is, like in Amerindian thought, construed as 'a bond rather than a division' (Walker, 2020: 148). Rather than being 'turned inwards' identity is 'turned outwards' (Césaire, 2003, no page number). Identity, self-hood, or personhood not only 'rests on a concept of the common' but also, and crucially, on one 'that is external, concrete, and collectively produced rather than abstract and innate' (Walker, 2020: 160). Identity, therefore, is here construed in relational terms, predicated upon the notion that 'nothing exists by itself, that everything interexists' (Escobar, 2018: 84). Identity is not asserted either *against* or *in spite of* others but *through* others. It is not given or fixed, but 'the result of the critical dialogue between diverse critical epistemic/ethical/political projects' (Grosfoguel, 2007: 212). Particularity does not confront universality as its other. The former is realized through the latter and *vice versa*.

Relational/coalitional identity of the form discussed here, then, presupposes pluriversality, that is, the affirmation of universality through the celebration of particularity or, put differently, the recognition that our universality, what we have in common, is difference. After all, 'it's hardly interesting to talk about what two things have in common unless they also have some differences' (Sayer, 2011: 100). A pluriverse, then, is a space in which 'diversity [is] a universal project' (Mignolo, 2000: 273). In a pluriverse the struggles against injustice inflicted on others become my struggles, not because I live like, or identify with, those others – this would entail a degree of homogeneity/universalism – but because my own liberation is, despite its singularity, inseparable from theirs. Pluriversality, therefore, allows one to 'move away the notion that you can only speak to those issues if you are a member of those groups' (Vaid, 1998: 100–1) and opens up the scope for deploying inclusionary identificatory practices in the struggle for emancipation.

Rethinking emancipation and overcoming the particularity/universality binary through a relational/coalitional conception of identity should not, however, be treated as a mere academic exercise or, as indicated earlier, as a mere attempt to remedy epistemic injustice. The concept of pluriversality has implications reaching far beyond epistemology. For, by capturing the essence of worldviews both radically different from, and resisting those making up, Global North thinking, it also provides a basis upon which to rethink social action and institutions beyond binary thinking and towards radical interdependence. The next chapters are devoted to revealing what such actions and institutions might look like. For now, though, suffice it to say that the concept opens up new ways of understanding socialist values like freedom and equality. For example, under the guise of pluriversality, negative and individualist conceptions of freedom are not conceivable. For, here, one's freedom is thought to be realized through the freedom of others. Freedom is construed as necessarily social and intrinsically connected to cooperation. Equality, on the other hand, is no longer associated with 'equivalence' (Walker, 2020) or the suppression of difference. What we instead find is a notion of equality whereby '[v]aluing the individual while still managing to connect individuals as a community' or 'maintaining tolerance alongside a heterogeneous, differentiated understanding of the general good' (Walker, 2020: 162), become possibilities.

Finally, under the guise of pluriversality, nature becomes a partner in emancipation. In Amerindian thought, for example, connectedness between humans, as well as between humans and non-humans, is not something to aspire to, but is instead 'given' (Viveiros de Castro, 2012: 126). Since, according to this body of knowledge, the 'original common condition of both humans and animals is not animality, but rather humanity' (Viveiros de Castro, 2012: 84), each living being is in a position to express a particular point of view. 'Humanity', then, is understood as 'a reflexive property of the subject position' (Viveiros de Castro, 2012: 106) and nature itself is 'an active subject' (Warren, 2000: 34). It follows that identification is a process that does not discriminate between the human and non-human world. Within the pluriverse, the nature/society binary is overcome. Freedom and equality are values reaching beyond the human world and, for this reason, presuppose the deployment of a logic of interdependence that, while recognizing difference, also entails a focus on the 'quality of relations, a principle of cooperation, and of responsibility to each other and to the earth, the forests, the seas, the animals' (Federici, 2019: 110). From the perspective of pluriversal emancipation, solidarity in action presupposes difference. It 'requires not just the affirmation of difference, but also sensitivity to the difference between positioning oneself *with* the other and positioning oneself *as* the other' (Plumwood, 2002: 202, emphasis in original).

Pluriversal emancipation, then, provides a sharply different account of the relationship between identity, particularity and universality from the one found in Global North conceptions of liberation, including the queer texts which have sought to resist binary thinking by rejecting identificatory practice. In the vision I formulated here, the logic of identification is harnessed for the ends of socialist values like freedom and equality. But because it is construed in relational terms, identity is not given or fixed, it is a dialogical process of becoming asserting the inextricability of our radical interdependence and difference. Identity is therefore central to building an internally differentiated 'collective we' (Collins and Bilge, 2016: 135) for the attainment of social freedom and equality without equivalence. Pluriversal emancipation counters the dispossessional tendencies of binary thinking by favouring a relational mode of identification presupposing a collectively empowering and life-affirming interdependence. It is to be distinguished, on the one hand, from an emancipatory vision presupposing 'projects of unity or merger' (Plumwood, 2002: 202) of the kind found, for example, in universalist emancipatory projects like in the working-class movement within the Global North. For, emancipation does not so much depend here on the capacity of different individuals to unite around the same goal as to recognize that their respective struggles depend on one another. On the other hand, it is distinguishable from the kind of disorientating indeterminacy found in post-structuralist accounts, which combine the ambiguity promoted by Anzaldúa with an outright rejection of identificatory practice. Instead, pluriversal emancipation envisions a form of liberation resting on an identity-ambiguity complementarity, that is, one that benefits from the open-endedness and potential relationality of anti-essentialism, while thriving on the self-affirming capacity for self-determination identity offers. No radical interdependence in emancipation is, after all, possible without the affirmation of differences/identities, that is, without creating the very basis for *inter*dependence.

The subject of pluriversal emancipation

So far, I explained why the concept of emancipation is central to an intersectional socialist project and exposed some of the features such a concept is expected to exhibit when conceptualized in pluriversal terms. I now turn to the task of conceptualizing the agent of change entailed by the proposed vision of emancipation. I shall explore some of the core features of this agent and ask whether it is effectively possible to speak of a *subject* of pluriversal emancipation. I start this discussion with an appraisal of Ernesto Laclau and Chantal Mouffe's seminal text entitled *Hegemony and Socialist Strategy*, for their work, which was originally published in 1985, remains one of the most complete and influential attempts to conceptualize the agent of change while grappling with the 'plural and multifarious character of contemporary social struggles' (Laclau and Mouffe, 2001: 2).

Laclau and Mouffe sought to breathe new life into Marxist thought by setting out to 'identify the discursive conditions for the emergence of a collective action ... struggling against inequalities and challenging relations of subordination' (2001: 153). Their work, therefore, echoes to some extent the task set out in this book and rests on a fundamental observation, namely, the emergence of a social world marked by 'the proliferation of widely differing points of rupture' and 'precarious character of all social identity' that lead to a 'blurring of frontiers' (Laclau and Mouffe, 2001: 171). This observation bears significant implications for the conceptualization of the subject. In fact, Laclau and Mouffe boldly conclude that the 'era of "privileged subjects" – in the ontological, not practical sense – of the anti-capitalist struggle has been definitively superseded' (2001: 87). As a result, Marxism, and socialist thought more broadly, must become more sensitive to the complex and highly differentiated character of domination marking contemporary societies and accept that:

> [t]here is no unique privileged position from which a uniform continuity of effects will follow, concluding with the transformation of society as a whole. All struggles, whether those of workers or other political subjects, left to themselves, have a partial character, and can be articulated to very different discourses. It is this articulation which gives them their character, not the place from which they come. (Laclau and Mouffe, 2001: 169)

In this short but dense passage, the two political philosophers make a range of highly significant claims about the contemporary subject of resistance. First, they reiterate their rejection of the idea that there can be one privileged or unique agent of change. Contemporary society, along with the forms of oppression it gives rise to, are so complex and diverse that it is only possible to speak of 'different subject positions' rather than a single subject of emancipation (Laclau and Mouffe, 2001: 87). Second, and following from the previous claim, the unity of the agent cannot be something that is given or determined by, say, one's 'position in the relations of production' (Laclau and Mouffe, 2001: 118), one's gender, or one's race. It is in a perpetual process of becoming – a unity lacking fixity and permanence. It takes the form of a continuously developing symbolic 'articulation' of emancipatory struggles lacking a 'unified and unifying essence' (Laclau and Mouffe, 2001: 181). Consequently (and finally), the identity of the agent of change, as well as the identity of the struggles composing it, result from the meaning(s) constructed through articulation, that is, through the 'construction of nodal points that partially fix meaning' (Laclau and Mouffe, 2001: 113), rather than from a particular position within society. Laclau and Mouffe have therefore offered a non-essentialist, non-reductionist and discursive conception of the agent of change.

Under such a reading, emancipation is thought to be led by multiple 'hegemonic subjects' (Laclau and Mouffe, 2001: 85), whose identity is determined by the outcome of the labour of discursive articulation. The subjects are effectively objects to themselves, to the extent that their identity has to be worked out, laboured upon, produced. But the outcome of this labour is never permanently fixed. There is a high degree of contingency affecting these hegemonic subjects, mainly because of the 'overdetermined' character of identity (Laclau and Mouffe, 2001). Indeed, to say that an identity is overdetermined is to regard it as the outcome, not of a single or particular position in society but, rather, as something 'constituted ... by every other aspect of social life' (Gibson-Graham, 2006: 55). For example, one's identity as a member of the working-class is constituted through more than the register of identity specific to class. It is overdetermined by other identity registers such as those specific to gender and race. But overdetermination manifests itself symbolically. It was in fact devised by Althusser to show that society has no essence, that the 'social constitutes itself as a symbolic order' (Laclau and Mouffe, 2001: 97), and that the identities making up the social are never fixed but continuously re-constituted and redefined. The task of the (symbolic) labour of discursive articulation is not to pin down or permanently fix an identity, for this would entail risking a fall into essentialism. Instead, it consists in constructing 'chains of equivalence' (Laclau and Mouffe, 2001: 182) between struggles, while recognizing the highly 'precarious and relational character of every identity' (Laclau and Mouffe, 2001: 99). A hegemonic articulation, therefore, does not suppress overdetermination; it is achieved through it. It works with it to achieve a 'system of relations' (Laclau and Mouffe, 2001: 86) in which a precarious 'equivalential articulation' is established between, for example, 'anti-racism, anti-sexism and anti-capitalism', while preserving the 'differential specificity' of each struggle 'with respect to the others' (Laclau and Mouffe, 2001: 182). Equivalence is therefore not sought at the expense of difference, for the 'logic of equivalence' is complemented, and to a degree counteracted, by a 'logic of autonomy' in articulation (Laclau and Mouffe, 2001).

At first glance, then, Laclau and Mouffe's approach to the agent of change appears to reflect many of the features of pluriversal emancipation identified in the previous section. Not only does it recognize and affirm the plural and relational character of identity in resistance, it does so by resisting the sacrifice of difference for sameness. However, upon closer inspection, their conceptualization of the agent of change reveals some notable inadequacies for the task set out in the present work. The first and most evident of those limitations is the highly abstract character of their conceptualization. While few glimpses of what a hegemonic articulation could concretely entail are provided by suggesting, for example, that it could connect anti-racist, anti-sexist and anti-capitalist struggles, very little, if anything, is said about the kind of relations and processes required for such an articulation. Could pre-existing decision-making processes and practices give rise to such an articulation? If so, what are they? If not, what alternatives must be constructed in order for the agent of change to be hegemonically articulated? While the authors refer to 'radical democracy', little is said about the way this is effectively expected to be brought to life.

Second, Laclau and Mouffe were not in a position to envision a bonding role for difference or adopt a vision of the social where division, opposition, and antagonism are not construed as given features of social existence. By proposing to create 'chains of equivalence', the problem they pose is a typically Western one, namely, to work out how to connect 'individual substances' (Viveiros de Castro, 2014: 126). To be sure, they do not propose to do so by entirely eliminating difference and favouring sameness over the latter. Given the open and indeterminate character of the social, chains of equivalence can only be expected to fix meaning temporarily, that is, to create a temporary '"alliance" between given interests' (Laclau and Mouffe, 2001: 184). For example, a chain of equivalence could be constructed between the anti-racist, anti-sexist and anti-capitalist struggles, where each retains its own specificity but is temporarily and symbolically allied with the others in a discourse articulated around the denunciation of welfare cuts as a source of increased socio-economic inequality. The logic of equivalence, therefore, echoes Michael Hardt and Antonio Negri's own adaptation of Spinoza's 'notion of parallelism' (2009: 343), which they apply to their conceptualization of collective action in the following manner:

> One of the most significant challenges of revolution today, then, which this parallelism of singularities suggests, is that revolutionary action cannot be successfully conducted or even thought in one domain alone. Without its parallel developments any revolutionary struggle will run aground or even fall back on itself. A revolutionary race proposition that ignores or even exacerbates gender hierarchies will inevitably be blocked, as will a class proposition that fails to keep up with its parallels in the racial domain. Multiplicity and parallelism set the standard for evaluating revolutionary politics today: the multiple parallel paths of liberation either proceed through correspondences or do not proceed at all. (Hardt and Negri, 2009: 343)

Laclau, Mouffe, as well as Hardt and Negri, seem to share many intersectionality scholars' view that the struggle for liberation ought to be articulated around more than a single axis. They employ terms like equivalence, parallelism, and correspondence in an effort to capture the search for commonality, which is essential for successful collective action and social transformation. Those terms, I would argue, are nevertheless underpinned by a kind of binary thinking incapable of affirming the radical interdependence entailed by pluriversal intersectionality. By turning to the work of feminists, including Black feminists, one finds a somewhat different and potentially more fruitful basis upon which to imagine pluriversal emancipatory action.

Patricia Hill Collins (2019), for example, proposed to think of collective action through the notion of 'flexible solidarity'. Here the aim is not limited to creating a chain of equivalence but to foster solidarity. It anticipates deeper bonds than those a mere attempt to establish an equivalence or parallel could achieve. It also anticipates a different role for relational difference than the one proposed by Laclau and Mouffe. Indeed, while the latter understood the search for commonality as a potential source of 'subversion' of relational difference or 'relational identities' (Laclau and Mouffe, 2001: 142), Collins viewed it as an extension of relational difference: as a 'necessary strategy for political action' (2019, 172) that contributes to 'the process of constructing truth' through 'a dialogical relationship among subjects who are differently situated within interpretive communities' (2019: 139). The Black Lives Matter movement, for example, deployed this logic of commonality in an effort to widen 'the circle of Black lives to incorporate Black trans people and others who face discrimination both within and outside Black communities' (Collins, 2019: 172). Thus, while Laclau and Mouffe understood relational identity as a matter of equivalence rather than radical interdependence, Collins envisioned bonding through difference and consequently understood identity as something achieved *through* others. It is possible to argue, therefore, that for Collins collective action does not so much result from merely asking what alliances could be constructed among different struggles – although this is of course a necessary part of such action – but from recognizing how struggles constitute one another. This is because intersectionality, as Collins and others understood it (see for example Yuval-Davis, 2009; May, 2015), sets out to achieve more than what overdetermination entails, that is, more than grasping how different social positions intersect to create symbolic alliances by overcoming given antagonism(s) between those social positions. Flexible solidarity makes explicit our radical interdependence. Under its guise struggles are connected, not as a result of constructing a chain of equivalence, but because they, like the identities associated with them, are thought to inter-exist. Flexible solidarity does not so much seek to overcome a separation or division as recognize a radical interdependence, such as the radical interdependence between Black feminist struggles and those of trans people.

The deployment of flexible solidarity in emancipatory action is, I wish to further argue, akin to what Silvia Federici (2019: 110) proposed to achieve in what she described as the 'reconstruction of the commons'. For, with it, we effectively come to assert our radical interdependence and 'refuse to base our life and our reproduction on the suffering of others' or 'see ourselves as separate from them' (Federici, 2019: 110). But it is not quite the 'becoming common' analysed by Hardt and Negri (2004). For, first, the 'common' of pluriversal emancipation is not so much 'the primary characteristic of the new dominant forms of labor today' (Hardt and Negri, 2004: xv) as the collective affirmation of the mutual constitution of struggles against domination. Second, while it is much like the 'multitude' insofar as the pluriversal agent of change is an 'internally different, multiple social subject', it is not merely based on what 'it has in common' (Hardt and Negri, 2004: 100). Like the concept of pluriversal emancipation discussed earlier, and like Laclau and Mouffe's concept of hegemony, Hardt and Negri's multitude entails a project of emancipation expected to resist sameness and whereby 'difference ... remains different' (Hardt and Negri, 2004: 99). However, also like Laclau and Mouffe, they understand bonds or connections as being established *in spite* of differences – through what struggles share or have in common – rather than *through* those differences.

The problem with this approach is that it does not sufficiently protect the project of emancipation against the pitfalls of Global North thinking, such as its universalist aspirations. Indeed, the construction of chains of equivalence or demand for a focus on what struggles share/have in common, could all-too-easily lead to a situation where, for example, the collective action of a working-class man and working-class woman could only be imagined by bracketing their gender. It risks turning into a 'project of unity or merger' with potentially oppressive universalist implications. Thus, despite seeking to preserve difference, the latter runs the risk of being construed as an interference to pluriversal thinking in collective action. Under the guise of pluriversal intersectionality and flexible solidarity, however, patriarchy and class oppression are understood and affirmed as mutually constitutive. It follows that class oppression cannot be fully understood without an analysis of patriarchy and *vice versa*. Consequently, no collective action could be envisaged without working out the given interdependence of different structures of domination. Here the collective action of a working-class man and working-class woman could only be imagined by bringing class into dialogue with gender, as co-constitutive elements of a coalitional subjectivity or 'dialogically constructed truth'. To conceptualize a pluriversal emancipatory subject, then, entails mobilizing collective action through a dialogue devoted to deploying flexible solidarity or, more specifically, making explicit the silent interdependence of struggles against domination.

But the subject is not, as already indicated, given and transcendental. Nor is it homogeneous. The subject in question does not exist *in itself*. It is worked out or produced and, for this reason, is an *object to itself* in the process of becoming a *subject in itself*. The process of subjectivity production involves a dialogical engagement between what Laclau and Mouffe would call 'differential positions'. Through this dialogue, diverse oppressed groups do not so much set out to find what they share or have in common as understand how they inter-exist in particular contexts or grapple with their contextualized radical interdependence. Outlets for this dialogical engagement could assume many forms, including a social movement and political party. But the search for the pluriversal subject is never complete. Like the 'multitude', it is 'not fixed or static but constantly transformed, enriched, constituted by a process of making' (Hardt and Negri, 2009: 173).

Furthermore, presupposing the possibility for an emancipatory subject and subjectivity need not entail expecting the agent of change to develop an essence. Essentialist approaches to the emancipatory subject akin to, for example, Marx's treatment of the proletariat as the revolutionary subject, have become rather outdated for very good reasons. Their reductionist tendencies mean that they risk reifying the agent of change, thereby failing to grasp the open, indeterminate, and complex character of the social world and, more specifically, domination. As the always-incomplete outcome of a dialogue, the pluriversal emancipatory subject might be best conceptualized as a set of 'coalitional identities of resistance' (Violet, 2002: 486) that are temporarily stabilized for the purpose of driving change. Those identities are essentially self-revelatory, to the extent that the relationality of both the self and structures of domination shaping the self's experiences of oppression is collectively elucidated and revealed to the subjects. As such, it corresponds to what Butler described as an 'emerging and unpredictable assemblage of positions' that 'cannot be figured in advance' (1990: 20). It is composed of selves 'who come into being, and can only come into being, on the occasion of relations with others, and so is located precisely in and as the relation to itself' (Butler and Athanasiou, 2013: 122). Coalitional identities 'are always partial, perspectival, and performative', in that 'they never encompass all dimensions of people's identities' (Chun et al., 2013: 923). They are a reality negotiated and temporarily stabilized by the diverse subjects dialogically engaged with one another. In the words of Audre Lorde herself (1993: 142), the pluriversal subject of emancipation entails 'the coming together of whole, self-actualized human beings, focused and believing, not fragmented automatons marching to a prescribed step'.

But rather than construing it as a strictly performative subject, that is, as the outcome of collective citational practices, the pluriversal subject of emancipation conceptualized here is better understood in structuralist constructionist terms: as an outcome of both objective structures and citational practices. Under such a reading, 'the cognitive structures which social agents implement in their practical knowledge of the social world are internalized, "embodied" social structures' (Bourdieu, 1986: 468). So, because the emancipatory subject opposes (objective) social structures that 'cannot be separated from mental structures' (Ritzer and Stepnisky, 2019: 200), the task of elucidating their mutual constitution rests, as noted earlier, on the subject becoming an object to itself. The subject, therefore, results from a set of representations that are constructed through dialogical engagement and the objective structures the dialogue in question exposes. In addition to overcoming the universality/particularity binary, then, the pluriversal subject of emancipation conceptualized here overcomes the subject/object binary.

It is also important that, in accordance with the treatment of non-human nature as a partner in emancipation defended in the preceding chapter, the subject of pluriversal emancipation be non-reducible to rationalist forms of communication. As Val Plumwood put it:

> Rationalist models which treat communication in intellectualist terms as an exercise in pure, abstract, neutral and universal reason, and which delegitimate the more emotional and bodily forms and aspects of communication, operate to exclude non-humans from full communicative status just as they exclude various human others accorded lower human status as further from the rational ideal. (2002: 191)

Included within the scope of its communicative toolbox, then, are emotional and bodily expressions. The pluriversal emancipatory subject is an embodied subject. It is therefore 'materialist' to the extent that it avoids 'spiritual remoteness [and] honour[s] the material and ecological bases of life' and 'counter-centric' in affirming the subjecthood of non-humans (Plumwood, 2002: 229). This is particularly important for a subject expected to counter dispossessional practices, which, in the process of depriving individuals of a range of symbolic and material resources, effectively transform human and non-human nature by cultivating subjectivities, shaping bodies, eliciting emotions, and extracting non-human nature (Butler and Athanasiou, 2013). Because dispossession affects the material, cognitive, and spiritual dimensions of life, a pluriversal subject of emancipation cannot be reduced to a merely rational existence.

Finally, in virtue of being marked by a process of 'becoming common' and coalitional subjectivity, the pluriversal subject 'contests dominant imaginaries' (May, 2015: 34). Because it is formed under the guise of pluriversal intersectionality and flexible solidarity, the pluriversal subject contests the 'atomized logics of liberal individualism' (May, 2015: 52), including the 'liberal model of agency' (May, 2015: 46) and the 'liberal notion of equality … premised on valuing sameness over difference' (May, 2015: 42). As such, it sheds light onto another world and is endowed with what Muňoz (1999) described as 'world-making' capacities. But it is questionable whether it could offer, as Muňoz (1999: 200) claimed, a 'utopian blueprint for a possible future'. While a positioning against dominant imaginaries opens up the scope for venturing beyond the given, the identity of the subject is not sufficiently stable to be able to perform a fully prefigurative role. Thus, while the pluriversal emancipatory subject drives change, it perpetually (re-)assesses the direction it ought to take, in the light of changing circumstances, such as new barriers to emancipation. This is in fact partly why a subject of change serious about emancipation must do all it can to avoid undermining the transformative force of its utopian energies, even after the process of change has begun to unfold (Abensour, 2008). This is indeed the only way the 'stubborn impulse toward freedom and justice' can be preserved; the only way to secure what Miguel Abensour (2008) called the 'persistence of utopia'.

Conclusion

Pluriversal intersectionality offers unique lenses through which a subject of emancipation can be conceptualized. While it provides a basis for thinking emancipation in holistic terms and across diverse struggles against domination, it also warns us of the dangers associated with universalist aspirations. But instead of falling into a separatist and particularist conception of political action, pluriversal intersectionality opens up the scope for departing from the kind of binary thinking that has pitted particuarlism against universalism, humanity against nature and subject against object. By bringing both queer and Indigenous scholarship into dialogue with one another, elements of a pluriversal conception of emancipation were offered. It was shown that identity affirmation constitutes an essential step towards, for example, the self-determination of colonized peoples. For this reason, it was argued that an emancipatory project serious about asserting the interdependence of struggles against domination must not reject identificatory practice. Instead, it must safeguard it against essentialist tendencies that divide society instead of affirming identities' inter-existence. A relational conception of identity was thus conceptualized based on a range of Indigenous perspectives whose (relational) ontology shares many affinities with pluriversal intersectionality. Under its guise, dialogue contributes to countering human-centredness, paving the way for 'the play of more-than-human forces' (Plumwood, 2002: 229). Through cognitive, affective, and bodily expressions asserted collectively humans and non-humans, then, do not so much seek equivalence as affirm their radical interdependence. Pluriversal emancipation, therefore, could be said to espouse some universalist and particularist aspirations, but understands their relationship in acutely different terms from those of many Global North struggles for emancipation. For, here, a subject emerges not as a result of a particular struggle imposing itself on others or different struggles united around a common project, but through the universal recognition of a radical interdependence necessarily grounded in difference. Difference/particularity is here the bond for collective action, not its barrier. It is affirmed as such through dialogue. In the following chapters I explore how such a radical interdependence can be given institutional form across a range of economic and extra-economic domains.

Work, Property, and Resource Allocation

Introduction

Since its inception, socialism has been inextricably tied to the labour movement and its critique of capitalist economic relations. Under the latter's guise, socialism is expected to offer an alternative to an oppressive, alienating, and exploitative economic life. But exactly what form this alternative ought to assume has been and continues to be debated within the labour movement. This includes questions regarding the nature and role of work, what constitutes genuinely socialist property relations or a form of allocation of resources capable of upholding pluriversal emancipation. In this chapter, I tackle those debates head on. But I do so by opening up the scope of those debates to discussions found outside of the labour movement. For, as Manning Marable put it 'the central questions confronting the Left aren't located within the Left itself but in the broader, deeper currents of social protest and struggle among non-socialist, democratic constituencies – in the activities of trade unionists, gays and lesbians, feminists, environmentalists, people of color, and the poor' (Marable, 1996: 278).

The task set out in this chapter shall therefore consist in bringing those 'deeper currents of social protest' into dialogue with socialist thought, in order to understand what they can offer the conceptualization of socialist economic relations. I begin the discussion by addressing the future of work – a debate figuring prominently within socialist thought. Here I deploy the intersectional lens to envision a counter-culture of capitalist work. This is followed by the conceptualization of a system of allocation of resources deriving from the latter counter-cultural vision and capable of institutionalizing radical interdependence. Finally, an alternative to the capitalist system of property is explored.

Collectivized emancipatory work

A central aspiration of the labour movement has been to give workers the chance to identify with their work and treat it as an outlet for self-actualization. Drawing on a critique of work akin to Karl Marx's own critique of alienation in his *Economic and Philosophical Manuscripts* (2000a), this particular aspiration treats work as an essential component of human life and potential source of autonomy and pleasure. Emancipation is here achieved *through* 'free labour'. Over the past few decades, however, many on the Left came to favour a vision of emancipation in which work would no longer play the leading role. Socialism, it is thought, ought to free individuals *from* work. This vision, most famously formulated by André Gorz (1994; 2012), takes stock of the increasing automation of work, bids 'farewell to the working class' as the agent of change and locates autonomy and self-actualization outside of the workplace. Paradoxically, this approach is, too, traceable to the work of Marx, particularly the *Grundrisse* (2000c), in which he depicts the replacement of human labour by machines as beneficial for the emancipation of the working class. Under this reading, then, the socialist struggle should devote its attention to creating a society where time spent at work is minimized and where emancipation is sought in activities other than work itself. Two contrasting, if not contradictory, approaches to the relationship between work and emancipation can therefore be observed within socialism. In what follows I formulate a vision of work informed by the deployment of the intersectional lens across a diverse range perspectives critical of the capitalist regime of work, both within and without the parameters of socialist thought. To begin with, let me further clarify the arguments on each side of the debate, particularly the kind of utopian insights they entail.

Work in socialist thought

In the socialist utopia depicted by William Morris in *News from Nowhere* (1995), the narrator, William Guest, wakes up in a world completely alien to him. In this world:

> all work is now pleasurable; either because of the hope of gain in honour and wealth with which the work is done, which causes pleasurable excitement, even when the actual work is not pleasant; or else because it has grown into a pleasurable habit ... and lastly (and most of our work is of this kind) because there is conscious pleasure in the work itself; it is done, that is, by artists. (Morris, 1995: 95)

Morris' utopia provides us with insights into the kind of work many proponents of the emancipatory labour approach had in mind. In it, workers do not fear losing a job they dislike doing, like wage workers under capitalism. Instead, they fear being 'short of work' precisely because work is 'a pleasure which [they] are afraid of losing' (Morris, 1995: 95). For Morris, socialism ought to address the problem of the degradation of work and workers found under the capitalist wage system and division of labour, and to do so not by moving beyond work but by changing its nature, as well as the function and terms under which it operates. Work, Morris thought, could and should give individuals the scope to realize themselves; work could and should become a creative activity, that is, one through which individuals can freely employ their faculties to the design and execution of tasks. However, this is not to say that machinery would be entirely excluded from work. It simply means that its use would be limited to '[a]ll work which would be irksome to do by hand' (Morris, 1995: 100). Machinery, here, does not so much replace work as help workers perform self-fulfilling work.

Morris' insights significantly inspired the work of another proponent of the emancipatory labour approach: G.D.H. Cole. The work of this key figure of the guild socialist movement is of particular interest here, not only because of its debt to Morris, but also because Cole provided detailed insights into the kind of economic institutions deemed desirable for releasing individuals' 'creative, scientific and artistic impulses' (Cole, 1980: 116) through work. He came to the conclusion that democratically organized associations, such as self-managed producer associations, would provide workers the 'fullest possible scope for creative activity' (Cole, 1950: 97). Organized around the principle of self-management, these associations are fertile ground for the kind of self-determination upon which creative work rests. They equip their members with the means to make autonomous decisions, albeit in cooperation with other workers. In fact, through associative actions, individuals do not 'cease to think of their own individual advantage', but treat 'the advantage of the whole association' as their own (Cole, 1950: 114). In doing so, associations remove the division of labour which Marx himself identified as a key obstacle to cooperation, as well as a source of alienation and oppression (Marx, 2000a).

But the goal of stripping work from the rigid separation of tasks entailed by the division of labour is not limited to removing obstacles on creativity at work. It also aims to increase variety and choice, as envisioned by proponents of job rotation. This particular form of work practice, also traceable to Marx's (2000d) work, is most fully conceptualized in the work of proponents of 'participatory economics' (Parecon). Here the focus is not so much on creativity – although it is highly compatible with it – as on the possibility 'for me to do one thing today and another tomorrow' (Marx, 2000d: 185):

Each actor does a job, and each job of course includes a variety of tasks. In rejecting current corporate divisions of labor, we decide to balance for their empowerment and quality of life implications the tasks each actor does. Every person participating in creating new products is a worker, and each worker has a balanced job complex, meaning the combination of tasks and responsibilities each worker has would accord them the same empowerment and quality of life benefits as the combination every other worker has. Unlike the current system, we would not have a division between those who overwhelmingly monopolize empowering, fulfilling, and engaging tasks and those who are overwhelmingly saddled with rote, obedient, and dangerous tasks. For reasons of equity and especially to create the conditions of democratic participation and self-management, balanced job complexes would ensure that when we each participate in our workplace and industry decision-making, we have been comparably prepared by our work with confidence, skills, and knowledge to do so. (Albert, 2003: 10)

What Parecon offers, then, is a more or less concrete insight into what emancipation through work entails in practice. What it entails is that workers ought to be able to perform a variety of tasks within a work environment they are responsible for managing with their co-workers in democratically organized associations. It thus entails recognizing that varied tasks lead to greater self-fulfilment. But it also means recognizing that there will always be unpleasant forms of work to perform. Instead of making fulfilling work a sphere exclusive to particular groups, Parecon seeks to make it available to everyone through the introduction of job rotation or complexes. As such, Parecon offers complementary insights to those of Morris and Cole, providing greater clarification on the kind of work practices entailed by the removal of the division of labour. With it, one finds an attempt to minimize drudgery by opening up access to self-fulfilling work through job rotation practices. In a sense, then, this approach is not entirely incompatible with the logic behind the end-of-work thesis. For the latter also intends to liberate humanity from drudgery. But while the emancipatory work thesis assumes the possibility and widespread existence of self-actualizing work facilitated by both a democratically organized workplace and job rotation, the end-of-work thesis proposes to abandon this sphere of action as a source of emancipation. This bears some non-negligible implications for the kind of institutions involved in the socialist re-organization of work, which will be addressed following a review of the key features of the emancipation from work thesis.

Although the positive assessment of work automation has run through a rather long line of thinkers, including 'Marxists, Keynesians, feminists, black nationalists and anarchists alike' (Srniceck and Williams, 2015: 86), it has gained particular momentum in recent years, within a context of precarity, increasing computerization of work tasks, the rise of artificial intelligence, and the proliferation of social media platforms. Some recent accounts include Srniceck and Williams' *Inventing the Future* (2015), Paul Mason's *Postcapitalism* (2015), and Aaron Bastani's *Fully Automated Luxury Communism* (2019). Although much has changed both at work and beyond since André Gorz bade farewell to the working class and declared the end of work, some clear parallels, intersections, and complementarities can be observed between his work and the more recent accounts mentioned earlier. But while all tend to agree on moving towards a post-work society, they do not all provide the same justification for thinking so, or offer identical insights on the re-organization of work.

Let me begin by addressing an aspect of Gorz's work, which makes his own position vis-à-vis the emancipation through work thesis all but clear and which will further illuminate the kind of society he envisioned. For this reason it is worth quoting his work at length here:

> In continuing to apply the idea of work-as-*poiesis* to tasks which in industry, particularly in the service sector, no longer have anything in common with the activities of material transformation and creation carried on by the toolmakers, boilermakers, metal-turners, masons and rolling-mill workers of the nineteenth century, one runs the risk of demanding that today's workers or employees regard as their 'means of personal fulfilment' precisely those tasks which prevent such self-fulfilment. The ideology of work, which argues that 'work is life' and demands that it be taken seriously and treated as a vocation, and the attendant utopia of a society ruled by the associated producers, play right into the hands of the employers, consolidate capitalist relations of production and domination, and legitimate the privileges of a work elite which, despite the existence of millions of unemployed, views a reduction in working hours which could create extra jobs as incompatible with its professional pride and ethic of productivity. (Gorz, 2012: 55)

Gorz wrote this passage at the beginning of the 1990s, at a time when it was becoming clear that the service industry had become the dominant supplier of jobs. But this was also the time when a new regime of production that came to be known as post-Fordism was transforming economic relations and, particularly, the workplace. Under this regime the search for self-actualization through work came to be harnessed for the ends of economic productivity. This marked the appropriation of 'work as self-realization' by employers, keen to maximize the economic performance of their businesses.

What this appropriation meant was that emancipation through labour was now irremediably subsumed under the 'ethic of productivity' and associated ideology of work. This explains why, according to Gorz, it has become counter-productive, if not dangerous, to locate the future of work in institutions as associations of producers, like those envisioned by the likes of Cole and Parecon proponents. How, then, is emancipation expected to be institutionalized for Gorz?

The operating principle of Gorz's post-work society is the notion that 'autonomy and self-fulfilment' must be realized 'through a freely chosen activity' outside of work (2012: 60). A key condition for opening up the 'possibilities of self-determined activity' (Gorz, 2012: 42) is to minimize work and envision emancipation in all other spheres of life. To this end, he advocated the reduction of working time and, later in his life, the introduction of a universal basic income (UBI) which would serve to maximize individuals' freedom from, to borrow Marx's famous phrase, the 'realm of necessity'. To achieve emancipation entails striving for a *'liberation of time,* by virtue of which social individuals should be able to emancipate themselves from the constraints of economic rationality embodied in capital' (Gorz, 2012: 20). However, this does not mean achieving emancipation by stripping society of economic rationality in a vein similar to the call of first generation critical theorist Herbert Marcuse (1969). Gorz's position is actually closer to second generation critical theorist Jürgen Habermas (1984 and 1987a) who envisioned a role for 'economic rationality' in society, albeit a highly reduced one. Like Habermas, he recognized the dangers associated with subjecting most domains of social life to the 'quest for maximum economic productivity' (Gorz, 2012: 32). Furthermore, for the French socialist, emancipation is not so much a matter of 'abolishing capital and the sphere of economically rational commodity activities', as finding 'a limited and subaltern function [for them] in the development of society' (Gorz, 2012: 20). Thus, like Habermas and proponents of emancipation through labour, Gorz recognized the perils of commercialism and, more specifically, economic rationality on self-determination. He also devoted a lot of his energy highlighting the environmental damages caused by a rationality that, to use Morris' own words, treats '"nature" as something external' to individuals and who, in turn, make it 'their slave' (1995: 187). For Gorz, the 'economic imperative of productivity' is antithetical to the 'ecological imperative of resource conservation' (Gorz, 2012: 32). Contrary to Morris and other proponents of the emancipatory work thesis, though, he did not seek to subsume work under a form of rationality more appropriate for treating this sphere of activity as one of self-determination. The latter would be sought outside of the confines of work. In short, he expected the distinctively socialist *'subordination of the economy to society'* (Gorz, 1989: 130, italics in original) to materialize, not by a complete re-organization of economic life as proposed by proponents of emancipation through work but, rather, by expanding 'spaces of autonomy in which economic purposes and commodity logic no longer prevail' (Gorz, 2012: 21).

Thus, despite formulating a damning diagnosis of work under late capitalism, Gorz did not propose a radical re-organization of economic relations. This is partly explained by his aversion towards an ideology of work as self-actualization appropriated by capitalist employers and the consequent rejection of economic democracy. Such a stance, however, is not shared by more recent proponents of the emancipation from labour thesis. For example, the likes of Bastani (2019) and Mason (2015) expect worker cooperatives and other forms of cooperative business models (Mason, 2015) to hold a prominent place in the future of work. For Bastani, the road to a post-capitalist society must involve a 'worker-led economy' relying on a system of 'socialised finance' (2019: 219). For Mason, the introduction of a basic income geared towards the reduction of working time must be complemented by a 'cooperative, self-managed, non-hierarchical' workplace (2015: 297). In both these visions of the future of work, then, the attainment of a post-work society is thought to involve increasing automation, a complete re-organization of economic relations around the principle of self-management, while expecting work to become 'more akin to play' (Bastani, 2019: 56). In those contributions, envisioning a post-work society is not antithetical to imagining a workplace reorganized around self-management. Benavav, therefore, unfairly charges contemporary proponents of the 'automation discourse' for failing to appreciate that 'the abolition of private property and monetary exchange in favor of planned cooperation' is 'the basic precondition for generating a post-scarcity world' (Benavav, 2020: 82). According to many post-work proponents, then, defending self-actualization through labour need not be opposed to the post-work project. One is nevertheless justified in questioning the coherence of a position whereby both full automation and workplace self-management are advocated. For, to take the former seriously means to make the latter redundant. In an effort to both remedy this confusion and deploy the logic of intersectionality to the formulation of a socialist utopia, I propose to step outside of socialist thought strictly speaking, and bring a range of perspectives in dialogue with some of the key issues addressed so far.

A particularly useful basis for assessing the future of work is the one informed by critical disability studies. I therefore propose to start answering some of these questions by addressing the standpoint of disabled people, as embodied in critical disability studies. In addition to the large-scale exclusion of people with disabilities from meaningful forms of work (Bates, Goodley, and Runswick-Cole, 2017), one key issue that is frequently raised in the scholarship in question is the problem emanating from the treatment of work as a basis for 'identity' and 'social membership' (Abberley, 1996). As Bates,

Goodley, and Runswick-Cole noted, '[w]ork is enabling' but also 'debilitates and exploits', and must therefore be treated 'with caution' (2017: 172). What tends to be highlighted in critical disability texts is the fact that many are not and will never be in a position to work and that, consequently, envisioning a society in which work is expected to serve as a basis for the all-round development of individuals risks excluding many disabled people. Here is how critical disability scholar, Paul Abberley, put it:

> The work-based model of social membership and identity is integrally linked to the prevention-cure-orientated perspective of allopathic medicine and to the specific instrumental logic of genetic engineering, abortion and euthanasia. Ultimately it involves a value judgement upon the undesirability of impaired modes of being. [T]he abolition of an individual's disablement is ultimately dependent and subordinate to the logic of productivity. (1996: 74)

Since Marxism and proponents of the emancipation through work thesis tend to fall within the parameters of the 'work-based model' described by Abberley in the earlier passage, they run the risk of reproducing mechanisms of oppression disabled people are subjected to under capitalism. Abberley and many other critical disability scholars, therefore, propose to draw inspiration from social movements and challenge individualism, productionism, and the 'production-based instrumental rationality' (Abberley, 1996: 75), which have all served to oppress disabled people under capitalism. Indeed, taken together, these orientations have shaped a conception of self-determination construed as an action – like 'cooking and eating' – undertaken 'without assistance', which fails to resonate with disabled people (Oliver, 1990: 91). They have underpinned 'a social system organised around the take-for-granted desirability of independence, work and physical normality' (Abberley, 1996: 64), and the consequent exclusion of disabled people from 'social production' (Abberley, 1996: 71). But, contrary to calls by several disability scholars, critical disability scholars are 'wary of drawing the conclusion that fighting oppression should involve our widescale inclusion in social production' (Abberley, 1996: 71). The fight in question is better served by, for example, re-organizing social life so that all individuals, including disabled people, have the 'ability to be in control and make decisions about [their] life' (Oliver, 1990: 91).

Reservations about the treatment of work as a sphere of self-realization are echoed in the work of Black feminist scholars like Patricia Hill Collins (2000). Definitions of what counts as participation in social production are not only formulated by non-disabled people. Those with the power to shape such definitions also tend to be white and male. The fact that white (non-disabled) men tend to be in better-paid and generally more fulfilling occupations than their Black (disabled) female counterparts, is here seen as a key reason why work is regarded as 'something for self' among white workers (Collins, 2000: 48). The history of Black labour, on the other hand, is a history of disenfranchisement, marked by patterns of what Dawson (2016) called 'expropriation' and 'super-exploitation', resulting in sharply different understandings of work from those found among white workers. Historically, it has been a lot more difficult for a Black worker to treat their work as a source of human worth than for a white worker. But despite lacking the material and cultural power to shape dominant conceptions of work, it is possible to find vibrant counter-cultural elements informing non-capitalist visions of work among, for example, Black Americans. With definitions 'that differed from public, market-driven, exchange-based community models', Black communities have often acted as places of 'collective effort and will', as evidenced by the fact that privatized conceptions of motherhood never succeeded in replacing 'communal child care within extended families' (Collins, 2000: 48). 'Notions of interpersonal relations' have indeed been central to the social life of Black people in the US and beyond (Collins, 2000: 48). Black women have effectively refused 'to obliterate the collective experiences, the knowledge, and the struggles that [they] have accumulated concerning reproductive work' and been instrumental in affirming what Silvia Federici calls its 'collectivization' (2019: 113). Solidarity and networks of mutual support have thus been central sources of human worth for those communities, as well as women more generally, who have in turn questioned the evaluation of 'individual worth by the type of work performed' (Collins, 2000: 48).

Critical disability, Black, and feminist scholars, therefore, shed further light onto the power relations framing existing conceptions of work. In addition to its bourgeois character, we found that the idea of work as a sphere of self-actualization tends to reflect the interests and experiences of white non-disabled male workers in the Global North. At first glance, then, it seems that deploying an intersectional lens leads one to conclude that one might be better to imagine the future of work through the emancipation from work thesis than its counterpart. But automation too is currently being harnessed for productionist purposes. For example, machines like computers have played a major role in making capitalism more responsive to the 'accommodation to ceaseless change' (Piore and Sabel, 1984). Like work as self-actualization in a post-Fordist regime, they have served the ends of economic performance.

Furthermore, it is important to note that the critique of the emancipation through work thesis offered by critical disability scholars does not tend to be complemented by an endorsement of a post-work utopia of the kind advocated by the likes of Gorz. In fact, Gorz's own approach to emancipation was an explicit target of criticism in Abberley's (1996) work. The latter takes issue with the fact that despite advocating the 'liberation of time', Gorz expresses demands for self-realization that fail to resonate with disabled people and even risk creating new conditions for disabled people's social exclusion (Abberley, 1996: 70). Gorz's post-work vision does not sufficiently break with the productivist paradigm of action. So, while critical disability scholars might take issue with the treatment of work as a sphere of self-actualization, they do share with the emancipation through work proponents the view that it is both possible and desirable to strip society of instrumental rationality. In fact, I wish to contend that despite not offering a definitive answer to the aforementioned questions, these contributions do hint at an important demand, that is, to re-organize economic life around a logic of action radically different from the one found in capitalist societies.

Ecofeminists, too, have warned against the post-work thesis which, they argue, tends to overlook the fact that several types of jobs, mainly undertaken by women, will never be automated. Maria Mies (2014a: 215), for example, noted that 'people still have bodies which need food and human care' that make complete automation impossible or, at least, highly undesirable. The 'paradise' of a leisure or non-work society, therefore, tends to ignore the necessity of caring practices which machines are not in a position to take on (Mies, 2014a). To be sure, this is something that even the most fervent advocates of full automation, such as Bastani (2019) and Srniceck and Williams (2015), recognize. Affective forms of work like social care or child care cannot be fully automated. For, machines are unlikely to develop the skills needed for such important work. So, if full automation is an impossible prospect, why then seek to achieve it? Furthermore, the 'technocratic utopia' in question is 'based on domination of nature, women and colonies' and will therefore do very little to address capitalist structures of domination beyond those affecting white male workers (Mies, 2014a: 216).

Finally, envisioning a post-work future could run the risk of seriously undermining 'the social function of work' (Jackson, 2021: 122). Given the 'endless replacing of people with machines' is currently driven by the pursuit of labour productivity, which reduces work to a mere value-creating activity (Jackson, 2021: 122). What one must do instead is to envision a different conception of prosperity, no longer cast as material wealth but in terms of 'health, employment, longevity, creativity, durability, fulfilment' (Jackson, 2021: 124). This, along with the alternative logic of economic action and rationality it entails, is understood by ecofeminists like Federici (2019) and Plumwood (2002) and environmentalists like Tim Jackson (2021), as a prerequisite for overcoming forms of domination within society and between society and nature. Thus, not only is full automation questioned here, it is also rejected in favour of a call for a 'labour of care and the work of craft and creativity' (Jackson, 2021: 124), akin to the emancipation through work thesis.

Thus, if we reject emancipation through work on the basis of its co-optation by capitalism, then we would also have to dismiss the possibility that machines hold the potential to emancipate us from work. This means that the debate about the future of work is best served not by framing the matter in terms of emancipation through work vs. emancipation from work, but by pitting emancipation against economic/instrumental rationality. It follows that rather than asking whether full automation is a more appropriate call than emancipation through work, it might be more appropriate to ask what work, stripped of instrumental rationality, would look like, or what conditions would optimize the production and deployment of machines for the subordination of the economy to society? Under this reading, both emancipation *through* work and emancipation *from* work could potentially complement each other in the quest for freeing humanity from the repressive and oppressive rule of instrumental rationality. Crucially, though, it must entail an alternative work culture, or what Mies (2014b: 320) described as a 'reintegration of culture and work, of work as both burden and pleasure'. It 'involves rejecting the notion that Man's freedom and happiness depend *on an ongoing process of emancipation from nature,* on independence from, and dominance over natural processes by the power of reason and rationality' (Mies and Shiva, 2014: 6).

This, I wish to argue, is best realized by pursuing two interrelated lines of action: the collectivization of work – in both its productive and reproductive form – and substitution of labour productivity by *social value* as the key measure of efficiency at work. To collectivize work means to move beyond the 'self-maximising and monological forms of rationality built on the model of the self as an isolated, atomistic self-contained individual' (Plumwood, 2002: 33). It means maximizing the scope for dialogue between workers, so that autonomous self-actualization is experienced as a collective endeavour and so that the freedom of each is aligned with the general social interest. Collectivizing work, therefore, entails bringing radical interdependence into work. It is akin to maximizing the scope for what Jürgen Habermas (1984) called 'communicative action' in economic relations, which economic democracy is rather successful at achieving (Dufays et al., 2020). But it must also do more than merely facilitate dialogue between workers. Collectivization must also include 'earth others' and recognize their 'agentic and dialogical potentialities' (Plumwood, 2002: 177) so that work and self-actualizing workers become 'receptive to the unanticipated possibilities and aspects of the non-human other' (Plumwood, 2002: 194–5) and work no longer raises humanity over nature. Finally, it means overcoming the 'distancing of production from reproduction and consumption' that has underpinned social and environmental domination (Federici, 2019: 109). To this end, reproductive work and consumption must be reimagined as collectivized spheres of autonomous self-actualization brought into dialogue with production (see next section).

The second line of action I propose to take for reimagining work on the basis of the intersectional lens deployed in this chapter is to subsume work under the principles of social value creation. This entails envisioning a logic of work in sharp contrast with the one upheld by the pursuit of labour productivity. According to the latter, work efficiency is measured in terms of how much economic value is created by a worker in a given period of time. It is driven by the distinctively capitalist logic of 'time is money'. The productionist approach to efficiency is strikingly monological, to the extent that the costs are measured by a given indicator, that is, labour productivity. The efficiency of social value, on the other hand, is measured in terms of whether a good or service meets a social need. To know whether a good/ service meets a need, those who supply those them must be in a position to know what the demand is. It entails bringing supply and demand into dialogue with one another. The social value approach to efficiency is, I contend, inherently dialogical and because a 'dialogical model' like this one 'requires a basic level of mutuality and equality, give and take, response and feedback' (Plumwood, 2002: 33), it is particularly well-suited for the task of collectivizing work and, crucially, bringing radical interdependence to life. Social value is to the dialogical model of work proposed here what labour productivity is to the capitalist model. Finally, by facilitating the creation of multiple information flows, this model 'offer[s] the best chance of effective action on ... ecoharms' (Plumwood, 2002: 90–1) and democratizes the processes through which definitions of the relationship between work, self-worth, and, of course, value, are developed. As such, it holds the potential for addressing concerns as diverse as those discussed so far in this chapter. What it does not do, however, is to promote full automation. While it does envision a role for machines, it recognizes that Global North science and technology are, to use Marcuse's (2002) qualification, 'ideological' insofar as they promote particular interests and ways of life at the expense of others, as most clearly illustrated by their impact on the environment and Indigenous populations.

The social value model, therefore, changes the conditions under which science and technology are produced and deployed, so that it can play a role not so much in freeing workers from work but, just like Morris himself had imagined, in giving workers greater scope for self-actualizing work. It is resolutely against drudgery, not work. For, like Jean-Philippe Deranty (2022), it insists on a 'reform [of] the world of work' (2021: 2) that recognizes the immense value and singularity of goods a correctly organized form of work can provide in the form of, for example, 'institutional networks protecting [workers'] interests and their welfare' (2021: 13). Social value creation, then, has an acutely liberating potential for workers. Through the relations of mutuality and reciprocity it presupposes, social value creation turns work into a sphere of radical interdependence and into a form of care, of the form envisioned by David Graeber (2018). This potential can nevertheless only be realized by addressing the macro-level of economic life and, more specifically, conceptualizing a system of allocation of resources driven by social value creation. I now turn to a discussion of this system, where I provide more detailed insights into the kind of institutions the utopia of work imagined earlier entails.

Dialogically coordinated allocation of resources

To start the discussion of the system of allocation of resources envisioned in this book, I thought I would return to Morris' *News from Nowhere*, in which it is possible to find some brief but valuable insights into the system of exchange social value creation could be expected to underpin: 'men make for their neighbours' use as if they were making for themselves, not for a vague market of which they know nothing, and over which they have no control. … So that whatever is made is good, and thoroughly fit for purpose. Nothing can be made except for genuine use' (Morris, 1995: 100).

Put simply, the drive towards the creation of social value entails ensuring that supply meets the needs of society at large. It means ensuring that sufficient information flows for producers to be in a position to meet the needs of consumers. It involves a process of satisfaction of needs whereby those supplying a good or service are conscious of the needs of those who will consume them. For, as anarchist scholar and activist Piotr Kropotkin plainly asked, 'before producing anything, must you not feel the need of it?' (2012: 158). To be sure, capitalism has been rather successful at meeting society's needs. In fact, capitalists themselves would claim that their success is largely attributable to the fact that they provide something consumers need or want. But unlike social value creation, the capitalist (free) market is driven by the principle of economic value creation. Under its guise, needs satisfaction is secondary: what drives the whole process is the profit motive or the fact that the producer can create economic value out of the satisfaction of needs. But to obtain those rewards, producers, or more generally those on the supply side of exchange, have to take risks. They enter exchange without the certainty that the good or service they provide will be needed, and many go bankrupt as a result of trying. This 'secondary uncertainty' (Devine, 1988) illustrates the acutely anarchic character of production which many critics have condemned and identified as a major source of 'macroeconomic instability' (Devine, 1988: 17). A key difference between social value creation and economic value creation, therefore, is the amount of information that those supplying goods and services are expected to hold about society's needs and the way those needs come to be defined. While the former requires vast quantities of information about those needs whose definition capital accumulation continuously expands, the latter thrives on precisely the opposite state of affairs, namely the competitive and self-interested behaviour that results from the scarcity of information about needs that are collectively defined. On the one hand, needs must be known *ex ante* and, on the other, they are known after a risk has been taken. Each form of value creation marks a different system of coordination. But before I tackle the system of coordination driven by social value creation in more detail, let me review some of the key shortcomings of a third, non-capitalist but actually existing and information-heavy system of allocation of resources, namely centralized command planning. This will help identify some key challenges an alternative to the capitalist market must be in a position to rise to.

Excursus: models of allocation of resources

What is often described as 'actually existing' socialism, as found in countries like Russia, Cuba, and China, was marked by a distinctive system of coordination that has mistakenly been regarded as the necessary route for the collectivization of production. Such a system could be summarized as follows:

> Central planning denotes the total body of government actions to determine and coordinate directions of national economic development. The process of central planning is composed of pre-plan studies and forecasts, formulation of aims for given periods of time, establishment of their priorities (order of importance), listing ways and means, and, eventually, the plan's implementation. (Kowalik, 1990: 42)

Under central planning, the satisfaction of needs is coordinated by the state and its various administrative branches. It is a collectivized form of production to the extent that it is managed by an institution – the state – thought to represent the interests of society at large. Key to the central planning, then, is the idea that a central and hierarchically organized institution is in a position to know, based on 'information on the economy's shape and tendencies at any given moment' (Kowalik, 1990: 45), what must be produced in order to meet society's needs. Unlike the capitalist market, which entails production for profit, this system of coordination involved 'planned production for use' (Devine, 1988: 10). As such, it replaced the anarchy of capitalist production underpinned by the 'invisible hand' of supply and demand with a 'central authority' responsible for devising production plans and formulating 'general guidelines' passed down to the relevant bodies more directly involved in the day-to-day production of goods and delivery of services (Kowalik, 1990: 45). The directives and indices comprised in those guidelines must be adhered to by local production units. It follows that '[t]asks named in an enterprise plan are both commands by a superior authority and obligations to supply enough resources to safeguard smooth cooperation' (Kowalik, 1990: 45). Central planning, therefore, 'presupposes some way of determining what production is socially useful, some way for that information to be communicated to production units and reasonable confidence that they will respond to it' (Devine, 1988: 10).

In an effort to ensure that guidelines are acted upon, planners also devised a range of incentives for the different production units. Targets, for example, would be used to reward and penalize both managers and workers of enterprises responsible for meeting society's needs (Devine, 1988). Incentives were in this sense deployed to secure the 'planned pattern of overall output', that is, to influence behaviour so that the 'general social interest' formulated by central planners and imposed on production unit is met (Devine, 1988: 62–3). In fact, such a system of incentives was deemed necessary precisely because what was presented as the 'general social interest' was effectively formulated by a handful of central planners imposing what they viewed as society's needs on managers and workers. Incentives were therefore a way of manufacturing consent for the general social interest.

For some time, the state socialist system of coordination proved rather successful, especially in terms of achieving full employment and low inflation. In fact, before it began to decline, the central planning coordination model managed to achieve a higher 'degree of macroeconomic control over the economy' than in capitalist economies (Devine, 1988: 79). But eventually the model came to exhibit some serious limitations, in terms of its incapacity to both meet society's needs and protect individuals' freedom. Let me start with the former. A key source of inefficiency in central planning can be found in the quantity of information required by planners, along with the way it was communicated. To devise their plans, administrators needed information that can only be known by those involved in local units of production, such as a single factory's productive capacity. They also needed to know how those local units' activities fit within the planned output. Given the scale of the information required by planners, they suffered from 'information overload' (Devine, 1988: 62). What is more, the information they obtained tended to lack the kind of detail required to be able to plan accurately, as a result of increasing aggregation as the 'information passes up the administrative hierarchy' (Devine, 1988: 61). But information was also distorted intentionally as enterprises deliberately under-estimated the costs of their activities to be able to be involved in the plan (Kowalik, 1990). A chronic lack of accurate information, therefore, undermined central planning's capacity to allocate resources efficiently.

But inefficiencies of the kind reviewed here developed amid the subjection of economic activities to political goals which, in turn, led to a highly 'inflated control system' (Kowalik, 1990: 47). On the one hand, workers, managers, and enterprises as a whole acutely lacked autonomy. For, what happened within local production units was effectively dictated by central planners through a range of indices and directives shaping producers' behaviour in such a way as to meet the plan's targets. On the other hand, when consumers did not face shortages, they were provided with 'poor-quality goods and a meagre product mix' (Kowalik, 1990: 47). This made it particularly difficult for state socialism to compete with the free market system, which proved increasingly capable of diversifying supply (Lane, 1996). Centralized command planning, therefore, severely restricted the autonomy for individuals *qua* producers and consumers. It is even possible to argue that, under its guise, the general social interest turned into a repressive force. One is in turn justified in asking whether production for use, that is, a satisfaction of needs directly attuned to the general social interest, could accommodate autonomy.

An answer to this question was given by proponents of a fourth type of system of allocation of resources, known as 'market socialism'. While the market's capacity to allocate resources efficiently and accommodate individual freedoms is emphasized, its detrimental effects are also highlighted. This is why proponents of this model of coordination effectively seek to socialize markets, that is, to create conditions capable of protecting individuals against the exploitation and inequality capitalist markets give rise to. Market socialists, in fact, think market forces are 'compatible with equality and self-government' (Devine, 1988: 83). A delicate balance between market forces, self-managed, and profit-maximizing enterprises, operating within a regulated economic environment, is here thought to secure the cooperative, autonomous, and efficient satisfaction of society's needs. But while it might succeed in alleviating some of the negative effects of market forces, the main system of coordination remains the invisible hand of the supply and demand mechanism. As such, market forces would continue to 'impose … an outcome on people, without addressing their perceptions that what they have been doing is undervalued' (Devine, 1988: 109). Regulatory controls might be able to achieve something akin to the 'organised stage' of capitalist development following WWII, such as a reasonably 'balanced regional development' and 'socially just redistribution of wealth and income' (Jessop, 2002: 61), but would not effectively rid the economy of its anarchic character. Economic agents would continue to be subjected to 'secondary uncertainty', albeit collectively. Furthermore, since profit-maximization would be expected to drive coordination, economic activities would continue to be guided by narrow self-interest. Thus, while it would address the problem of inefficiency marking centralized command planning, market socialism would not eliminate the kind of 'antagonistic social adjustment' found under capitalism (Devine, 1988: 109), and would fall short of creating conditions sufficiently auspicious for self-determination. It would create an environment in which 'decision-makers [have] no choice but to maximize the bottom line' and ignore any 'human effects that did not bear on costs and revenues ... or else risk competitive failure' (Albert, 2003: 70). One the one hand, then, one finds a centralized command planning system that not only found it impossible to gather enough accurate information to be able to allocate resources efficiently, but also severely restricted, if not totally eliminated, the scope for self-actualization. On the other, one finds a market socialist system that has been rather successful at allocating resources, but thrives on the kind of adversarialism and uncertainty that stifle human and more-than-human flourishing. While I would not dare contend that it is possible to find a perfect system of coordination, I am certainly confident that alternatives capable of addressing these problems are both desirable and possible. One fruitful avenue, particularly suited for social value creation, is what I chose to call the system of *dialogical coordination*.

Dialogical coordination

To envision such a system I draw on a range of contributions,[1] which were formulated more or less explicitly as a critique of actually existing systems of coordination such as those discussed earlier. Those contributions do have much in common, but also exhibit some non-negligible differences. In what follows I review the features that are most relevant to the issues raised in this chapter and conclude by offering my own conceptualization of dialogical coordination. It must be noted here that the term 'dialogical' was chosen to highlight the fact that the allocation of resources is, in large part, the outcome of negotiations between diverse actors directly affected by the process. It therefore serves to emphasize both the conscious and deliberative character of this form of coordination and to throw into sharp relief its affinity with pluriversal intersectionality, particularly the notion of radical interdependence.

An important first feature of this system is its decentralized character. Proponents of dialogical coordination reject the view that the task of determining what is socially useful – of creating social value – must be centrally determined. For example, guild socialist G.D.H. Cole warned against the perils of an 'omnicompetent State' (1980: 32). According to him, societies have become far too complex and differentiated for a central institution like the state to act as its representative or, put differently, to know what society needs. Instead, he envisioned a system of coordination that 'involves and implies the extension of positive self-government through all [society's] parts' (Cole, 1980: 13). Put concretely, this entails workers 'enjoying real self-government and freedom *at [their] work*' (Cole, 1980: 49, emphasis in original), and being empowered to deliberate on what counts as socially useful production. This is echoed in Devine's work, whose model of 'negotiated coordination' involves a 'multiplicity of decentralized, autonomous decision-making units' (1988: 13), thought to be a much more appropriate system than central planning for achieving 'the conscious shaping of economic activity' (1988: 5) entailed by social value creation. Thus, rather than a super-imposed set of guidelines based on inaccurate information about society's needs and local units' productive capacity, resources come to be allocated on the basis of negotiations between actors directly involved in the process of satisfaction of needs, such as producers and consumers.

This leads me to a second key feature, that is, dialogue. While many socialist utopias inspired by Marxism have tended to focus on the re-organization of production, proponents of dialogical coordination recognize, as Kropotkin himself did, that it is equally important to devise a system that involves the 'study [of] the needs of individuals' (2012: 158). For, after all:

> [a] man [sic] is usually either a miner or a railway-man, and not both; but he consumes coal, uses the railways, and only limits the variety of his consumption by his lack of opportunity. But in both the essential social differentiation is not that between individuals but that between interests or concerns, that is, between types of production and consumption. (Cole, 1980: 81)

According to Cole, any system of satisfaction of needs must grapple with the fact that the interests of individuals *qua* producers differ sharply from those of individuals *qua* consumers, and that both sets of interests could even end up opposing one another. For example, demands emanating from consumption could exert significant pressure on production and interfere with producers' autonomy. Thus, since '[w]orkers create the social product' and '[c]onsumers enjoy the social product' (Albert, 2003: 91), both must be in a position to engage in a dialogue. Such a dialogue is in this sense key to arriving at 'individually and collectively determined needs' (Devine, 1988: 5) so that needs are met without undermining the self-determination of both producers and consumers. To this end, each side would negotiate with one another through democratically organized associations of producers and consumers. But in addition to safeguarding the satisfaction of needs against the tyranny of the capitalist market and central planners, dialogue between the different units directly involved in the satisfaction of needs addresses the problem of information faced by centralized command planning. For, since communication and information flows no longer need to reach a centre, they are effectively stripped of a range of factors undermining the accuracy of the information used to allocate resources. In fact, 'through conscious social decisions and action', dialogue 'enables more effective use of society's productive resources, in accordance with collectively and individually determined preferences, than would be possible without it'

(Devine, 1988: 13). It provides a 'procedure, a form of social organization, that enables people to make most effective use of the possibilities open to them to achieve their objectives' (Devine, 1988: 13). With dialogue, the invisible hand of the market is substituted by the visible negotiations between producers and consumers. The iron fist of planners comes to be replaced by the self-determined actions of dialogically coordinated economic agents.

A third key feature follows from dialogue and consists of the kind of outlook dialogical coordination is expected to foster. Cole, for example, anticipated his alternative to the capitalist market to involve 'the substitution of service to the community for service for private profit' (Cole, 1946:10). Under its guise, the satisfaction of needs would be driven by an 'impulse of free and unfettered service' (Cole, 1917:302), replacing feelings of greed and fear with the rewarding sense that one has made a 'direct and useful contribution' to society (Cole, 1980: 89). Here, producers would no longer 'seek to thwart [consumers, but instead] be eager to elicit and respond to them because [they] will have the strongest of social motives for doing so, and no sufficient motive for doing otherwise' (Cole, 1980: 89). Dialogical coordination, then, could be said to generate 'information through a transformatory process in which concern for others as well as for oneself is encouraged and reinforced' (Devine, 1988: 191–2). For this reason, it could most certainly be compared to Joan Tronto's (2013) 'caring democracy', which partly aims to entrench the norms of action associated with caring practices in economic relations. Thus, by framing the pursuit of personal freedom as something inextricably tied to the pursuit of freedom of other producers and consumers (Albert, 2003), dialogical coordination serves as a basis on which to bring radical interdependence to life.

Finally, recognizing that the efficient allocation of resources depends on a system capable of coordinating resources and needs within and across spaces of action, proponents of this alternative system of coordination tend to envision a coordination between producers' and 'consumers' organizations at every stage, local, regional and national' (Cole, 1980: 91). Representatives would be elected by members of producer and consumer associations to negotiate at each of those levels. What consequently 'emerges is a network of representative bodies and administrative structures responsible for different functional activities with varying territorial extensions – local, regional, national, and perhaps eventually also international' (Devine, 1988: 142).

But while these features are shared between the different approaches to dialogical coordination I briefly reviewed earlier, some notable divergences are notable. For example, while both Parecon proponents and Devine insist on the value of 'participatory' or 'democratic' planning respectively, Cole's guild socialist phase was marked by a rejection of planning of any form.[2] For the former two, planning is not antithetical to the 'maximisation of positive freedom' (Devine, 1988: 13). In fact, according to Devine, planning of a democratic form is not only an essential basis for 'agreed and socially constructed definitions of the social interest' (1988: 234), but is also a fundamental condition for freedom. This is due to the fact that it equips all relevant economic actors with knowledge about what can and cannot be done under a given set of resources and needs. As such, a democratically planned economy is thought to give those actors the kind of control that could enable them to flourish as producers and consumers. So how does democratic planning concretely operate? What exactly is being planned and how? These questions are best answered by exploring the work of Parecon proponents like Michel Albert (2003) and Robin Hahnel (2016), who provided detailed insights into the kind of allocation of resources entailed by participatory planning. Here is how Albert himself depicted the process:

> In participatory planning every actor (individual or council) at every level will propose its own activities, and, after receiving information regarding other actors' proposals, and the response of other actors to its proposal, each actor makes a new proposal ... And similarly, each production 'actor' proposes a production plan. Workplaces enumerate the inputs they want and the outputs they will make available. Regional and industry-wide federations aggregate proposals and keep track of excess supply and demand ... As every individual or collective worker or consumer participant negotiates through successive rounds of back and forth exchange of their proposals with all other participants, they alter their proposals to accord with the messages they receive, and the process converges. There is no center or top. There is no competition. (Albert, 2003: 128)

Producers and consumers alike formulate plans based on what they need/ desire. However, rather than strictly reflecting their individual interests, those plans are negotiated with other actors, be they producers or consumers. Through dialogical coordination, plans are both individually and collectively determined, aligning each person's own interest with the general social interest. It starts with each actor thinking 'about her or his plan for the year' (Albert, 2003: 136), like a consumption actor making 'proposals for private goods such as clothing, food, toys etc'. (Albert, 2003: 128). But it ends with the associations of producers or 'Neighbourhood councils', as Albert (2003) and Hahnel (2016) call them, approving such requests on the basis of information provided by both consumers and producers.

It must nevertheless be noted that the detailed insights discussed earlier are specific to the Parecon literature. What the likes of Albert and Hahnel have done, and others fell short of doing, was to envision what dialogical coordination would look like in practice. Given the emphasis on 'democratic planning' and 'negotiated coordination', placed by Devine in his work, it would not be unreasonable to assume that the details of his own model would closely resemble those of Parecon proponents. But the more details one provides, the more vulnerable their contribution becomes. One particularly pertinent criticism of Parecon planning was formulated by Erik Olin Wright (2016a) in an exchange with Hahnel (2016) about alternatives to capitalism. Here the late American sociologist takes issue with the need for households to submit a plan for the year in advance and for having to seek approval from the neighbourhood councils. Wright (2016a) expresses his unease and incomprehension at the thought of requiring consumers to both plan a year's worth of consumption and be required to have their personal choices of goods and services approved by a consumer council. Indeed, while he sees no problem in giving such councils a key role in planning for public goods, Wright finds it difficult to see how one's personal consumption choices could affect other consumers and therefore require negotiation. This is, in my view, a fair and important charge levelled at the model conceptualized by Parecon advocates. For, it is rather difficult to expect each consumer to plan, even very sketchily, what they will need for a year. In his response to Wright, Hahnel (2016) insists that consumers will be able to use the information communicated through the first plan as a basis for all future plans and, as such, would not be as burdened with planning as one might expect. But the response, along with the expectation for individuals to formulate personal consumption plans miss the mark. On the one hand, they tend to assume that individuals will only slightly deviate from their original consumption plan every year. This, I think, constitutes an under-appreciation of the volatility of needs marking most individuals' life. For example, what good does the original plan become when someone chooses to move home more or less unexpectedly? Such a change is likely to disrupt one's consumption activities in a significant manner. In fact, one's personal circumstances can regularly and rapidly change, thereby undermining the usefulness of the plan and efficiency of coordination. Thus, to be genuinely useful, plans must be flexible to such an extent that they would not be called plans anymore.

On the other hand, and following on from the earlier reservation, individual plans of this sort run the risk of encroaching on individuals' freedom. For, while the plan might be, in part, individually determined, it could eventually act as a repressive force in cases where individuals wish to deviate from what they originally planned to consume. In turn, it would also risk giving consumer associations like neighbourhood councils too much control in the personal affairs of individuals. But this particular problem with personal consumption raises a more general issue with the phenomenon of planning that many libertarian socialists like Pierre-Joseph Proudhon[3] and G.D.H. Cole fervently', condemned, that is, the evolution of the plan into a diktat. For, a plan – whether negotiated or not – can only become useful if it is complied with, and compliance can quickly turn into servitude once circumstances change. There is therefore something inherently inflexible about all forms of planning, which is why Cole suggested that the role of consumer associations should be limited to making 'articulate and definite the consumers' needs and desires' (Cole, 1980: 89). They would mainly serve as outlets through which consumers' interests are communicated to producers. But he went further and proposed yet another measure to prevent coordination from developing into a repressive force: the representation of the consumer 'must be a specific, functional, *ad hoc* representation' (Cole, 1980: 85). Rather than being required to formulate a plan and seek approval for it, consumers would be free to communicate their needs to functionally differentiated consumer associations, representing their interests on an *ad hoc* basis. How, then, would Cole expect society's needs to be known and resources to be allocated efficiently without a plan?

Cole falls short of providing a clear answer to this immensely important question. The best one can do is to draw on some of Cole's broad principles, which shall form the basis of the position I wish to defend in this chapter. I would in fact contend that contemporary developments such as the emergence of digital technologies, have contributed to making Cole's own model of dialogical coordination a more realistic prospect than ever before. Evidence for this can be found in initiatives like Brazilian online organic food business Raizs, which seeks to minimize food waste by strengthening the bonds between direct food producers and consumers through an on-demand service for its organic products. Here digital technology and machine learning is effectively used to measure consumer demand and ensure that harvest production is optimized by matching that demand as closely as possible.[4] Unlike Wright's (2016b) pluralist position, Cole does not anticipate the market system to play a role in coordinating production for personal consumption. Both what he called 'personal and domestic consumption', as well as '"collective" consumption' must, according to Cole, be subjected to some form of negotiations. The key difference with Albert and Hahnel's proposals, however, is that this need not involve a plan. What could here take the place of the negotiated plan and the market is a system relying on digitally stored information about consumer preferences existing alongside consumer associations, not dissimilar from existing systems such as loyalty cards or algorithms. But instead of being privatized, commercialized, and used to manufacture demand for more goods, those technologies would be made available to all relevant producer and consumer associations, in such a way as to ensure that resources are allocated efficiently. A consumer data body or various consumer data bodies, each, for example, specific to a particular industry, would therefore take responsibility for devising data collection mechanisms like a data consumption card or an online profile that we would all be using to consume goods and services. But, as just emphasized, needs and desires tend to change and vary. Consistent with the role of consumer associations envisioned by Cole and his *ad hocery* principle, consumers would, when needed, choose to communicate their preferences to their representatives who would propose new products or services to producers. Dialogue would therefore mainly drive innovation and safeguard 'certain specific concerns of the consumer, mainly in connection with quantity and quality of production, adequacy of distribution to meet volume and variety, and price of sale' (Cole, 1980: 88). It would also ensure that goods are produced and services are offered if there is use for them. The model of dialogical coordination proposed here, therefore, envisions allocating resources through the combined deployment of big data collection methods and negotiations between democratically organized producers and consumers.

But, so far, I have limited to scope of my analysis of the system of coordination to a rather narrow range of actors. For, while production and consumption are central spheres of interest for the allocation of resources, the latter directly affects and is directly affected by another range of interests that the aforementioned spheres do not necessarily capture. As Devine put it:

> For economic democracy to be real, the detailed use of socially-owned means of production at the local, or sub-system, level must be controlled by those most directly affected by their use at that level. This clearly includes those who work with the means of production in individual workplaces and enterprises. However, other categories of people also have an interest, including users of what is produced, the community in which the workplace is located, the society as a whole in the case of large scale enterprises, groupings concerned with equal opportunities and environmental effects, and possibly others. A way has to be found to enable all with an interest in how particular means of production are used to be involved in the decision. (1988: 132)

While organizing producer and consumer groups democratically increases the chance of addressing issues like discrimination or the environmental impact of economic activities, such an organization may not constitute a sufficient guarantee for the inclusion of such matters in negotiations. Some way of allowing those interests to be involved in dialogical coordination must therefore be found. For example, such 'user groups' could be represented on 'the governing bodies of production units', if only to provide a 'safeguard against the tendency that people have to perceive things primarily from their own standpoint, even when they are genuinely committed to doing what is best for the overall interest (Devine, 1988: 221). Alternatively, such user groups could, in virtue of their non-economic character, form their own associations and negotiate with producer associations to communicate 'the vital spiritual and physical demands of the people' (Cole, 1980: 110). This last proposed feature, therefore, is essential for bringing the pluriversal character of emancipation to life. For, it ensures that decisions making up the allocation of resources develop a relational and dynamic character by grounding them in the intersection of diverse standpoints brought into negotiation with one another, and effectively turning the system of coordination in '*a world where many worlds fit*' (Escobar, 2018: xvi, emphasis in original). The model of dialogical coordination recognizes that individuals inter-exist, namely that their needs, from the personal to the collective, are realized not in competition with others but *through* them.

Such a triangular system of dialogical coordination envisions a conscious allocation of resources with the potential to overcome a range of tensions or contradictions brought about by capitalism, not least between producers and consumers and between the sphere of production and reproduction (see Chapter 6). In so doing, it not only changes how humans relate to one another but also how they relate to the non-human world. As many have pointed out, envisioning a system of allocation of resources that no longer relies on the destruction of the biophysical environment must involve overcoming the 'contradiction between producers and consumers' (Mies, 2014b: 299) underpinning capitalist productionism. It must move beyond economic value creation and towards the creation of social value through the recognition of the 'dialectical relation between production and consumption' (Foster et al. 2010: 395). Because it rests on and cultivates communal forms of production and consumption 'aimed at the genuine needs of communities' (Foster, Clark, and York, 2010: 398–9), dialogical coordination has the potential to foster attitudes focused on 'human relationships, sensuous experience, and qualitative development' (Foster, Clark, and York, 2010: 395) and accommodate the kind of caring practices favourable for radical interdependence across the human world and between the human and non-human world.

Thus, in addition to removing the need for the formulation of repressive plans, dialogical coordination provides a basis for the collective formulation and realization of the general social interest that is sensitive to earth others. Under its guise, dialogue serves the purpose of communicating needs and desires likely to change the quantity and quality of resources and ensuring that negotiated distribution volumes and prices are met. In this sense negotiations are expected to complement information-gathering technologies in formulating the general social interest and ensuring that dialogical coordination successfully creates social value through its allocation of resources. Social value is effectively realized through the formulation and realization of a general social interest negotiated by democratically organized and autonomous producer associations, consumer associations, and user groups. But the conceptualization of economic life under intersectional socialism would not be complete without a discussion of the way ownership is expected to be organized and experienced. I therefore conclude this chapter by providing insights into the kind of property relations potentially suitable for bringing pluriversal emancipation to life.

Property

In what follows I predominantly set out to conceptualize a form of property orientated towards social value creation and compatible with the operational principles of dialogical coordination. Before tackling it, however, a few words must be said about the form of property marking capitalist relations, along with the values underpinning it. For, to understand existing property relations and be in a position to conceptualize an alternative to their capitalist form, it is essential to grasp them as something more than a set of rights enshrined in law. The private property regime dominating capitalist societies is inextricably tied to the 'ideology of "possessive individualism"' according to which 'every aspect or attribute of the subject, from its interests and desires down to its soul' are construed as 'properties that are owned by the individual' (Hardt and Negri, 2004: 203). Under its guise, relations between individuals, as well as between humans and more-than-humans, come to be subjected to economic rationality. Ownership turns into a competitive pursuit framed by relations of power and manipulation, where others, be they human or non-human, are treated as either adversaries or resources. To privatize property means to exclude. It is an inherently divisive regime of property under whose guise some are able to thrive at the expense of others.

Furthermore, the history of privatization, as various practices of expropriation have shown, is a history of dispossession and oppression. Enclosures in England, for example, have not only given landowners exclusive access to land while denying workers free access to their means of subsistence and opening the door to environmentally destructive practices. As the land got privatized and capitalism came to dominate social life, men were turned into poorly paid wage-labourers, Indigenous populations were dispossessed of their land, and women came to be 'increasingly confined to reproductive labor', thereby finding it 'more difficult than men to support themselves' (Federici, 2004: 74). Combined with the inhumane practices of enslavement of African and Indigenous Americans and other dispossessional practices like the gentrification of Times Square in the 1990s (see Chapter 3), the aforementioned practices of expropriation became constitutive of capitalist domination. They served as means for division, dispossession, oppression, and, ultimately, rule.

But the entrenchment of private property in society could not have been possible without its legitimation by 'the idea of the self as an indivisible, bounded unit of autonomous agency' (Bollier and Helfrich, 2019: 39). In fact, without it, capital accumulation itself would be deprived of its very *raison d'être*. For, the drive to accumulate ever more material resources could only be sustained by turning it into a matter of personal success or, put differently, by ensuring that some can claim exclusive access to such resources. The move from 'property ownership ... oriented toward exchange value' towards one where 'possession [is] focused on concrete use and use value' (Bollier and Helfrich, 2019: 222), that is, social value creation, must therefore involve more than a mere economic change. As the discussion on dialogical coordination showed, it must involve thinking differently about the way we relate to ourselves and earth others. As such, it involves anticipating new social relations. This task, I shall argue, can be further served by drawing on the concept of the 'commons', which underpins three possible forms of property: public ownership, common ownership, and relationalized ownership. Before I address them, let me explain what is meant by 'commons'.

Writing about contemporary social movements, Donatella della Porta noted the 'new discovery of "the commons" as spaces in which the common goods are to be managed through the participation of all those affected by them' (della Porta, 2015: 140). While it might be more appropriate to speak of a rediscovery than a new discovery (Federici, 2004; Linebaugh, 2008; Standing, 2019), della Porta is right to highlight the role the commons have recently played in resistance, particularly in the prefigurative opposition of capitalist values and practices. Before capitalism took hold, though, a document known as the *Charter of the Forest*, a long-forgotten companion document of the *Magna Carta*, safeguarded the rights of individuals in England to access and use the land freely so that they can secure their means of subsistence. In one of its clauses, for example, the charter states that '[e]very freeman may in his own woods have eyries of hawks, sparrow hawks, falcons, eagles, and herons; and he may also have honey that is found in his woods' (Cited in Linebaugh, 2008: 9). Here, the commons seem to refer to a '*a conception of people's relation to property and the land*' (Federici, 2019: 79, emphasis in original). So, what exactly are the 'commons'? What kind of counter-culture do they entail and how can they inform the conceptualization of property relations?

While some have interpreted the commons as a set of natural resources used in common and also known as 'common pool resources' (Olstrom, 1990), others have emphasized their extra-economic and extra-environmental character, preferring to speak of 'commoning' rather than 'commons' (see for example Linebaugh, 2008; Patel, 2010; Bollier and Helfrich, 2019). This terminology was chosen to highlight the fact that the commons are much more than mere resources and that, in fact, the concept could shed light on new ways of thinking through which the non-human world ceases to be regarded as an object to be manipulated and mastered. Since the 'commons are living social systems through which people address their shared problems in self-organized ways' (Bollier and Helfrich, 2019: 17), they involve practices marked by the 'willingness to spend much time in the work of cooperation, discussing, negotiating, and learning to deal with conflicts and disagreement' (Federici, 2019: 96). As such, commoning 'involves a web of social relations designed to keep our baser urges in check, fostering different ways of valuing our world, and of relating to others' (Patel, 2010: 97). In virtue of being 'based on a *deep relationality* of everything' (Bollier and Helfrich, 2019: 41), it underpins a system of relations particularly suited for bringing pluriversal emancipation to life. It opposes the hierarchical, competitive, individualist, and divisive relations marking the capitalist property regime with horizontal, cooperative, communal, and relational ones. More specifically, it 'vests all property in the community and organizes labor for the common benefit of all' (Linebaugh, 2008: 6).

As just mentioned, it is possible to conceptualize three forms of property regime emanating from this system of social relations. While each provides an alternative to private property, they do not all fully succeed in bringing pluriversal emancipation to life. This is not to say that they cannot hold a valuable place in an intersectional socialist utopia, but simply to contend that they do not provide a sufficient basis upon which to design an alternative to private property that thrives on relationality and dialogue. Take, for example, public ownership. This property regime involves the national ownership of some industries and 'promotes long-term planning of the economy, helps to provide modernising infrastructure, quality health and social care, and to combat climate change' (Labour Party, 2017: 5). Favoured by central command planning economies, state ownership works towards the general interest but 'inevitably moves the means of production … into the public domain, the sphere of politics' (Devine, 1988: 123). Decisions, therefore, tend to be centralized, with power in the hands of a small political elite. So, while on the one hand, such a form of property does oppose the individualist and competitive ethos upheld by private property, it falls short of accommodating in any sufficient manner the horizontal and cooperative inclinations entailed by commoning practices. For this reason, if public or state ownership were to play a part in an intersectional socialist utopia, it would have to be done through an increase of its 'democratic accountability' (Labour Party, 2017: 5). But even an improvement of this sort would never be sufficient to foster different worldviews and relations. Centralization could far too easily become the preferred way of managing public property. Public ownership, therefore, presents some serious difficulties for designing a property regime suitable for pluriversal emancipation.

The matter becomes more complex when the other two forms of property are examined. For, common ownership and relationalized ownership do display all of the features involved in commoning practices. According to Bollier and Helfrich (2019), however, the former falls short of overcoming some key problems associated with private property. What, then, is common property? This form of property can be found across the world. It can assume diverse forms, ranging from a worker-owned cooperative to communal arrangements such as those found in many Indigenous communities of Latin America (Richards, 1997). Broadly speaking, a common property regime involves 'rights and duties of a group of individuals to one another with respect to a resource held collectively' (Bremner and Lu, 2006: 501). It therefore refers to a system of shared or collective ownership and rather than restricting access to, say, a single individual as in the case of private property, it restricts it to a group. Here, in fact, lies the reason why Bollier and Helfrich found this regime of ownership problematic:

> What we are suggesting is that collective property is only modestly different from personal property. There is no difference in principle between the two. It helps to realize that the etymology of the word 'private' traces back to the Latin word *privare*, meaning 'to deprive'. Individual and collective property rights both authorize the *right to deprive*, or exclude others from use of the property. (2019: 218)

Thus, while common property is less exclusive than private property, it operates on exclusionary terms, to the extent that it just slightly broadens access and use of property. After all, as McKean pertinently pointed out, 'common property is shared private property' (2000: 36). The fact that ownership is shared, often even equally so, among members of a group and that the group, like worker-owned cooperatives, is run democratically, do not seem to constitute strong enough reasons for Bollier and Helfrich to regard common property as a fruitful way of giving life to radical interdependence. Something seems to be missing, such as safeguards against domination and limits to use. For example, the system in question does not in itself eliminate competitive relations between common property groups and prevent, say, a cooperative, from dominating others. But both environmentalist activists insist that they 'are not naively suggesting that all property should instead be open to anybody at any moment, without limitation' (2019: 218). Instead, they conceptualized an entirely new regime of property expected to circumvent the problem of exclusion/domination, while refraining from advocating fully open access to property. They called it 'relationalized property':

> Relationalized property is a novel class of socio-legal governance and provisioning that partially or completely neutralizes exclusive ownership rights over things regarded as property. People decide to adopt a relationalized property regime and manage shared wealth through Peer Governance; the regime is not imposed

on them. It enables forms of interrelated possession of property that is life-enhancing and strengthens relationships – with each other, the nonhuman world, past and future generations, and the common good. (Bollier and Helfrich, 2019: 88)

So, while like common property, wealth is shared, 'no individual or collective can own absolutely' (Bollier and Helfrich, 2019: 150). An example they give is the Movimento Sem Terra (MST) movement in Brazil, in which farmers are given access to the land in a manner akin to the rights protected by the *Charter of the Forest* in England. Here, for example, each farmer can freely choose what to do with their respective plot of land but none of them have the right to sell this land individually, for their 'use of the land is wrapped up with their belonging to the movement' (Bollier and Helfrich, 2019: 150). With relationalized ownership, then, no difference is made between individual and collective interests – both are effectively aligned with one another to pave the way for a system that protects property 'from both internal capture and external alienation' (Bollier and Helfrich, 2019: 220).

Interestingly, however, many of the examples given by the two advocates of relationalized ownership can actually operate within the confines of the common property regime. Bollier and Helfrich even give the example of Park Slope Food Coop in New York, a worker cooperative which they particularly praise for the fact that everyone can choose to become a member-owner of the organization (2019: 242). Such a voluntary basis of membership/ownership is for them an essential precondition for circumventing exclusion/domination. Indeed, as Federici noted, '[e]qual access to the necessary means of (re)production must be the foundation of life in the commons' (2019: 93). Park Slope is nevertheless a cooperative, that is, an organization owned and run by its members. What can therefore be inferred from their analysis is that systems of common property could, under the right conditions, become a form of relationalized ownership. In fact, I wish to contend that what they call relationalized property is effectively a form of common property best operating within a non-capitalist environment. Let me now show you the reasoning behind this claim and, thereafter, draw the contours of a regime of property suitable for the intersectional socialist utopia formulated in this book.

In their fairly detailed conceptualization of relationalized property, Bollier and Helfrich insist that the owned resource must cease being subjected to the 'capitalist practice of allowing those with greater money to out-govern and control others' (2019: 220). To this end one must seek its removal from market relations and de-commodify possible forms of property like land. Instead of experiences marked by power and control, relationalized property would foster a sense that the use, access and experiences of particular resources, be they 'lands, waters, forests, systems of knowledge, capacities for care' (Federici, 2019: 93), are shared. Relationalized property fosters sociality and solidarity. It cultivates, and indeed relies upon, a sense that one's access to a resource is not achieved at the expense of another individual. Such a state of affairs can only be achieved through three key requirements: that membership to an organization responsible for managing a particular resource be open and voluntary, that ownership of the resource be shared, and that decisions about the resource in question be made democratically. But such conditions are not antithetical to common ownership. For, if common ownership operates within a system orientated towards a dialogically coordinated social value creation rather than within a free-market system marked by competitive economic value creation, then equal access to the means of (re)production becomes a much more realistic prospect. Social value creation does indeed provide a fruitful basis upon which to reimagine property in relational terms. Furthermore, rather than being the property of individual workers, rights of ownership under a common property regime 'are vested in the workers as a collectivity' (Dahl, 1985: 142). As such, they do not possess rights of ownership individually and must, consequently, seek discussion and negotiation. Crucially, they 'lack most of the rights thought essential to private property, such as rights to possess, use, manage, rent, sell, alienate, destroy, or transmit portions of the enterprise' (Dahl, 1985: 151). Common property, therefore, holds the potential to display many of the features Bollier and Helfrich identified with relationalized property. The latter is essential for achieving pluriversal emancipation, for it is key to bringing to life the notion that 'nothing exists by itself, that everything interexists' (Escobar, 2018: 84) within property relations. But while a relational property regime does not yet exist, its nuclear and incomplete existence can be located in existing forms of common property such as those discussed earlier and which hold the potential to be developed into relationalized systems.

This is not to say that other forms of property would not be expected to exist alongside it. Indeed, there is no reason to believe that personally owning an everyday consumer good of some form like clothing or furniture would be incompatible with shared ownership of the means of (re)production. It would nevertheless be unreasonable to assume that all resources used by individuals *qua* consumers must be privatized. For example, some goods that are currently privatized in many parts of the advanced capitalist world, like education, roads, information/knowledge and healthcare, would become public goods. While some of those goods lend themselves to common ownership, others might benefit from becoming state property. For this reason, it would be reasonable to anticipate a role for public ownership for goods whose quality and quantity is best secured by the financial power of the state: goods that are not only socially desirable but also require long-term planning and the modernization of large infrastructures. But while their ownership would be public, that is, owned by the state, their management/ administration would be, wherever possible, local and democratic. It would therefore be more appropriate to speak of a majority form of property, the relationalized property regime, and minority forms like private and public ownership, confined to specific resources and uses. Crucially, though, a utopia envisioning pluriversal emancipation must be in a position to imagine a system of property relations appropriate for social value creation. Its guiding principle must therefore be to transform property in such a way that one owns not *against* or *in spite of* others but *through* others, as in the case of relationalized property.

Conclusion

Envisioning an economic life capable of turning pluriversal emancipation into a reality requires one to imagine institutional forms auspicious for radical interdependence. What I sought to achieve in the preceding discussion is to show what such relationality could look like in work, the system of allocation of resources and property. Through the deployment of an intersectional lens taking us through the knowledge projects like those of critical disability studies and Black feminist thought, one can begin to reach beyond the tension between emancipation through work and emancipation from work found in socialist thought. Lying at the intersection of this dialogue between different critical approaches to work, could be found a conception of work underpinned by social value creation. It was shown that in virtue of orientating production towards a form of use/general social interest defined and realized collectively, social value creation holds the potential for bringing radical interdependence to life. It could help transform work in such a way as to align individuals' interest with collective ones through the democratization of the workplace and favouring the re-organization of work over its (automated) demise.

Social value creation, it was further agued, is best realized within a dialogical system of coordination giving producers, consumers, and user groups the possibility to negotiate the general social interest or, put differently, to allocate resources based on a dialogue between different democratically organized interest groups affected by this allocation. Dialogical coordination, as I proposed to envision it here, makes explicit the function and necessary complementarity of different economic agents and organizations. In this sense it is directly informed by the principle of radical interdependence.

Finally, social value creation could serve as a basis for designing an alternative regime of property that would supplant the exclusionary system of private ownership with an inclusionary system of relationalized property capable of minimizing, if not even eliminating, exclusive control by an individual or group over resources that can be subjected to commoning practices. Intersectional socialist economic life is therefore inherently self-actualizing, democratic, cooperative, and inclusive. But for such a re-organization to be possible, the sphere of reproduction, too, must be rethought, along with its relationship to production. For as indicated in this chapter, such economic changes require a more fundamental change in culture and social relations. In fact, it requires us to rethink how economic life relates to reproductive activities and move beyond the capitalist sexual division of labour.

On the 'Production of Life' and Labour of Care

Introduction

Reports of rape and domestic abuse towards women rarely lead to convictions. The police and the courts, which are male-dominated institutions, often fail to pay heed to the voice of women (Farris and Holeman, 2015). They either deny that the statements made by women are true or that the matter they report is of public significance. In fact, police officers often treat domestic violence as a private matter, unwilling to accept that what happens in the home should be of public concern (Farris and Holeman, 2015). A hierarchy of significance is therefore built around the private/public split, which, as will be further explored next, also operates as basis for patriarchal domination.

But the split's implications are visible beyond relations between men and women. Take, for example, the *Lawrence and Garner vs. Texas* ruling in the US. While it made history by ruling that consensual sodomy does not constitute a crime, this sexual act had to take place behind closed doors, in the private sphere. Decriminalization of same-sex adult sodomy was predicated upon its privatization. Here the treatment of an act as something private appears to constitute progress for queer people. But as Jasbir Puar (2007) noted, it effectively marked an attempt to remove queerness from public sight and, consequently, to regulate it. Because the legal case involved a Black American (Tyron Garner), the ruling also contributed to the homonormativization of black male subjects and their inclusion within the 'national body politic' (Puar, 2007: 136). By homonormativizing queer Black subjects, then, the ruling does not so much liberate them as impose a (homo)normativity on them. In short, it further universalizes heteronormative domesticity. What such an analysis of the ruling helps shed light on, then, is not only the co-constitution of heteronormativity, capitalism, and white supremacy but the central role of the capitalist sexual division in supporting capitalist domination. It follows that in addition to imagining an alternative economic life, an intersectional utopia must also envision a world beyond the capitalist sexual division of labour.

The task of this chapter consists in envisioning the operations of radical interdependence within what Honneth (2017) called the 'sphere of love, marriage and the family'. But as it will entail altering the relationship between the private realm and its public counterpart, it will also include a clarification of the re-organization of the economic sphere discussed in the preceding chapter. The insights offered here aim to breathe new life into the way the relationship between the two spheres in question is reimagined and draw largely on contributions emanating from ecofeminism, queer of colour critical theory, and critical disability studies. What follows, in fact, rests on a core presupposition, namely that an expanded conception of capitalism requires one to formulate a critique of the capitalist sexual division of labour and that the latter entails both a critique of political economy and normativity. It therefore echoes some of the presuppositions found in Roderick Ferguson's brilliant *Aberrations in Black* (2004), in which we are reminded of the necessity to complement a critique of economic oppression with a critique of the way ideas and behaviour come to be normalized. I begin by complementing the intersectional analysis of capitalist domination provided in Chapter 2 by making explicit how the formal separation between a private and a public sphere of action came to underpin capitalism's development and how it, too, came to uphold capitalist domination. I then turn to the task of affirming the mutual dependence of productive and reproductive life, which the capitalist sexual division of labour contributed to erasing. Finally, alternative kin relations are envisioned.

The capitalist sexual division of labour

The emergence of a private sphere, construed as the domain of social life almost exclusively devoted to reproductive activities, leisure, consumption, and intimate relations, standing outside the realm of economic and political life, is a relatively novel invention. This development is inextricably tied to the spread of capitalist relations, particularly the commodification of labour power through the introduction of wage labour (Horwitz, 2015), the domestication of women (Federici, 2004; Mies, 2014a), the separation of state and civil society, and the institutionalization of a bourgeois sphere of public opinion-formation with the potential to influence political decision-making (Habermas, 1989). These developments have effectively served the differentiation and separation of two spheres of activity, each governed by its own logic of action. While there are several different meanings in the sociological and political science literature for the words 'private' and 'public', the former shall be used in this book mainly to refer to the sphere of personal life and to all matters deemed by bourgeois society irrelevant to, or indirectly affecting, public life or the general social interest. 'Public', on the other hand, shall refer to both economic and political life, that is, the sphere of activity in which decisions are, under capitalism, thought to affect the general interest in a direct manner.

Under the public sphere's guise, the efficiency and productivity of a worker's labour must be optimized, and the public use of reason for rational deliberation freed from natural impulses. In virtue of its indirect contribution to economic and political life and overtly intimate character, domesticity came to be construed by the bourgeoisie as a burden; as a barrier to economic performance and rational decision-making. To be able to optimize economic value creation and rational argumentation, workers and participants in rational-critical discourse were expected to be freed from the 'burden' of child-rearing, emotional attachment and the like. The separation of the public sphere from its private counterpart is therefore a separation of decision-making activities with the power to shape society from the realm of intimacy and domesticity, where decisions are only expected to affect personal relations. It is also a separation between two sets of behavioural norms. Performance in each of these spheres of action is indeed assessed on the basis of distinct, if not antagonistic, normative yardsticks. In private life, for example, the capacity to nurture and care for others is construed as a strength. In public life, such character traits are thought to interfere with economic value creation and rational argumentation, and are consequently regarded as a weakness (Benería, 1999; Acker, 2004). Each sphere, therefore, celebrates distinct norms of behaviour. I must note that in this chapter, I mainly draw on feminist critiques of the private/public split and therefore place a predominant focus on the economically productive side of public life, that is, the decision-making activities devoted to material production. The political dimension of the public sphere will be dealt with in the following chapter. This is why in what follows I regularly refer to the private/public distinction as one between reproduction and production. The norms of behaviour I shall be referring to therefore speak of the private sphere as the realm of reproductive life and the public sphere as the realm of material production.

But the distinction in question is much more than a mere difference in the way individuals are expected to behave in each of the two spheres. The separation of productive from reproductive life could in fact be said to frame and uphold a vast system of structures of domination. A first and rather well-documented set of structures within the feminist literature are those associated with patriarchal domination. Here the distinction between private and public norms of behaviour is not limited to a difference in the way people are expected to behave. It is effectively a 'gender-coded' distinction underpinning the 'reproduction of different and unequal lives of women and men, and … the reproduction of images and ideologies that support difference and inequality' (Acker, 2004: 25). This is explained by the fact that the separation took the form of a sexual division of labour assigning the responsibility for production to men and for reproduction to women and, crucially, that capitalism prioritizes economic value creation, that is, production, above all else. The separation of production and reproduction, therefore, turned into a source of inequality between men and women once a system that thrives on this separation and places a premium on capital accumulation became dominant. This structure of domination manifests itself in the fact that housework is unpaid or treated as a non-economic form of labour and that the kind of paid jobs women do are 'viewed as the result of women's reproductive activities' (Benería, 1979: 203).

But it also manifests itself culturally or ideologically, through capitalism's tendency to reward what has come to be regarded as a masculine form of behaviour, namely one that is rational-calculative, 'aggressive, ruthless, competitive, adversarial' (Acker, 2004: 29), while punishing nurturing inclinations that capitalist relations have constructed as distinctively feminine and irrational. Such gendered norms of behaviour are in turn naturalized in the form of gendered biological properties, according to which men are born rational beings with the natural inclination to accumulate capital and women are irrational creatures predisposed to care and nurture. The private sphere has even tended to be ignored by political theorists, like the social contract theorists (Pateman, 1988) or many of the early socialists (Honneth, 2017). In their work society seems to be reduced to a single sphere, that is, the public sphere. The only visible social actors are men; the only free agents are men. What those texts take for granted and end up reproducing, then, is the construction of the separation between the public sphere and the private sphere as a separation between freedom and subjugation, respectively. What they fail to account for, therefore, is the entire system of domination upon which the organization of society into a public and private sphere rests on: 'sexual contract' (Pateman, 1988). It is through the implicit formulation of the latter that men are set free to lead society and women are expected to support them. It is also through this contract that the capitalist sexual division of labour naturalizes gender differences.

There is yet another, albeit less widely studied (Federici, 2004; Mies, 2014a), way in which the production/reproduction separation has contributed to patriarchal domination under capitalism. Under this reading, the role of men in 'gain[ing] control over the reproductive capacities of women' is emphasized (Mies, 2014a: 69). This position is most fully developed in the work of ecofeminists Maria Mies (2014a) and Silvia Federici (2004) who have brilliantly shown how the witch hunt taking place across Europe in the 18th century was both essential for capitalism's entrenchment in society and key to 'controlling women's sexual and reproductive behaviour' (Mies, 2014a: 69). Here is how Mies described the developments in question:

The witch hunt had not only the direct disciplinary effect of controlling women's sexual and reproductive behaviour, but also the effect of establishing the superiority of male productivity over female productivity. These two processes are closely connected. The ideologues of the witch hunt found no end in denouncing the female nature as sinful ('sin' is synonymous with 'nature'), as sexually uncontrollable, insatiable and ever ready to seduce the virtuous man. What is interesting to note is that women were *not yet* seen as sexually passive or even as asexual beings, as was the case later in the nineteenth/twentieth centuries. (2014a: 70)

Thus, in addition to excluding women from wage labour and constructing them as weak and vulnerable, the capitalist sexual division of labour subjugated them to the reproduction of the workforce and regulated their sexuality (Federici, 2004). Since this confinement to unpaid reproductive work unfolded alongside the commercialization of economic life, including the privatization of land, it had the effect of worsening their conditions of existence. For, it was not until the firm entrenchment of capitalist relations that women came to be pacified to such an extent and were denied, like their male proletarian counterparts, 'access to the commons and other communal assets' which had provided them with their own means of subsistence (Federici, 2004: 97). Capitalism was in fact highly successful in 'reducing women to a double dependence: on employers and on men' (Federici, 2004: 97). The capitalist separation of productive and reproductive life is, from the standpoint of women's experiences, a case of acute dispossession. This is what led Federici (2004: 64) to describe capitalism as responsible for 'more brutal and insidious forms of enslavement' than feudalism.

Once one begins to grasp the role of the sexual division of labour in patriarchal domination, one can begin to appreciate the role of institutions like marriage and the nuclear family in structuring oppression among women and beyond. Michel Foucault (1978: 122), for example, highlighted the heteronormative family's function as 'instrument of political control and economic regulation' ensuring the compliance of individuals' sexual behaviour, particularly of the poorer classes, with bourgeois norms. More specifically, the nuclear family, which is based on 'imaginary identifications with opposite and asymmetrical masculine or feminine positions' (Hennessy, 2000: 25), ensures the reproduction of the workforce by naturalizing heteronormativity and demonizing homosexual identity, unless the latter can accept its assimilation within 'dominant heteronormative assumptions and institutions' (Duggan, 2003: 50). As D'Emilio (1993) compellingly demonstrated, the capitalist sexual division of labour contributed to the creation of sexual identities harnessed for the ends of capital accumulation. But, in the process, it demonized particular behavioural traits, such as those associated with femininity and non-monogamous homosexuality. The gentrification of Times Square in New York offers a particularly vivid and tangible demonstration of this phenomenon through the eradication of loci and practices of the 'public sexual culture' on which the members of the queer community relied to express their sexual identity (Warner, 1999: 179). This is reinforced by the ruling of the 2003 *Lawrence and Garner vs. Texas* case discussed earlier, which concluded that same-sex practices did not constitute a crime as long as they take place behind closed doors. These developments effectively served to discipline those individuals by not only physically removing their sexual practices from the public eye but also by ensuring their assimilation within 'the dominant culture of privacy' (Warner, 1999: 179). The capitalist separation of production and reproduction, along with the institutions it has given rise to, have thus created conditions particularly favourable for integrating patriarchal domination and heterosexism.

Similar tendencies are at work in the capitalist oppression of disabled people, some of which have already been discussed in Chapter 5. Of particular interest here, however, is the role played by the production/reproduction split in pathologizing impairment. Like women, disabled people have been constructed as 'mad, bad and ill' (Goodley and Runswick-Cole, 2010: 274). This is explained by the way impairments come to be interpreted under an economic regime that rewards economic performance and punishes forms of behaviour that fail to conform to the productivist ethos. Critical disability scholar Michael Oliver (1990: 71) in fact noted that 'the experience of disability, like experience generally, is structured by the "ideology of masculinity"' under capitalism. Because impairments often limit disabled people to contribute to material production, they tend to be treated not only as different but also as unproductive and sick (Barnes, 1996). They fail to match the 'abled-bodied ideal' culturally produced by capitalist societies (Barnes, 1996). Their impairment is also medicalized and, as such, reduced to individual biological properties (Oliver, 1990). They are seen as unable to free themselves from natural constraints and act as rational economic beings. In short, they are, like women and queer people, ideologically and materially condemned to a life in the private sphere.

There is nevertheless a non-negligible risk associated with analysing patriarchal oppression, capitalist ableism, and heterosexism mainly in terms of exclusion from public life. As the work of Black feminists and queer of colour critics has shown, the operations of oppression induced by the capitalist sexual division of labour do not necessarily follow a logic of confinement to the private realm of social life. In fact, doing so runs the risk of overlooking a range of oppressive conditions affecting particular groups, like queers of colour. The latter do not only experience an exclusion from the public sphere but are also often expulsed from the home by their heteronormative parents (Ferguson, 2004: 2), as vividly depicted by the first scene of the ground-breaking series on Black ballroom culture *Pose*. The same problem goes with focusing on the plight of the middle-class housewife. Such a focus distracts one from fully grasping how particular groups of women experienced oppression, not as a result of their exclusion from public life, but because of their acute exploitation within it (hooks, 1984; Collins, 2000). Here gender, race, and class work together to produce acute forms of oppression. To be sure, both Mies (2014a) and Federici (2004) recognized and explicitly highlighted how gender and race were 'constitutive of class rule' (Federici, 2004: 64). For instance, primitive accumulation did not merely create a capitalist class hierarchy and proletarianize vast segments of the population across the Global North, it also entailed the formation of sharp divisions and forms of servitude articulated around gender and race, with the effect – among many others – of fragmenting the nascent working class (Federici, 2004). But what a shift towards the experiences of Black working-class women offers is a fuller understanding of the implications of the production/reproduction separation for this particular group. Indeed, on the one hand, the formal split between a sphere of paid work and unpaid reproductive work does not apply to many American Black working-class women. While their work has historically been unpaid, it was not confined to the private sphere (Collins, 2000). For example, 'U.S. Black women worked without pay in the allegedly public sphere of Southern agriculture and had their family privacy routinely violated' (Collins, 2000: 47). The nature of these women's experiences cannot therefore be adequately captured by the concept of housewifization found in many feminist works like those of Mies and Federici.

On the other hand, the capitalist sexual division of labour is essential for understanding how the experiences of Black women in the Global North are constructed. Such constructs tend to depict this group as 'deficient' in gender terms (Collins, 2000). Since they tend to work in the public sphere, Black women have to compete with men and consequently 'become less "feminine"' (Collins, 2000: 47). Thus, while framing the experiences of Black women with the critique of housewifization falls short of adequately grappling with the material dimension of their oppression, it is an essential step for understanding its ideological articulation. Such insights are immensely important not only for grasping the way capitalist oppression operates but also to be able to envision an alternative to capitalism. They do not only alert us to the pernicious material and ideological consequences of the production/reproduction split, but also encourage us to see beyond the fixed character of this split. In turn, they open up the scope for thinking of an alternative relationship between production and reproduction and even help rethink what counts as productive and reproductive life.

However, the implications of the capitalist sexual division of labour for racial oppression do not end here. As already shown in Chapter 2, racial domination in the Global North is inextricably tied to colonial rule. In fact, as Mies compellingly argued, the pacification of women through the split between production and reproduction is itself directly connected to colonization:

> It is my thesis that these two processes of colonization and housewifization are closely and causally interlinked. Without the ongoing exploitation of external colonies – formerly as direct colonies, today within the new international division of labour – the establishment of the 'internal colony', that is, a nuclear family and a woman maintained by a male 'breadwinner', would not have been possible. (Mies, 2014:a 110)

Both the witch hunt in the Global North and colonial rule by the Global North have entailed the brutal subjugation – at times even extermination – of women and Indigenous communities respectively. Both have been possible by constructing women and Indigenous peoples as 'disorder or unreason' (Plumwood, 2002: 105) and confining them to particular spheres of action – unpaid reproductive labour for white women in the Global North and unpaid productive labour for colonized populations (Quijano and Ennis, 2000; Dawson, 2016). The disciplining of those groups therefore depended on opposing the oppressor's qualities to those of the oppressed and, in turn, devaluing the latter. In both cases, then, it is possible to observe a division or separation, both material and ideological, turning into a basis for inequality and domination. In both cases, one finds the shadow of the formal separation of private/unreason and public/reason, which the white male bourgeoisie brutally imposed on societies both within and outside of the Global North to gain control over the reproductive capacities of women and of the re/productive capacities of colonized peoples. But as we will now see, it was also instrumental in gaining control of natural resources.

Indeed, while the liberation of production from the 'burden' of reproductive work contributed to deep divisions and forms of servitude articulated along class, gender, (dis)ability, and race lines, it also put to work a logic of environmental domination. The latter, Mies (2014a: 71) contends, was 'first established between men and women and men and nature'. This is because the process through which men and women are differentiated is one and the same as the process differentiating humans from nature. The separation of productive/public life from reproductive/private life was, after all, part of a commercialization of economic life driven by imperatives of efficiency and productivity which turned nature into a source of economic value creation, thereby raising humanity above nature. This process of separation and subjugation, which marked the advent of modernity and the victory of capitalist relations over feudalism, constituted the core object of Carolyn Merchant's ecofeminist critique of the scientific revolution. Here is an extract of her work, which was highly influential among ecofeminists:

> Central to the organic theory was the identification of nature, especially the earth, with a nurturing mother: a kindly beneficent female who provided for the needs of mankind in an ordered, planned universe. But another opposing image of nature as female was also prevalent: wild and uncontrollable nature that could render violence, storms, droughts, and general chaos. Both were identified with the female sex and were projections of human perceptions onto the external world. The metaphor of the earth as a nurturing mother was gradually to vanish as a dominant image as the Scientific Revolution proceeded to mechanize and to rationalize the world view. The second image, nature as disorder, called forth an important modern idea, that of power over nature. Two new ideas, those of mechanism and of the domination and mastery of nature, became core concepts of the modern world. An organically oriented mentality in which female principles played an important role was undermined and replaced by a mechanically oriented mentality that either eliminated or used female principles in an exploitative manner. (Merchant, 1990: 2)

The subjugation of women by men was made possible by confining women to nature. Correspondingly, the subjugation of nature by humanity was supported by the feminization of nature, that is, by treating nature as a source of disorder and chaos that be brought under control. The two processes are therefore inextricably linked through the ideological construction of women and nature as belonging to the private realm of chaos, disorder, and irrationality; as objects of control and manipulation. Under capitalist relations, the bourgeoisie's attempt to withdraw white women from productive life and pacify them did not simply mean laying the groundwork for a despised (homo)sexuality, the oppression of disabled people, and the expropriation of racialized populations both within and outside of the Global North, it also meant gaining control over nature.

The sexual division of labour is therefore a relatively new invention, which, without shifting the analysis away from the bourgeois standpoint, could appear to constitute a rather benign and even highly progressive achievement. This is because without deploying an intersectional lens, one would be forgiven to think that the emergence of a private sphere of intimate relations withdrawing women and children from the toil of productive life marks a humanization of the '*most deeply interpersonal of all human institutions*' (Horwitz, 2015: 98, emphasis in original), namely the family. However, under the surface of this seemingly humanizing development lies a much more troubling reality. The distinction between rationality and irrationality, order and chaos, monetary and non-monetary relations, paid and unpaid work, competing and nurturing, and so on, entailed by the split of production and reproduction becomes a subjugating force under a socio-economic system that effectively favours behavioural traits associated with economic value creation over those connected to reproductive life. Once this component is included within the scope of the analysis, it becomes possible to see the emergence of the bourgeois family as something rather different from a humanizing development. What is instead highlighted is its role in social control and, more specifically, its deployment by the bourgeoisie as a means to secure efficient economic value creation and impose a rationalist-productivist ethos on society through the material and ideological disciplining of the working class, women, homosexuals, disabled people, colonized peoples, and the mastery of nature. This should not however be a cause for pessimism; quite the contrary. What I hope has been made clear in the earlier analysis is that what is understood as private/reproduction and public/production under capitalism is not, after all, fixed or absolute. It is, as already mentioned, a rather novel phenomenon often resisted by Black women, the queer community and Indigenous communities struggling against colonizers, among others. In what follows I conceptualize some possible avenues for moving beyond the structures of domination discussed earlier.

From the capitalist sexual division of labour to the 'production of life'

In Chapter 5 I explored possible avenues for the re-organization of economic life along intersectional socialist lines. I also argued that the economy ought to be reimagined around social value creation, that is, by measuring the efficiency of economic activity in terms of whether a good or service meets a social need. In this chapter section, I complement the conceptualization of the relationship between production, consumption, and user groups offered in the fifth chapter by shedding light on the relationship of those components of dialogical coordination with reproductive life. I take particular issue with the disciplinary effects of the production/reproduction split, especially the silencing of multiple groups' voices through their confinement to the latter sphere. Let me start, though, by taking stock of Silvia Federici's own explanation for patriarchal domination in capitalist society, as this will help grasp the core issue at hand when setting out to imagine an alternative to the capitalist sexual division of labour:

> the power differential between women and men in capitalist
> society cannot be attributed to the irrelevance of housework

for capitalist accumulation – an irrelevance belied by the strict rules that have governed women's lives – nor to the survival of timeless cultural schemes. Rather, it should be interpreted as the effect of a social system of production that does not recognize the production and reproduction of the worker as a social–economic activity, and a source of capital accumulation, but mystifies it instead as a natural resource or a personal service, while profiting from the wageless condition of the labor involved. (2004: 8)

At the heart of male domination under capitalism lies the exclusion of reproductive work from what counts as social production or, to be more precise, from the sphere of activity thought to be devoted to realizing the general social interest. This separation, which also marks a split between reason and unreason, culture, and nature, and so on, is, as shown in the previous section, also a basis on which other forms of domination have been produced and/or reproduced. Reproductive work's confinement to the private sphere effectively corresponds to its devaluation as an activity that, in virtue of not making a direct contribution to capital accumulation, is not sufficiently important to be rewarded financially. Particularly striking here, then, is that despite being a vital sphere for the reproduction of the workforce and, consequently, for acting as an 'indispensable background condition for the possibility of capitalist production' (Fraser, 2014: 61), reproductive life is treated as value-less. Even its commodification is unable to overcome such a denigration, as evidenced by the experiences of carers, nannies, and other paid reproductive workers. In reality, since capitalism itself is the problem, it is unreasonable to think that extending capitalist relations is part of the solution. Attention should instead be devoted to a radical re-organization of the relationship between production and reproduction beyond capitalism's parameters. This, I wish to argue, is a precondition for ensuring that, to borrow Mies' (2014a: 210) terminology, the 'colonizing divisions' underpinning capitalist domination are finally stripped from social life.

Central to such a re-organization is the task of redefining what counts as social production and imagining the institutional forms capable of reflecting and upholding such a redefinition. It entails 'revising institutional boundaries' (Fraser, 2020: 10) in such a way as to end the devaluation of reproductive life. A set of institutional boundaries have already been revised in the preceding chapter, where economic life was opened up to include the kind of decision-making processes capitalism had historically confined to the political sphere. The task at hand here is nevertheless of a different nature. It must involve, as Federici argued, putting 'an end to the separation between the personal and the political and between political activism and the reproduction of everyday life' (Federici, 2019: 112). This does not however mean 'abolish[ing] any separation between public and private life' (Tronto, 2013: 17). What it means is that one must redefine the boundaries of each of those two spheres, that is, to rethink what counts as private and public.

Politicizing the personal

The starting point for this ambitious but necessary task ought to be the rallying slogan of second wave feminists in the 1960s: 'the personal is political'. The slogan was predominantly aimed at ensuring that women's suffering, whether in the form of domestic violence, their confinement to the private sphere or the general devaluation of reproductive life, is regarded as much more than a strictly personal issue. This suffering must instead be treated as something connected to a wider system of male domination. It follows that precisely because of this connection, the 'personal' ought to be treated as matter of collective responsibility. To politicize the personal therefore entails resisting the silencing of patriarchal domination. It means making visible what the private/public split had rendered invisible. It means ensuring that the interests of those involved in reproductive life are recognized as the interests of society at large. Ultimately, then, it means turning much of what capitalism has historically treated as private and personal into matters of public interest and collective responsibility. Politicizing the personal turns what might be regarded as a domestic matter for which individuals are personally responsible to a 'larger social problem' (Shah, 2002: 121) involving the responsibility of society at large. Strikingly, the fact that, as a socio-economic system, capitalism has been unable to give material and ideological recognition to the fundamental importance of reproductive life seems all the more incomprehensible once the demand to politicize the personal is taken seriously. It is a key step towards exposing the irrationality of an institutional order that denigrates reproductive work and towards recognizing the latter as the 'material basis of our life' (Federici, 2019: 196).

What, then, does politicizing the personal mean in concrete terms? What kind of institutional re-organization is expected from such a demand? To answer those questions I draw inspiration, once again, from the work of feminists, most notably Federici's (2019) own, particularly her demand for 'collectivising reproductive work'. Under such a reading, politicizing the personal entails redefining 'our reproduction in a more cooperative way' (Federici, 2019: 112). It entails re-organizing everyday life around the same principles as those identified for the re-organization of economic life, that is, to bring it under collective, even democratic, control (Devine, 1988: 156), while cultivating the 'impulse of free and unfettered service' (Cole, 1917: 302). But while such a re-arrangement might at first glance seem unreasonable, impracticable, and entirely utopian, the organization of reproductive life as a collective process was something that had existed for centuries prior to the emergence of capitalism, through networks of mutual care and support provided by the extended family or the local community (Federici, 2019: 111). Calls for the 'communalization of housework' (Federici, 2019: 110) have in fact been central to the feminist tradition, at least in the US. They find some of their contemporary manifestations in phenomena like 'othermothers' in Black American communities. Othermothers can be another member of one's family or friend sharing the responsibility for child-rearing with the blood mother (Collins, 2000). Through this practice children are not regarded as property or possession (hooks, 1984: 144). For this reason, it challenges the values and norms of behaviour associated with 'prevailing capitalist property relations' (Collins, 2000: 182) and in effect collectivizes a sphere of activity that those relations had privatized. Little seems therefore new in Honneth's (2017) demand for envisioning the operations of social freedom in the sphere of reproduction. For feminists have themselves frequently insisted on creating conditions whereby individuals 'realize their capacity for freedom as members of a free social community' (Honneth, 2017: 28). Calling for the politicization of the personal through the collectivization of reproduction is effectively to assert and affirm the inherently collective character of reproductive life.[1] It is, ultimately, about recognizing that child-rearing, housework duties, and so on, are constitutive of the general social interest and, in virtue of being so, can and must be democratized and brought under the scope of social value creation. Finally, it entails operationalizing radical interdependence, that is, to cultivate self-actualizing reproductive practices guided by the spirit of mutuality, reciprocity, and complementarity.

The task of collectivizing reproduction also rests on the possibility for, as bell hooks (1984) herself noted, direct co-parents to cooperate and 'define the work of fathering and mothering in the same way' (1984: 137). This is essential to ensure that parenting is equally shared between them. Under the existing private/public split, men are 'socialized to avoid assuming responsibility for childrearing' (hooks, 1984: 139). Women, on the other hand, believe that child care is their responsibility (hooks, 1984: 140), despite their mass entry into the workforce. What is needed to overcome this highly unequal state of affairs is a set of measures that can help change both the reality and ideological construction of the male breadwinner. The task of collectivizing reproduction must in this sense be democratized partly by ensuring that negotiations between co-parents on such matters as career choices and parenting are institutionalized. One possible avenue for this could be, as briefly mentioned in the preceding chapter, the creation of formal channels through which matters regarding reproductive life are, like matters regarding consumption, brought into dialogue with matters regarding productive life (and, of course, consuming life). User group associations, for example, could provide co-parents an institutional basis on which to cooperate and delimit, together, their respective sphere of activity in relation to work, child-rearing, and housework patterns. Because reproductive issues affect and are affected by production and consumption practices but are not reducible to them, the former must be brought into dialogue with the latter spheres of action. Doing so would effectively serve to turn reproductive issues into what are today considered public issues, that is, into matters of collective responsibility.

Guiding such a re-organization is Mies' own concept of the *'production of immediate life'* (2014a: 217, emphasis in original). Devised in an effort to rethink the relationship between production and reproduction, the concept seeks to redefine what counts as social production in terms of a *'production of life'* and instead of the 'production of *things and of wealth'* (Mies, 2014a: 217, emphasis in original). Bringing reproductive issues, in the form of user group associations (see Chapter 5), into dialogue with productive life therefore means ensuring that they are incorporated into what counts as social production or the general social interest. This is not, however, achieved by privatizing and commodifying reproductive activities in a manner akin to neoliberal practice, but by radically reimagining the *raison d'être* of material production. To suggest that it must be redefined as the 'production of life' essentially entails '[o]bserving society from the point of view of the activities that ensure its reproduction' (Deranty, 2022: 5). It expands the notion of production to include those involved in reproductive life but, crucially, also those 'contributing to social reproduction [that] do so without individuals seeking to achieve such an aim', like the mere fact of collectively remembering past experiences and keeping particular 'values and norms alive' (Deranty, 2022: 5–6). In sum, the collectivization of reproduction must, on the one hand, ensure that parenting, housework, and other reproductive activities are shared by different members of the community, whether or not they belong to the nuclear family. Extending the practice of othermothering or making available collectively run day care centres to parents are among possible ways of achieving this. On the other hand, it must entail institutionalizing cooperation between co-parents in such a way as to facilitate the negotiation of personal career projects and reproductive issues collectively. Achieving this could involve ensuring that, for example, parenting associations and producer associations are brought into dialogue with one another to delimit the scope of their members' involvement in their individual career plans, parenting activities, housework, and the like. This, I contend, could constitute an important step towards treating reproductive issues as matters of public interest and redefining social production as the production of life in both economic and extra-economic forms.

Before I show in greater detail how the proposed utopian demands are expected to overcome the capitalist sexual division of labour, let me discuss a final set of measures that could help 'politicise the personal'. These relate to the public sphere, that is, the space in which public opinion in society comes to be formed and norms come to be legitimated (Habermas, 1989). An extensive treatment of the public sphere will be offered in the next chapter. Suffice it to ask, here, what role such a sphere could have for consolidating the redefinition of production and reproduction. I wish to argue that these developments could be best achieved through the institutionalization of a 'space in which citizens deliberate about their common affairs' (Fraser, 1992: 110) and are in a position to shape the norms, schemes of perceptions, and discourses affecting their own identity. In the case of unequal parenting, such discursive spaces would enable their participants to shape public opinion in such a way that parenting and housework are no longer assumed to be the mother's responsibility. Subordinated groups, like women and queer groups, 'have repeatedly found it advantageous to constitute alternative publics' (Fraser, 1992: 123), because they provide a basis on which new schemes of perception, norms, and discourses could develop. In this sense, user groups of the kind discussed in Chapter 5 could constitute such publics. But as I will show shortly, most associations within the system of dialogical coordination conceptualized in this work could involve norm-legitimation and public opinion formation. This is because, like Durkheim (1984), I expect the associations in question to develop a moral character.

At this stage, a note on the kind of relationship between the economy, culture, and norms, or between what Habermas (1984; 1987a) called the 'system' and 'lifeworld', expected to develop in this re-organization of production and reproduction seems in order. For, by proposing to integrate public opinion formation and other processes of norm-legitimation with material production, the proposed re-organization goes against the grain of the highly influential German philosopher's vision of emancipation. First, let me be clear and say that it would be highly unreasonable and indeed mistaken, given Habermas' treatment of norm-legitimation and cultural reproduction as public matters, to suggest that the private/public and lifeworld/system split mirror one another. Habermas' analytical distinction between system and lifeworld cannot be equated with the distinction between production and reproduction. This is partly because under the modernist model embraced by Habermas, norm-legitimation (lifeworld) is understood as something unfolding outside of both production and reproduction. Engaging with the Frankfurt School member's work will nevertheless help clarify the utopian vision of the relationship between production and reproduction whose contours are drawn in this book.

Central to his critical theory is the differentiation of a sphere of 'communicative action' serving the development of identity, culture, and norms, from an 'instrumental' sphere of action devoted to material production and administration. Such a differentiation marks the emergence of modernity and is construed by Habermas as a progressive achievement. In fact, according to him, the uncoupling of actions orientated towards mutual understanding from instrumental or strategic forms of action is, we are told, the only possible route for achieving autonomy in a complex and highly differentiated society. This, it must be noted, led him to be critical of anarchism and other systems of thought likely to erode the separation through the 'willingness to solve problems and coordinate action through mutual understanding' (Habermas, 1996: 481). According to him, the idea of 'a society made up entirely of horizontal networks of associations' in a manner akin to the one offered here, is today unworkable 'given the regulatory and organizational needs of modern societies' (Habermas, 1996: 481). One could nevertheless argue that what has become particularly unrealistic is the prospect of maintaining an institutional design that has served, and today seems incapable of ending, the legitimation of a productivist economic model responsible for the destruction of the biophysical environment. Habermas does not even question 'the emancipation from seemingly "natural" constraint' (1987b: 311) marking the 'system', preferring to envision safeguards against the system's encroachment on the lifeworld to imagining an economic life beyond the domination of the biophysical environment.

I nevertheless wish to argue that reimagining the production/reproduction relationship as well as the severe environmental problems facing the world today urge us to rethink this position and seek ways to coordinate economic action through mutual understanding. They force us to question the existence of an economic life stripped of orientations towards mutual understanding. Dialogically coordinated and democratically organized associations of the form discussed in this work provide a fruitful basis for moving beyond this (Dufays et al., 2020). In addition to serving material production, they can make a direct contribution to discourse formation by 'developing the deliberative skills of individuals or by providing the voices that constitute public agendas and debates' (Warren, 2001: 114). They open up a space for discursive interaction within the production of life and consequently equip the system of allocation of resources, the workplace, and other components of social production with the communicative resources to shape and legitimate norms, as well as formulating interpretive schemes and value standards. To redefine production and reproduction in terms of the production of life as proposed here entails, therefore, a redefinition of the relationship between lifeworld and system.

The task of politicizing the personal or publicizing the private, however, is not the only avenue for re-arranging the relationship between production and reproduction. Part of this task could involve rethinking the norms of action making up public life. The mere fact of redefining what counts as material production into the production of life is an important step in this direction. For, it forces a realm of action and norms of behaviour traditionally construed as 'private' into public life and, in doing so, forces the normative criteria of action to change. Put more concretely, once reproductive activities become a function of material production, the nurturing and caring norms of behaviour associated with them come to challenge those of other, historically public, activities like material production. This is akin to what Nancy Fraser (1994: 611) envisioned as making 'women's current life patterns the norm'. As such, they could be said to 'feminize' the public sphere, to the extent that women have been almost exclusively responsible for reproductive life under capitalism. But there is no guarantee that the treatment of reproductive activities as a matter for the general social interest will necessarily lead to a 'feminization' of public life. Doing so could instead entail subsuming such activities under imperatives of efficiency and productivity. For socialists and many advocates of social justice, like Black radicals and ecofeminists, the prospects of emancipation depend on institutionalizing values of mutual care, cooperation, and equality within public life. They depend on 'feminising' the public sphere. It is therefore important to imagine ways in which such values could become dominant in public life.

Feminizing the public

I propose to undertake this task by drawing on Zenzele Isoke's (2013) 'politics of homemaking' and Joan Tronto's (2013) concept of 'caring democracy'. Drawing on the experiences of Black women's politics of resistance in the New Jersey city of Newark (USA), the concept of 'homemaking' refers to a range of practices 'articulated affectively through discourses of care, belonging, affect, and relationality rather than through logic, objectivity, and rationality' (Isoke, 2013: 80). It constitutes a field of contestation of capitalist practice and means to 'creatively confront and transform multiple structures of domination' (Isoke, 2013: 78). In so doing, Black women activists have created a space – a 'home' – within a hostile environment; a space wherein individuals are not only attentive and provide care to others, but also build 'enduring affective relationships to the physical environment' (Isoke, 2013: 80). The politics of homemaking could be said to involve practices that cultivate the kind of radical interdependence marking pluriversal emancipation. Such practices are in fact an important reminder that it is possible to create spaces capable of *building the will to resist* (Isoke, 2013: 80, emphasis in original) capitalism through the cultivation of caring norms of behaviour and redefining the boundaries of private and public life.

With her concept of 'caring democracy', Tronto (2013) could be said to offer a systematization of the 'politics of homemaking' discussed in Isoke's work. Despite saying little about the institutional forms such a re-organization of public life entails, Tronto offers some rather powerful insights into a democratic life articulated around care. Recognizing that such a re-organization is 'essential' (Tronto, 2013: 172) for achieving social justice and going 'beyond the current default of explaining all aspects of human life in economic terms' (Tronto, 2013: 10), she proposes the widespread institutionalization of caring practices or, put differently, of 'people's interdependence' (Tronto, 2013: 45):

> [d]ependence marks the human condition from birth until death. What makes us free, actually, is our capacity to care and to make commitments to what we care about. This is a kind of choice, but it is not choice understood simplistically. It requires action rather than consumption. It requires engagement with others. It is often not presented to us, or does not seem to come to us, as a choice. When people make commitments, aware of and yet regardless of the constraints around them, and hold to those commitments, then we can define them as making a free choice. But I do not know a better way to think about freedom. (Tronto, 2013: 94)

Tronto's utopian insights presuppose a radically different reading of freedom than the one upheld and ideologically constructed by the capitalist sexual division of labour. While the latter is instrumental in imposing a vision of (inter)dependence as a barrier to freedom, Tronto sees the two as inextricably tied. Freedom entails dependence and *vice versa*. The reason for thinking so is that, in her view, there is no stronger instance of freedom than the act of choosing to care for or depend on someone else. In this sense, we must embrace dependence and make care a core value of the re-organization of public life. More concretely, this entails ensuring that sufficient space is made in public life for the free, conscious, equal, and collective 'allocation of social and individual responsibilities' (Tronto, 2013: 63). What Tronto therefore offers is a way of further clarifying the operations pluriversal emancipation in the production of life and ensuring that decision-making processes – both economic and political – are in a position to foster the 'impulse of free and unfettered service' imagined by G.D.H. Cole (1917). Caring means to serve, and to do so in a free and committed manner. The triangular model of dialogical coordination – production, consumption, and user groups – proposed in this work is, I wish to argue, particularly well-suited for operationalizing 'caring democracy', given the place held by self-managed practices in each of the aforementioned spheres of action and in the mediation of their interaction. What it offers are possible avenues for institutionalizing 'widely diverse and thorough democratic processes of agreeing and disagreeing' (Tronto, 2013: 45), that is, ample space for negotiating caring responsibilities.

Under such a reading, the production of life involves the dialogical coordination of different associations complementing one another in the formulation and realization of the general social interest. Those associations are not expected to compete with one another for their survival. Each performs a particular function and, consequently, offers something others cannot offer. To say that they do not compete does not mean, however, that disagreements will end. Different associations might disagree on what counts as the general social interest. But central to the model proposed here is the way those disagreements are resolved. In the spirit of 'free and unfettered service' and caring for others, priority is given not so much to what Habermas (1998: 37) called 'the unforced force of the better argument' as to the affirmation of those associations' difference and mutual dependence. Put differently, resolutions are expected to result from attempts to understand what kind of singular contribution/commitment each association can make to one another in the formulation and realization of the general social interest. For, by organizing the production of life around a dialogue whereby each association makes explicit its own demand on the basis of the function it performs within the overall satisfaction of needs, dialogical coordination also makes explicit those associations' difference *and* complementary necessity. Instead of sacrificing difference in favour of commonality, the general social interest is here formulated and realized by asserting difference as the basis of collective action. Difference is expressed in terms of function. Function is a basis for care to the extent that it brings mutual dependence into sharp relief. While rethinking the relationship between production and reproduction through the *politicization of the personal* entailed collectivizing and publicizing reproduction and rethinking both production and reproduction as mutually dependent halves of the 'production of life', the *'feminization' of public life* proposed here consists in institutionalizing caring practices in production. Through those two avenues the relationship between production and reproduction is not only redefined, it is also reorganized in such a way as to uphold radical interdependence as the *dialogically coordinated production of life*.

This is facilitated by the fact that each association – production, consumption, and user group – could be said to represent a different counterpublic to the extent that they continuously seek to redefine, collectively, ways of thinking and being in the world through their contribution to the formulation of the general social interest. Different counterpublics might develop different normative strands for both the nature and distribution of caring responsibilities. What is nevertheless crucial in order to maximize their participants' autonomy, is to give them scope for expression and representation in the production of life and to ensure that dominant discourses are continuously challenged and reshaped. This is particularly important for questioning, for example, the gendered division of labour and liberating women from the assumption that they bear responsibility for childcare. The institutional avenues for re-organizing production and reproduction offered here are in fact expected to do more than merely serve the emancipation of women. For, given the mutually constitutive character of the different structures of domination making up capitalist life, and consistent with pluriversal emancipation, their liberation is inextricable from the liberation of other oppressed groups. Take the case of the queer community. Queer scholar Michael Warner (1999; 2002), for example, grounded the sexual autonomy of members of the queer community not in making the same rights as heterosexuals available to them, but in opposing the bourgeois private/public split. To this end he envisioned the consolidation of a discursive space or 'queer counterpublic' wherein queer people are able to 'imagine and cultivate forms of the good life that do not conform to the dominant pattern' (Warner, 1999: 112). Rather than assimilating the community in question within the dominant heteronormative way of life through the accumulation of civil liberties, he anticipated this community to play an active role in shaping social life. As a counterpublic institutionalized in the form of user association in dialogue with producer and consumer associations, it can participate in the production of life while engaging in the 'the public elaboration of a social world that can make less alienated relations possible' (Warner, 1999: 171–2). A queer counterpublic marks a 'critical relation to power' (Warner, 2002: 56) with the potential to 'supply different ways of imagining stranger sociability and its reflexivity' (Warner, 2002: 121). It asserts the 'world-making' character of an inherently anti-individualist queer culture (Berlant and Warner, 2002). It equips members of the queer community with the means to exert some control over the means of representation, formulation, and realization of the general social interest. As such, it liberates the voice of a currently subordinated group, while opening up a horizon of possibilities for thinking about the meaning and practice of care in the production of life.

But the redefinition and re-organization of production and reproduction proposed here is also intended to serve the emancipation of disabled people. Like women and queer people, disabled people will be able to communicate their needs in the production of life and actively shape interpretive schemes through their participation in, for example, user groups representing their interests as well as the democratically organized associations of producers and consumers. Crucially, they would be equipped with the means to contest the productivist ethos instrumental for their oppression under capitalism and contribute to the definition of a general social interest and self-determination no longer articulated around the individualist 'able-bodied ideal' of capitalist social production. It must be noted, however, that what is being envisioned here cannot be equated with what is known as the 'normalization' of disabled people in the disability literature, that is, with the task of merely giving those individuals 'valued social roles' to counter social devaluation (Fulcher, 1996). The problem with such a project is that disabled people are expected to be assimilated within the dominant productivist culture, rather than offering their own normative strand. Under its guise, they are not expected to 'challenge dominant cultural images' (Oliver, 1990: 77) but to internalize them. Instead, by politicizing the personal and entrenching caring practices in public life, the model proposed here helps make disabled people's interests and schemes of perception more visible, equipping them with the means to contest the dominant productivist discourse and directly participate in the realization of the general social interest.

Furthermore, through the re-organization of the relationship between production and reproduction, the way humanity relates to the biophysical environment is also expected to change. This is something Isoke (2013) sought to highlight in her work by anticipating the creation of 'enduring affective relationships' with nature through the politics of 'homemaking'. By creating institutional avenues for recognizing production and reproduction as mutually dependent halves of the production of life, a logic of radical interdependence treating nature as a partner in emancipation is set in motion. For, it re-organizes production and reproduction in such a way as to affirm a 'different way of being in the world and different ways of knowing and acting' (Bollier and Helfrich, 2019: 4), that is, our relationality with human and non-human others that capitalist relations had repressed. Collectivizing reproductive life and ensuring that public life is governed by orientations towards mutual understanding and care, serve to cultivate the kind of collective responsibility that is needed for maximizing 'the range of sensitivity towards earth others' (Plumwood, 2002: 177). Put concretely, it means that the different associations will formulate the general social interest and participate in the production of life, based on a much more empathetic relationship with the non-human world and through the recognition that what is good for me must also be good for earth others. It means moving beyond the material and ideological basis for the domination of nature.

Such developments could, too, affect the material and ideological basis for colonial and racial supremacy. Resting on the construction of Indigenous communities as racialized, uncivilized, and inferior others close to nature, the imaginary on which this supremacy rests is antithetical to a way of being and knowing asserted through radical interdependence. Colonialism and racism are supported by a logic of othering, according to which the freedom of the colonizers/whites must be realized at the expense of the freedom of the colonized/non-whites. Both therefore rest on divisions, exclusions, and hierarchies that the practices discussed earlier actively serve to dismantle. Governed by a sociological 'principle of non-domination' (Fraser, 2020: 11), these practices redefine the relationship between freedom, dependence, and care in such a way that they become constitutive of – as opposed to antagonistic to – one another. Central to the intersectional socialist utopia is the operationalization of a form of freedom that, instead of presupposing a reconciliation of formally competing interests, sets out to affirm a given, albeit latent, state of mutual dependence. This is ensured by turning the formulation of the general social interest into a space for collectively negotiating caring responsibilities; for treating our mutual dependence as something given, but yet-to-be-affirmed. Thus, instead of seeking to operationalize an antagonistic and zero-sum conception of freedom construed as something alien to care but familiar with supremacist thinking, intersectional socialism's institutions seek to emphasize each association's function and complementarity to one another in the formulation of the common good. It organizes the production of life in such a way as to make explicit each association's respective function in, and contribution to, the general social interest. The capitalist logic of othering and mastery is replaced by an institutional logic of mutuality, reciprocity, and complementarity.

The re-organization of production and reproduction offered here, therefore, involves expanding the scope of norms of behaviour capitalism confined to the private sphere and ensuring that, in addition to serving economic life, democratic control also serves reproductive life. Such a utopian vision draws on a range of really-existing practices – past and present – as well as diverse resistant knowledges, such as ecofeminism, Black feminism, and queer of colour critique. The practice of othermothering, for example, serves as a guide for collectivizing parenting practices. Mies' notion of the 'production of life' helps redefine what constitutes the general social interest and recognize reproductive work as the material basis of life. Uniting these ideas and practices is the logic of mutuality, reciprocity, and complementarity, echoed in Cole's (1917) 'impulse of free and unfettered service' and Tronto's (2013) 'caring democracy'. But, since those developments entail the expansion of spaces of discursive interaction beyond what Habermas called the 'lifeworld', they force us to rethink the relationship between communicative action and material production. While Habermas might have insisted on preserving their differentiation, practices like those involved in worker cooperatives signal that coordinating the production of life through mutual understanding is both a possible and desirable goal. Dufays et al., for example, argue that '[c]ooperatives, and probably other types of organizations that simultaneously pursue social and economic goals, create a space at the intersection of the system and the lifeworld, where communicative action can develop through the enhancement of lifeworld resources, as a vehicle of the system' (2020: 978).

While thinking of organizations pursuing economic goals and acting as counterpublics might be anathema to Habermas, it is indispensable to any attempt at ensuring participatory parity in the production of life. It is instrumental for creating both the material and ideological basis upon which to strip social life of the logic of othering and mastery responsible for diverse systems of oppression under capitalism. The different associations making up the intersectional socialist system of dialogical coordination thus contribute to the production of life *and* shape the normative fabric of social life through the 'disidentification' (Muñoz, 1999) with capitalist norms. They contribute to both material and symbolic production. But what does this all mean for institutions like marriage and the family? What are the implications of such macro-level developments for the realm of intimate life? In what follows I answer those questions by envisioning a system of kin relations beyond those instrumental in supporting capitalism.

Rethinking kin relations

Despite capitalist relations' acute tendency to devalue reproductive work, the latter has been an indispensable instrument of capital accumulation. This is not only because such work is essential for the reproduction of the workforce. It is also explained by the important role played by two institutions found within the private sphere, marriage, and the family, and around which kin relations serving the interests of capital are articulated. The rights afforded by marriage, for example, have provided property with the legal protections 'serving as a dense transfer point for land and inheritance' (Hennessy, 2000: 64). But it has also directly served the interests of property and capital by providing the ideological justification for the capitalist sexual division of labour and ensuring that the 'labor of renewing labor power ... take[s] place primarily in the home and [is] naturalized as the responsibility of women' (Hennessy, 2000: 64). It is through their role of wife that women came to be excluded from public life under capitalism. Marriage has, in the sense, been actively involved in creating favourable conditions for the entrenchment of capitalist property relations, capital accumulation, and patriarchal domination.

The bourgeois family is the system of kin relations underpinned by the legal protections afforded by marriage. Like marriage, it is an inherently heteronormative institution to the extent that it serves as (hetero)sexuality's 'privileged point of development' (Foucault, 1978: 108), naturalizes heterosexual norms of behaviour, and contributes to the regulation of sexual behaviour in society. Of particular importance for the task set out here, however, is the bourgeois family's 'forced combination of the principles of kinship and cohabitation' (Mies, 2014a: 104). For, it was partly through this combination that women's withdrawal from 'public' matters and their confinement within a 'private territory' (Mies, 2014a: 104) could be ideologically constructed and the subjugation of women to reproductive work was legitimated. Thus, it is also through their role as blood mothers that women have been, and continue to be, expected to take responsibility for reproductive work. It must nevertheless be noted that many within the Global North do not identify with the kinship model institutionalized by marriage and the family. Whether they have actively sought to resist what they regard as an oppressive kinship system or simply created an alternative set of kin relations in the face of acute socio-economic pressures, those groups, along with many Indigenous communities outside of the Global North, have developed practices signalling the possibility of redefining kinship beyond its hetero-bourgeois form.

Among Black American women, for example, othermothers have played an essential role in supporting single blood mothers in reproductive work. While often involving blood relatives outside of the nuclear family in such activities as child-rearing, these forms of community-based caring practices have also involved what one might call 'fictive kin' (Collins, 2000: 179). Developed in order to cope with less than favourable socio–economic conditions and resist oppression, the practice of othermothering provides a window into a world of relations 'expressing ethics of caring and personal accountability' beyond blood or biological relations (Collins, 2000: 192). As such, it opposes capitalist relations not only by rejecting the construction of children as property or possession but also by opposing the 'separateness and individual interest as the basis of either community organization or individual self-actualization' (Collins, 2000: 192). Instead, it is grounded in an altogether 'different value system' (Collins, 2000: 192) affirming the kind of relationality and mutuality presupposed by pluriversal emancipation, that is, by realizing one's freedom through others. Othermothering could therefore be said to constitute one possible route for envisioning alternative kin relations with the capacity to operationalize radical interdependence.

This practice, along with the values it rests on and kin relations it gives rise to, is reflected in the queer community's own kin relations, especially those of queer of colour men. Take, for example, William Hawkeswood's (1996) study of 'gay black men in Harlem'. Here we are shown very similar ways of extending kinship to members of a community 'who share the same aspirations, sense of security, friendships, and sexual preferences' (Hawkeswood, 1996: 64). Like many Black American women, Black queer men in Harlem and beyond have developed their own system of kin relations in the face of adversity. They:

> refer to their community, this collection of interrelated social networks, as their 'family'. This conceptualization enhances the emotional meaning of their membership in the group, or gay community, and is expressed verbally by the members in the use of kinship terms for each other. 'Mother', 'sister', 'brother', 'aunt', 'uncle', 'cousin', 'husband', and 'children' are all commonly used to indicate the status of an individual in the gay community or the fictive kinship relationship between the speaker and another person. The sense of belonging to such a family invokes a loyalty to other members of the gay population. This loyalty is comparable to the loyalty expressed toward real kin and kinship groups in Harlem. (Hawkeswood, 1996: 64)

A particularly vivid example of this can be found in the Black ballroom culture in major US cities like Detroit and New York. Here, support networks are organized around what is called a 'house' led by a 'father', or 'mother', and competing with one another at different balls throughout the year. But such 'houses' are much more than simple groups preparing their members for ballroom competition. They act as support networks for their members who, often rejected by their biological families due to their non-heteronormative practices, have come to 'forge alternative kin relations and ties' (Bailey, 2013: 80). Houses are, in this sense, like families preparing their members for competition on the ballroom floor and, equally importantly, 'serving as a space not only for friendship but also for nurturing, affirmation, belonging, and conflict' (Bailey, 2013: 100). While ballroom culture might at times recreate some of 'hierarchies and regimes of exclusion' (Bailey, 2013: 27) found in social life, it provides the different members of 'houses' with multiple opportunities to engage creatively with the formation of their gender and sexual identity through ballroom performances.

Thus, it is not difficult to appreciate why, as Marlon Bailey highlighted, the kin relations forged within and through ballroom culture act as an 'important form of individual and communal self-fashioning' (2013: 24). Combining self-expression and strong community ties, ballroom 'houses' ensure that their members do not simply personally gain from their involvement in such kin relations but also contribute to making other members' lives better (Bailey, 2013: 210). Like the othermothers discussed earlier, self-actualization is not here construed as an individual endeavour but as something relational and grounded in relations of mutuality. For instance, a house mother like Blanca Evangelista in the TV series *Pose* does not only provide spiritual and material support to her 'children', but can also gain materially and spiritually from their work on the ballroom floor, especially when competitors succeed in winning multiple categories. The work involved in forging kin relations is, too, inextricable from the work invested in the ball performances. Black ballroom culture, therefore, does not simply redefine kin relations, it redefines what a home is, along with the boundaries between private and public.

This is what led Bailey to conclude that '[b]allroom culture forces a reexamination and expansion of the meaning of labor' (2013, 209), echoing the work of di Leonardo (1987) on kinship. What ballroom culture does, in its own unique way, is recognize the work invested in forging kin relations by rewarding individual participants as members of a particular house. 'Kin work', that is the 'maintenance and ritual celebration of cross-household kin ties' (di Leonardo, 1987: 443) is here understood as a 'category of labor' (di Leonardo, 1987: 449). In fact, ballroom performances necessarily involve kin work to the extent that support for the preparation of performances directly depend on the kin relations of each 'house'. Like in small-sale societies, '[o]ne cannot ... speak of labor that does not involve kin' here (di Leonardo, 1987: 449). For this reason, we are confronted with an alternative to the capitalist split between the private and public, productive and reproductive work, and between work and family. We are given insights into possible ways of making kin work, namely the labour of care, visible, as well as rewarding it. In fact, I would argue that, like othermothers, US Black ballroom culture sheds light onto the meaning of work entailed by rethinking production/reproduction as the production of life and a concrete example of the way kin work and the caring practices it entails could be recognized, valued, and extended.

But in this book I wish to do more than merely suggest that socialist institutions could draw inspiration from existing practices of the kind found in particular communities like queers of colour or Black women. I also want to offer insights into what this might mean for institutions making up the production of life under intersectional socialism. In the case of kin work I want to suggest, like di Leonardo (1987), that work, family, and community are not separate spheres of life but can, and indeed do, depend on one another. To offer a redefinition of production/reproduction into the production of life is to recognize and affirm the mutual dependence of those spheres. Kin work is here therefore thought to be as important and valuable to the reproduction of social life as the work involved in economic production. In fact, it is understood as part and parcel of economic production, which, under intersectional socialism, is organized around caring practices. In short, what is effectively being proposed here is to treat kin work and more conventional forms of labour as mutually constitutive. Concretely, this means ensuring that workplaces and other domains of public life value and cultivate kin work, so that they can contribute to the deconstruction of the 'self-interest/altruism dichotomy' (di Leonardo, 1987: 452) and further entrench radical interdependence.

What, then, does the earlier discussion of kin work mean for the home and, more specifically, for such institutions as the family and marriage? As othermothers and ballroom 'houses' demonstrate, a family need not be organized around biological ties. Families can also be formed on the basis of shared interests, loyalty, and mutual support. What is therefore being proposed here is to create the normative space for the development of alternative (non-biological and non-heteronormative) definitions of the family. Intersectional socialism must be so organized that a plurality of models is defined and recognized. This, I contend, could be achieved through, for example, the work of user groups or even within producer and consumer associations. All have the potential to serve as public spheres, but while the former might organize for the purpose of legitimating particular worldviews like those revolving around kinship, the latter would tend to engage with such demands on how to live through the prism of their function as particular associations of consumers or producers. Empowering groups like Black women or Black queer men to define and legitimate norms in democratically organized associations could thus help ensure that the labour of caring, that is, kin work, is not reduced to relations between blood relatives.

An intersectional socialist utopia must therefore set out to achieve more than a mere opening up of heteronormative practices and rights to individuals previously excluded from them. It must do more than merely give the queer community the right to marry. For, this effectively serves to assimilate this community within the dominant heteronormative culture instead of equipping it with the means to redefine what counts as family. This, Lisa Duggan powerfully argued, results in what she calls 'homonormativity' or a state of affairs in which '[t]here is no vision of a collective, democratic public culture or of an ongoing engagement with contentious, cantankerous queer politics. Instead we have been administered a kind of political sedative – we get marriage and the military then we go home and cook dinner, forever' (Duggan, 2002: 189).

Asserting the value and importance of kin work is a political act (di Leonardo, 1987). It entails giving particular groups, often silenced and oppressed, the capacity to assert their own value patterns, change their material conditions, and contribute to redefining institutions like the family. Accordingly, it is not difficult to appreciate how practices devised in order to cope with and/or resist oppression within the Black working-class community can contribute to the liberation of the queer community and women. Kin work of the form found in the practices of othermothering and Black ballroom culture 'houses' does indeed open up the scope for marginalized groups to find their own means for self-actualization and to achieve it through a logic of mutuality. Kin work could in fact be regarded as 'a means of altering their ways of *being* in the world and of creating an *alternative world* altogether' (Bailey, 2013: 19).

Furthermore, once attention is turned to regions outside of the Global North one comes to appreciate the role such kin work could play in human to non-human relations. Take, for example, the notion of kinship found in many Amazonian communities. Here dialogue, even humanity, are 'conceived of as a position' (Vilaça, 2002: 349). This means that all living creatures have the potential to be human. As Viveiros de Castro (2012) took great care to show, they are all different subjects 'who apprehend the world from distinct points of view related to their bodies' (Vilaça, 2002: 351). What such subjects eat, their habits and social relations, all play a role in changing their bodies, which, in turn, change their position and determine their humanity. Given kinship is determined by social relations rather than biology, and all earth beings are capable of humanity, kin work, or the labour of caring, is something members of those Indigenous communities engage with in their interactions with members of both their own species and other species. Engaging in kin work in this way, that is, by 'experiencing kinship across the species barrier' (Charles, 2014), opens up an horizon of possibilities for rethinking society's relations with nature. Drawing on Indigenous forms of knowledge, Val Plumwood's (2002) own 'intentional recognition stance' rests precisely on the achievements of interspecies kin work. For, in order to 're-animate nature both as agent in our joint undertakings and as potentially communicative other' (Plumwood, 2002: 177), we, humans, must first be in a position to be receptive to nature and sensitive to its demands. We must be in a position to care for nature. Thus, if, as Plumwood argued, 'the real ... challenge at this level of interspecies communication is for we humans to learn to communicate with other species on their terms, in their own languages, or in common terms' (Plumwood, 2002: 189), then it is through the labour of caring, nurturing, and loving that this challenge can be risen to. Kin work could therefore be expected to play an important role in overcoming diverse relations of domination, including those between humanity and nature.

Finally, to extend kin work in that way entails normalizing particular attitudes and forms of behaviour that, particularly under the guise of the neoliberal principle of responsibility, tend to be demonized and denigrated. Redefining what counts as kin relations can, too, open up the scope for what Paul Abberley considered a core component of a critical theory of oppression, that is, to 'assert ... the value of disabled modes of living' (1987: 17). While it would be unreasonable to suggest that all carers and those they care for develop kin relations, the task of caring for someone involves the kind of supportive and nurturing attitudes essential for the development of those relations. What recognizing kin work as valuable and significant also allows for, then, is the re-assertion of 'collectivist notions of work as the product of family and group involvement' (Oliver, 1990: 44), which capitalism had eclipsed. By individualizing work and locating it outside of the realm of kin relations and the home, capitalism created both the material and ideological conditions for the oppression of disabled people. To recognize kin work as a category of labour is an important step towards re-creating collectivist notions of work, independence, and freedom, sharing much greater affinity with the experiences of disabled people than the self-interested and personally responsible agent of capitalist life.

Conclusion

To take capitalist domination seriously requires one to tackle the sexual division of labour imposed by the bourgeoisie on society. This, in turn, means extending the scope of our analysis beyond the confines of economic life and offer utopian insights into the re-organization of production and reproduction. Such insights, I argue, involve rethinking what effectively counts as productive and reproductive life. Construed as activities devoted to what Mies called the 'production of immediate life', production and reproduction are here thought to be equally central to, and mutually dependent on, the reproduction of social life in general. But it was also shown that such a reconceptualization is predicated upon institutional re-arrangements guided by a logic of mutuality, reciprocity, and complementarity or, to use Cole's terminology, a 'spirit of free and unfettered service'. Put concretely, this entails bringing reproductive work under democratic control in such a way that caring responsibilities involved in such work are shared. User group associations embodying the function of different reproductive activities, such as a parenting association, could here be brought into dialogue with representatives of relevant producer associations to ensure that those responsibilities are fairly distributed. It also entails ensuring that material production itself is reorganized in such a way as to entrench norms of behaviour excluded from public life under the guise of capitalist relations. It was argued that to anticipate a production of life organized in the outlined terms means rethinking the meaning of labour to include the kind of work invested in forging kin relations. To envision a world organized around the relational logic of radical interdependence means ceasing to treat work, family, and community as separate spheres of action and, consequently, recognizing the value and importance of kin work beyond the confines of intimate life. Intersectional socialism comprises a range of institutional mechanisms like dialogical coordination which facilitate and reward the labour of caring.

This chapter, in short, aimed to develop issues already raised in Chapter 5, such as those related to the nature of work or the organization of economic life. Its main contribution nevertheless consists in showing that a re-organization of economic life such as the one suggested in that chapter cannot be imagined without rethinking the way it relates to other domains of social life like reproductive work or, as I will now show, political life.

7

Beyond the Modern Liberal-Capitalist State

Introduction

Following persistent Indigenous peoples' demands for recognition of their rights, the Canadian state introduced the Constitution Act of 1982, which recognized 'existing aboriginal and treaty rights' and laid the groundwork for the 1995 recognition of their 'inherent right to self-government' (Coulthard, 2014: 2). The move ostensibly marked a change in the relationship between the Canadian state and Indigenous peoples away from the distinctively colonial denial of their right to self-determination. On the face of it, the Canadian state appears willing to put an end to the dispossession of Indigenous peoples through the constitutional recognition of their rights. A state, it seems, can exhibit enough reflexivity to transform itself and challenge its own role in domination. The extent to which it has succeeded in doing so is nevertheless debatable (Coulthard, 2014).

In fact, a core question I wish to tackle in this chapter is whether the modern liberal-capitalist state can indeed transform itself in such a way as to secure pluriversal emancipation or is condemned to acting as an organ of domination. Capitalism, it was shown, must be understood as a 'complex and multifaceted system of domination' (Bohrer, 2018: 64). I wish to argue here that the same can be said about a more specific, albeit just as complex, institution at the centre of capitalist domination: the modern liberal-capitalist state. As a central coordinating body within the capitalist order, the state plays a key role in securing the conditions for the system's reproduction. The question regarding the fate of the state in an intersectional socialist utopia will be answered by deploying an intersectional lens. First, though, one must be in a position to understand what the state consists of, that is, its nature. I therefore propose to engage with an old but highly relevant debate between Ralph Miliband and Nikos Poulantzas on the nature of the capitalist state. This will serve as a basis for framing the discussion of the state through the lens of other resistance knowledge projects like feminism and anti-racism. It will be argued that instead of rethinking the state, this socio-political institution must be rejected as a model for institutionalizing pluriversal emancipation. This is due to its inextricability from structures of domination. The latter discussion is followed by the conceptualization of an alternative to the state comprising something akin to a commune and a system of functional representation. In the last section, I address the international dimension and defend the re-organization of international relations around international functionalism. This, it will be shown, constitutes a particularly suitable mode of political organization for institutionalizing radical interdependence at the international level.

The state, capitalism, and domination

In the 1960s and 1970s, sociologists Ralph Miliband and Nicos Poulantzas engaged in a critique of the capitalist state that became highly influential within Marxist circles. The discussion centred around a range of issues such as the role the state plays vis-à-vis capitalism, whether the state is necessarily capitalist or simply an instrument of the dominant interests at any one time. Behind those issues lies a fundamental question each of the two theorists claims to answer differently, that is, can the state change to serve the interests of the dominated groups or must an entirely new set of institutions be designed to serve this purpose? Miliband's own answer to the question is clear: the state can indeed be transformed. Since the state is regarded as the 'guardian and protector of the economic interests which are dominant in them' (Miliband, 1969: 265–6), all that needs to change are the interests in question for the state itself to change. The socialist state, he further argued:

> requires the achievement of real power by organs of popular representation in all spheres of life, from the workplace to local government; and it also involves the thorough democratization of the state system and the strengthening of democratic control upon every aspect of it. But it nevertheless also means that state power endures and that the state does not, in any strong sense, 'wither away'. (Miliband, 1983: 68)

Since this approach presupposes a transformation driven by the appropriation of the state apparatus by the dominant group, I chose to call it the theory of *state co-optation*. For Poulantzas (1969), however, there is more to the nature of the state than the mere control exerted by the dominant class. According to him, 'the relation between the bourgeois class and the State is an *objective relation*' (1969: 73, emphasis in original). The state is not so much a set of institutions a class needs to control in order to rule society at large but an essential function of the capitalist order. Thus, when Poulantzas writes that the state is *'precisely the factor of cohesion of a social formation and the factor of reproduction of the conditions of production of a system* that itself determines the domination of one class over the others' (1969: 73, emphasis in original), I take it to mean that the state is a function of class domination and that its *raison d'être* is to serve the capitalist system of domination. It follows that the state is, at bottom, an organ of domination and cannot be expected to change vastly enough to become an organ of liberation. This is why Poulantzas concluded that one cannot simply take the state apparatuses 'in hand as they are and merely chang[e] their function' (1969: 78). One must instead smash the state (Poulantzas, 1978). Whereas Miliband offers a theory of state co-optation, Poulantzas offers one of *state supersession*.

Their different diagnosis on the nature of the capitalist state, therefore, leads them to draw different conclusions about its future. Both are nevertheless united in their focus on class as the key structure of domination. The interests the state serves are here primarily construed as class interests. They therefore tell us little about the way the capitalist state relates to power relations beyond those articulated around class. Understanding how the state relates to different structures of domination under capitalism, however, can help us shed further light on the extent to which the state is inextricable from its role in domination. I would even argue that it can help us settle the debate about the nature and future of the state. For this reason, I propose to deploy an intersectional lens and engage with critiques of the capitalist state emanating from feminist, anti-racist, and decolonial thought.

A particularly fruitful work to begin this exercise with is Catherine MacKinnon's (1989) feminist theory of the state. Critical of both Marxist and Marxist-feminist critiques of the state for the primacy assigned to class in their analysis, MacKinnon undertook the task of probing the 'relation between the state and society within a theory of social determination specific to sex' (1989: 159). Put more concretely, she sought to show that since gender is 'a social system that divides power' and within which men dominate, it is also a 'political system' of male domination (MacKinnon, 1989: 160). Because men dominate society, they also dominate the state. The latter is thus characterized as 'male' to the extent that the 'law sees and treats women the way men see and treat women' (MacKinnon, 1989: 161–2). She illustrates this issue with the example of rape laws. The fact that men are a lot more likely to rape than women forms 'the material conditions of their epistemological position' (MacKinnon, 1989: 176), on the basis of which laws are formulated. The laws in question therefore end up reflecting the standpoint of men, that is, the schemes of perception of those who are more likely to rape than be raped, masquerading as conventions. She concludes by asserting that in 'male supremacist societies, the male standpoint dominates civil society in the form of the objective standard – that standpoint which, because it dominates in the world, does not appear to function as a standpoint at all' (1989: 237).

But to claim that the state protects the interests of men in that way tells us little about the prospects for state transformation. It tells us little about whether the state can be re-modelled to protect the interests of women or is an inherently male system of domination. One gains greater clarity on MacKinnon's position once her proposals for change are accounted for. For the feminist theorist, what seems at issue here is the standpoint from which laws, and the activities of the state more generally, are grounded in. Whether the state is an organ of male domination or not thus depends on whether 'statutes … work to end or reinforce male supremacy, whether they are concretely grounded in women's experiences of subordination or not' (MacKinnon, 1989: 248). Her theorization of the state, therefore, envisages the possibility for a change in the way the state operates – a change of epistemological position from which the state acts and a change of the interests it seeks to protect. This view could consequently be said to side with the idea that the state can be changed if the group controlling it changes and could in this sense be brought within the scope of the theory of state co-optation.

According to Wendy Brown (1995), however, there is something more fundamentally masculinist about the state and state power. For example, the modern liberal-capitalist state's 'bureaucratic order', she claims, is fundamentally masculinist, for the forms of 'technocratic control' on which it is founded are 'socially masculine … insofar as the ultimate value is control, and the uncontrollable as well as that which is to be controlled … are typically gendered female in the discourses' (Brown, 1995: 193). Changing who controls the bureaucratic machine will not, therefore, change the fact that the machine rests on instrumental rationality and is a 'particular expression of a [masculinist] will to power' (Brown, 1995: 193). Under Brown's reading, then, the state appears highly unlikely to change. Described as 'an incoherent, multifaceted ensemble of power relations and a vehicle of massive domination' (Brown, 1995: 174), it inevitably naturalizes and normalizes the powerful and their interests, while pathologizing and demonizing the dominated (Brown, 1995: 167). The modern liberal-capitalist state is therefore akin to a system of domination. This is why Brown concludes that seeking liberation through the state can only lead to 'innately contextual and historically specific, hence limited, forms of freedom' (1995: 7). The latter, she argues, echoes what Marx (2000e) called 'political emancipation', that is, a liberation from particular constraints that leaves the more fundamental and structural bases of domination intact. Abortion rights and the rights for same-sex couples to marry are two examples of political emancipation, for they can be enshrined in the law without undermining the wider heterosexist structures. It follows that in order to achieve 'human emancipation', that is, the more 'thoroughgoing and permanent' (Brown,

1995: 7) form of freedom, one must cease 'looking to the state as provider, equalizer, protector, or liberator' (Brown, 1995: 196). Human emancipation, therefore, requires us to venture beyond the state – it requires us to adopt the theory of state supersession.

We are here confronted with a similar dilemma to the one observable in the Miliband/Poulantzas debate. At first glance, then, venturing into feminist critiques of the state seems to fall short of shedding further light on the future of the state in an intersectional socialist utopia. However, the mere fact that the state is masculinist and can reflect and promote the interests of men as well as the bourgeoisie – of the male bourgeoisie – is itself an important step towards understanding what the state is and could become. Indeed, first – and rather obviously – it tells us that the scope of its domination is not restricted to class (or, as we will see, gender) or that the state's active role in domination is not reducible to its co-optation by the dominant class interests. Second, and following on from the previous observation, it appears to provide further evidence that the domination channelled by the state might be better understood as something that is inherent in the state rather than as something incidental. If that were indeed the case then the idea that emancipation rests on superseding the state seems a more sensible one to defend than the view that the state could be transformed to support it. Addressing the issue of race will help gain greater clarity on the matter.

David Theo Goldberg's (2002) work on race and the state provides an in-depth analysis of what he chose to call the 'racial state'. In it, Goldberg boldly claims that race is:

> integral to the emergence, development, and transformations (conceptually, philosophically, materially) of the modern nation-state. Race marks and orders the modern nation-state, and so state projects, more or less from its point of conceptual and institutional emergence. The apparatuses and technologies employed by modern states have served variously to fashion, modify, and reify the term of racial expression, as well as racist exclusions and subjugations. (2002: 4)

The values, practices, and institutions making up the state, along with the interests it seeks to protect, are shot through with race. Race, itself 'the centerpiece of a hierarchical system that produces differences' (Hall, 2017: 32), is therefore constitutive of what Goldberg (2002) consequently chose to call the 'racial state'. Such a state can take different forms, which means it is more appropriate to speak of 'racial states'. But what such a type of state is characterized by is its historical engagement in the 'constitution, maintenance, and management of whiteness' (Goldberg, 2002: 195) in the form of, for example, a colonial state or, more recently, the (neoliberal) colourblind state. Under such a reading, the state does not merely reflect the interests of the powerful; it is constituted by them and constitutive of them. Goldberg explicitly rejects MacKinnon's own theorization for failing to grapple with the complexity with which the state and dominant social relations are articulated (Goldberg, 2002: 6) but praises Poulantzas for recognizing that the state occupies an '"objective" structural position in virtue of reproducing an historically specific and internally contradictory mode of production, locally and globally' (Goldberg, 2002: 102). If we extrapolate the latter observation to the issue of racial relations, we come to the conclusion that just like class and gender, those relations are not a 'condition external, prior in ontological logic, to the state' (Goldberg, 2002: 6) and that the state is a system of domination in itself. In sum, if race, itself a category of domination, is integral to the constitution of the state, then domination itself is integral to the state. Emancipation from racial domination must consequently entail emancipation from the (racial) state.

What to make, then, of the state's overtly progressive achievements? How can we make sense of the fact that the state has put an end to chattel slavery, eliminated segregation laws, introduced abortion laws, and institutionalized welfare mechanisms? Do those achievements not demonstrate that, after all, the state can serve liberation? As briefly indicated earlier, a progressive achievement might provide greater freedom within a system of domination but does not tend to liberate individuals from the system in question. Instead, it contributes to maintaining domination. Take, for example, Indigenous peoples' relationship to the modern liberal-capitalist state, especially the recognition paradigm of rights marking its latest structural transformation. Here one finds colonial states forced:

> to modify [themselves] from a structure that was once primarily reinforced by policies, techniques, and ideologies explicitly oriented around the genocidal exclusion/assimilation double, to one that is now reproduced through a seemingly more conciliatory set of discourses and institutional practices that emphasize our *recognition* and *accommodation*. Regardless of this modification, however, the relationship between Indigenous peoples and the state has remained *colonial* to its foundation. (Coulthard, 2014: 6)

Colonial powers recognizing Indigenous peoples as peoples with rights – the basis of the recognition paradigm – is not sufficient to move beyond the colonial relationship between those peoples and colonial powers. Key, here, is who does the recognizing. Just like Espinosa and Bustamante-Kuschel (2022) observed, one finds here a rather clear case of restricted liberation. For, while the voice and rights of Indigenous peoples have been increasingly recognized by modern liberal-capitalist states, their worldview is such that it is incompatible with the individual property rights enshrined in liberal states' law. So, instead of being given genuine sovereignty, or the power to shape the liberal state's laws, institutions and practices, it has limited their political agency and integrated 'Indigenous peoples into the liberal *bios*' (Espinosa and Bustamante-Kuschel, 2022), that is, as liberal political subjects. To have a voice and to be given rights, then, Indigenous peoples must effectively embrace liberal values and abandon the hope of shaping socio-political life in their own image. Recognition entails assimilation.

Similar observations can be made regarding the anti-racism of the neoliberal state. Here we find state actions contributing to 'the incorporation of racial difference into the knowledge architecture' (Melamed, 2011: 32) through the cultural celebration of '*openness, diversity, and freedom*' (Melamed, 2011: 43, emphasis in original). However, in this particular 'racial formation' (Omi and Winant, 2014), multiculturalism is cultivated alongside law-and-order initiatives disproportionately affecting people of colour and a state-sanctioned 'hyperextraction of surplus value from racialized bodies and ... a system of capital accumulation grossly in favor of the global North over the global South' (Melamed, 2011: 42). Multiculturalism does not eradicate racism (Lentin and Titley, 2011) but silences race at the public-administrative level (Goldberg, 2009) while tolerating 'racially exclusionary preferences' (Melamed, 2011: 221) in private. Such a 'nonredistributive antiracism' (Melamed, 2011: 4), then, contributes to the legitimization of an economic system that dispossesses racialized groups. Taking stock of the different racial formations marking a country like the US, Melamed (2011) notes that whether the state actively participates in overt racial domination as it did under the Jim Crow laws or seeks to celebrate cultural difference, it seems unable to tackle the structural causes of racism. The state, therefore, is 'fundamentally white supremacist and ill-equipped for antiracist projects' (Bracey, 2015: 562). But as we have seen so far, it is also inherently bourgeois, masculinist, and generally better at assimilating groups than genuinely empowering them. One is consequently better off seeking to institutionalize pluriversal emancipation in an altogether different set of socio-political institutions and adopt the theory of state supersession.

But what does this discussion reveal about the nature and operations of the modern literal-capitalist state's power? What role does the state play within the dispossessional architecture of the capitalist order? Just as it is a vehicle of domination, the state is a vehicle of dispossession. By this it is meant that the state plays an essential role in creating an environment favourable for dispossessional practices. It does so through legal, material, and symbolic means. For example, by giving same-sex couples the right to marry, the state makes the institution of marriage available to all and, in the process, alters the material conditions of those couples (through tax benefits), while assigning same-sex marriage the same semiotic value as marriage between members of the opposite sex. But whichever right the state grants and whichever law it passes, it is essential to remind ourselves that they are ultimately decided by the state, that is, by a system of domination shot through with, and at the service of, the interests of the powerful. Once this is accounted for, one can begin to appreciate the dispossessional character of those apparent achievements. In the case of same-sex marriage, enshrining it in the law eventually became a possibility because, on the one hand, the institution of marriage is itself shot through with bourgeois material interests, as reflected in the tax benefits it offers. Symbolically, marriage – whether same-sex or not – is shot through with heteronorms, which naturalize the values, behaviour and lifestyle associated with heterosexuality. The state either overtly dispossesses particular groups by denying them rights, as was the case prior to the same-sex marriage law, or ostensibly equalizes those rights, while implicitly reproducing existing power relations, as is the case after the introduction of the same law. In either case, the state's dispossessional character lies in the 'universalization of the particular interest of the dominant' (Bourdieu, 2014: 183) by denying the dominated the possibility to shape the laws in their own image. Even when the state chooses to tax the rich to the extent witnessed during the post-WWII phase of capitalist development, it does so to induce consent to a socio-economic system that continues to exploit and de-skill male workers (Braverman, 1974), excludes women from the sphere of production (Friedan, 2010), and super-exploits black women (hooks, 1984). Thus, in addition to reproducing the conditions for material inequality, the state dispossesses the dominated of the capacity to articulate the laws around their own system of values. Under the guise of the modern liberal-capitalist state assimilation is akin to dispossession.

For French sociologist Pierre Bourdieu, however, the (symbolically) dispossessional character of the modern liberal-capitalist state goes even deeper. It does not merely seek to universalize and legitimize the interests of the dominant or 'justify their existence as dominant, it is far more than this. The state structures the social order itself – timetables, budget periods, calendars, our whole life is structured by the state – and, by the same token, so is our thought' (Bourdieu, 2014: 183).

The state is here said to play a key role in the production of meaning and, consequently, in shaping common sense based on the socially dominant's own system of values. What we come to regard as normal and acceptable behaviour and dismiss as objectionable and improper is, Bourdieu argues, in large part due to the actions of the state. The state is not just capable of printing money, taxing citizens, and punishing them, it is also 'an instance that constitutes the world according to certain structures' (Bourdieu, 2014: 183). The world it constitutes is one of 'hierarchies' and 'principles of hierarchization in conformity with these hierarchies' (Bourdieu, 2014: 183). As such, the state is not just a system and vehicle of domination, it is also responsible for structuring society around domination.

Such bold critiques of the modern liberal-capitalist state are echoed in the work of libertarian socialists and anarchists, who tend to subscribe to the theory of state supersession thesis. Take, for example, the work of G.D.H. Cole. Under his reading, the state is omnipresent or, as he put it, 'its functions are practically universal and unlimited' (Cole, 1920). It is not only too big, unwieldy, and remote to be able to represent individuals' interests adequately, state power is also far too centralized. This is because the form of political (parliamentary) representation marking the modern liberal-capitalist state is, as Cole (1920: 103) put it, a 'false theory of representation'. According to Cole and many anarchist thinkers, the idea that one person can represent another or several others is flawed. Indeed, '[n]o man can represent another man, and no man's will can be treated as a substitute for, or representative of, the wills of others' (Cole, 1920: 103). Since each person is 'a centre of consciousness and reason ... an ultimate reality' (Cole, 1920: 106), representation cannot avoid super-imposing the reality of the representative onto the represented. As a result, its democratic character, its very capacity to embody a collective will is, to borrow Bourdieu's (2014: 6) own words, a 'collective fiction, a well-founded illusion'. Through its remote parliament, occasional elections, as well as through its grip on the education sector and its media influence, the state manufactures the collective will it claims to embody and represent. Alongside the hierarchies it contributes to creating and sustaining, then, the state produces an illusory political community, in which the citizen 'is robbed of his real life and filled with an unreal universality' (Marx, 2000e: 53). Alongside its 'technologies of antirelationality' (Gilmore cited in Melamed, 2015), the state seeks to re-connect what has been severed in the social world. But without eliminating the divisions making up the social (and largely upheld by the state itself), the state can only be expected to create a political community artificially. Genuine democracy and pluriversal emancipation can, in turn, only be achieved through the 'abolition of the State' (Bakunin, 1970: 84).

What form the socio-political institutions of the intersectional socialist utopia drawn in this book could take will be explored in the next section. Suffice it to say here, though, that since domination is integral to the institutions of the modern liberal-capitalist state, those institutions must be rejected to pave the way for a pluriversal collective will. After all, as Audre Lorde (2018) warned us, 'the master's tools will never dismantle the master's house'. What political architecture pluriversal emancipation necessitates will be discussed next.

Functional representation, the commune, and the 'politics of difference'

The chief problem with the modern liberal-capitalist state is not only that it operates as a system of domination, but also its tendency to masquerade as a democratic system or, to borrow Marx's (2000e) own term, as a 'heaven' of freedom and equality. So, while it is acutely exclusionary, it somehow succeeds in garnering legitimacy as an ostensibly inclusionary political community. Its illusory character as a democratic political community becomes plain to see once attention is paid to the voices shaping the general social interest, the liberties the state chooses to protect and the groups it systematically prosecutes. The class, patriarchal, racial, and colonial character of the state is a reality often concealed by the abstract universality of liberal political rights, as illustrated by the legalization of same-sex marriage. What is therefore needed, Marx tells us, is to re-organize the relationship between economic and political life in such a way that the community, freedom, and equality embodied in the state cease to be abstractions for the 'individual man [sic] in his empirical life' (2000e: 64), or cease to be a reality for a few – white middle-class men – and an illusion for the many. This, I will argue, necessitates a pluralist conception of politics or 'politics of difference' (Young, 1990), that is, a form of political life that is attuned to, stands on, and upholds difference, and therefore ceases to sacrifice it in favour of a necessarily abstract universality.

In previous chapters, I provide insights into economic life and its relationship to reproductive life in an intersectional socialist utopia. Such insights were guided by the principle of radical interdependence at the core of pluriversal emancipation. To this end I emphasized the importance of creating an institutional space for associative life in the economy and in the form of producer, consumer, and user group associations. This, I want to argue here, entails not only adopting a rather different conception of publicity from the one Habermas appears to idealize in *The Structural Transformation of the Public Sphere* (1989), but also moving beyond the very relationship between economic and political life marking the modern liberal-capitalist state. The bourgeois public sphere discussed at length by Habermas, for example, emerged on the basis of historically unique circumstances: 'The social precondition for this "developed" bourgeois public sphere was a market that, tending to be liberalized, made affairs in the sphere of social reproduction as much as possible a matter of private people left to themselves and so finally completed the privatization of civil society' (Habermas, 1989: 74).

The formal separation of political and economic life capitalism brought about created a space for 'the practice of rational-critical discourse on political matters' (Calhoun, 1992: 9). Through it, individuals – almost exclusively white bourgeois men – would engage in a 'debate over the general rules governing relations in the basically privatized but publicly relevant spere of commodity exchange and social labor' (Habermas, 1989: 27). It also acts as counterweight to the state in virtue of developing forms of public opinion that can be critical of existing political practice. The public sphere thus became an essential component in the formulation of the common good within the capitalist order or, as I chose to call it in this book, of the general social interest.

For this reason, the bourgeois public sphere was depicted by Habermas (1989) as central to the democratic life of modern liberal-capitalist states. But once one looks closely at its mode of operation, one quickly comes to appreciate its non-negligible shortcomings as an engine of democratic deliberation, even before its perversion by commercial interests and the social democratic state. Precisely because of its function as a single sphere of public opinion formation mediating a political life (universal) formally separated from economic life (particular), the work of the public sphere was devoted to overcoming the tensions between private interests and matters of public concerns. It did so on the basis of a rational consensus guided by a universalist logic paving the way for a 'democratic generalization of interests' and 'universalistic justification of norms' (McCarthy, 1992: 64). Participants in the public sphere were expected to devote their attention to what they regarded as matters of 'public' interest. What defined them as private individuals, such as their social position, their individual desires, needs and values, all had to be bracketed to let the force of the better argument drive the formation of a consensus around the general social interest.

The bourgeois public sphere, therefore, rested on a distinctively modern-capitalist binary between private/particular and public/universal, where only the latter half of the binary was deemed worthy of incorporation within the general social interest. Because of this, and since it emerged following the separation of political and economic life, the public sphere could be said to be enmeshed in a system of modernist-capitalist binaries structuring social life. It is therefore integral to the complex system of capitalist domination structured by those binaries. Despite its ostensibly democratic function, the bourgeois public sphere has operated along exclusionary lines, not only reflected in the fact that it eventually turned into 'the power base of a stratum of bourgeois men who were coming to see themselves as a "universal class"' (Fraser, 1992: 114), but also because its universalist aspirations inevitably 'negate difference' (Postone, 1992: 168). Consequently, the bourgeois public sphere formulates the general social interest by neutralizing difference.

In this sense it is antithetical to the logic of pluriversal emancipation, which celebrates difference and treats it as inextricable from the general social interest. What, then, happens to the bourgeois public sphere within an intersectional socialist utopia? As already indicated earlier and discussed in more detail in preceding chapters, the process of opinion formation/ norm-legitimation would no longer be concentrated in the hands of a single public sphere but distributed among different publics within a system of dialogical coordination. This is, first, because the relationship between economic and political life marking capitalism would be significantly altered in an intersectional socialist utopia. Rather than a democratic process of opinion formation ostensibly abstracted from, but actually perverted by, economic relations, the process in question will be integral to material reproduction. This is to ensure that the kind of attentiveness and openness entailed by radical interdependence are given institutional form in the very practices upon which the realization of the general social interest depends. Reconciling orientations towards mutual understanding with strategic forms of action, or bringing the lifeworld within the system, to use Habermas's own terminology, is the best safeguard against the colonization of the former by the latter. Second, a multiplicity of publics, each with scope to shape the general social interest, provides subordinated groups a space in which to express and assert their difference. Here, each public – as it appears in producer, consumer, and user group associations – is akin to the kind of 'inclusive democratic communities' anticipated by Patricia Hill Collins (2017: 37) in her model of participatory democracy. For, rather than bracketing status differentials, those publics will provide a space for making sense of 'both individual and collective experiences [their members] have within hierarchical power arrangements' (Collins, 2017: 28). They are embodied in voluntary democratically organized associations involved in the dialogical production of life and, as such, equip subordinated groups with the means to 'formulate oppositional interpretations of their identities, interests, and needs' (Fraser, 1992: 123) within the very same decision-making processes as those involved in material production. Put differently, individuals are here said to articulate decisions on how they want to live (*formulation* of the general social interest) with decisions aimed at meeting society's needs (*realization* of the general social interest). This is why, like Fraser (1992: 135), I argue that 'self-managed workplaces, child-care centers, or residential communities ... could be arenas of both opinion formation and decision-making'.

Ensuring the institutionalization of publics within the production of life, thus, constitutes one core component of the pluralist approach[1] to politics I formulate in this chapter. A second, equally important component, is functional representation. While parliamentary representation rests on the notion that one person can represent the will of many others within a given geographical constituency, functional representation re-organizes politics around issues individuals are interested in, that is, around vocation:

> The essence of functional democracy is that a man should count as many times over as there are functions in which he is interested. To count once is to count about nothing in particular: what men want is to count on the particular issues in which they are interested. Instead of 'One man, one vote', we must say 'One man as many votes as interests, but only one vote in relation to each interest'. (Cole, 1920: 115)

Each association – producer, consumer, or user group – is devoted to the realization of a particular set of interests or function/vocation. Representation is said to be functional to the extent that the singular interests of an association are themselves represented politically, at the local, regional, and national levels. Furthermore:

> Through vocational associations, those working in one area will have the power to organise their discipline. Teachers will have, for instance, the authority to decide upon the curricula, the length of the lessons, and so forth. Moreover, individuals could establish civic associations, for example for their spiritual needs. There is thus not only a radical-democratic but also an epistemic argument for functional organisation, because persons would have only participatory rights in areas of which they possess know-how. (Holthaus, 2014: 864)

Under parliamentary representation, a member of parliament represents a very broad range of citizens and is responsible for dealing with an equally broad range of economic, social, cultural, and environmental issues within a given constituency. The tasks facing those representatives are therefore pretty much insurmountable as one person cannot be expected to represent everyone's interests, let alone accumulate sufficiently extensive expertise to be able to deal with such a broad range of local issues. What functional representation does is overcome those problems by ensuring that those making decisions affecting voters have the requisite expertise for representing their interests.

But in addition to enhancing the quality of democratic decision-making, functional representation ensures that political life accommodates pluriversal emancipation. Here, politics is not so much governed by universalist aspirations as by ensuring the complementarity of functions in the 'social organisation of production' (Cole, 1920: 155). For, each of those functions contributes something distinctive to the social organization of production. Functional representation, therefore, channels difference in such a way as to accommodate radical interdependence. Under a capitalist regime, political life seeks to abstract itself – rather unsuccessfully – from the conflicting economic interests making up society. Under an intersectional socialist regime, political life channels the functional interdependence of different associations involved in the dialogical production of life into itself, all in an effort to secure the coordination of the realization of the general social interest. Functional representation, on the one hand, 'affirms the public and political significance of social group differences as a means of ensuring the participation and inclusion of everyone in social and political institutions' (Young, 1990: 168). On the other, it ensures that difference becomes the basis of complementarity, not conflict. As a concept pluriversality presupposes the existence of different, albeit radically interdependent, worlds – of different standpoints and experiences of the world. Functional representation does not seek to stifle this plurality but to accommodate it by giving institutional form to the complementarity of differences.

But given the vast range of representative bodies such a model entails, a high degree of integration and coordination will be necessary. In other words, relations between different components making up the general social interest will need to be regulated. For example, an overarching body will be needed to introduce laws determining the respective spheres of operation of each of the different bodies. A body will also be needed to allocate 'material and labour' (Cole, 1980: 144–5) wherever those are necessary at any one time. Those functions would not, however, be performed by a state, which for anarchists and libertarian socialists cannot be anything other than an 'instrument of coercion' (Cole, 1980: 122). The overarching body cannot be abstracted from the functional bodies but must instead be composed by their representatives. It must therefore act as continuation of principles of self-management making up the economic sphere – not as its counterweight. For this reason it is best described as a 'commune', that is, a political body that 'acquires the character of a community in which the working man [sic] maintains direct control over various aspects of his social existence' (Pasic, 1975: 38). As the coordinating political body of an intersectional socialist utopia, the commune would therefore consist not of a 'single association, but a combination of associations, a federal body in which some or all of the various functional associations are linked together' (Cole, 1920: 134). The commune would thus take on a local, regional, and national/societal form.

G.D.H. Cole (1980: 127–8) identified five functions for the commune, which could help with the coordination and integration of the production of life in an intersectional socialist utopia. First, one finds the financial functions. Here the commune would allocate 'the communal labour-power and the provision of capital' (Cole, 1980: 145) among the different functional bodies. It would act, too, as a court of appeal in case of disagreements between functional bodies, administer extra-functional town affairs like the extension of town boundaries, and perform a coercive function by funding and administering the police. However, the matters of collective responsibility such as 'housing, water, communications, public health and the environment, education, training and recreation, science and the arts, and health and welfare' (Devine, 1988: 213) do not fall fully within the commune's remit. This is because the latter's core functions should be limited to coordination and integration, and avoid a direct involvement in the satisfaction of needs of the kind observed in state socialist countries like the USSR. In other words, what falls within the scope of the production of life, of the activities directly contributing to the realization of the general social interest, cannot fall under the commune's own remit.

It is nevertheless important to note here that it would be unrealistic to assume that political life would be entirely stripped of all centralized activities. While decisions regarding such large-scale issues as the environment, inequality, and education are matters of collective responsibility which functional representatives at the local, regional and societal levels would play a key role in addressing, they must also be steered by a centralized decision-making body responsible for ensuring that decisions are implemented equally and in common. This body is akin to a central government, comprised of ministers, representing the different functions making up the system of dialogical coordination and periodically elected by functional representatives at the societal level. But macro-level decisions made by this group of functional ministers would be directly informed by the radical interdependence asserted through dialogical coordination. They would lie at the intersection of groups whose interests are directly affected by the issue in question. Macro-level decisions aimed at reforming education, for example, would be informed by a dialogue between the educator user group and pupils user group in dialogue with associations of producers. The decision to, say, extend the teaching of mathematics to all pupils up to the age of 18 could therefore emanate from needs interpreted and coordinated by functional representatives of those associations at the local, regional, and societal levels. Conversely, functional ministers could initiate negotiations themselves before putting decisions out to consultation with local, regional, and societal representatives of the relevant bodies, as in the case of Zapatista/Chiapas system (Martell, 2023). To be sure, tensions between collective/individual and societal/local needs will always exist in any system that recognizes the need for centralized macro-level decision-making mechanisms. But the system proposed here is aimed at minimizing those tensions. It is aimed at radically democratizing decision-making processes, including some necessary but circumscribed centralized forms of governance. In the proposed vision, centralized macro-level decision-making processes are not abstracted from, but are embedded in, a system of functional representation of democratically organized associations at the local, regional and societal levels. They are aligned, as far as it is possible, with a pluriversal collective will.

The commune and functional ministers cannot, therefore, be strictly compared to a state – socialist or not – despite necessarily manifesting statist tendencies such as those discussed earlier. For, while the commune does perform legal and coercive functions like a state in its attempt to coordinate and integrate functional bodies, it is so organized that economic functions fall outside its remit. The commune is not expected to plan production by dictating individual firms controlled by the state bureaucracy the quantity they are expected to produce. The commune is not a state taking control of the economy. It is simply a coordinating body that sets out to create the financial, administrative, and legal conditions for the dialogical coordination of the production of life. The commune could therefore be said to provide the 'framework for the ... horizontal integration and coordination of self-managed social activities' (Pasic, 1975: 38). But it remains decentralized to the extent that the bulk of this work will not fall into the hands of a centralized legislative body but, mainly, in those of the regional representative bodies (Cole, 1920), or what Mikhail Bakunin (2002) called 'provincial parliaments'. It is in those intermediate (regional) bodies that human affairs are small enough to resonate with the represented and big enough to matter and make a difference to large sections of the population. But it must be noted that this should not be incompatible with other versions of communalism such as the 'libertarian municipalism' proposed by Murray Bookchin (1999). Here the locus of political life is the more local municipality – the town. This level of political decision-making is not antagonistic to the model proposed here. The interactions of municipal life envisioned by Bookchin could indeed constitute the local layer of the commune. It is the level of assemblies comprising functional representatives of local associations working together to tackle local human affairs. Also, unlike the parliamentary democratic representation, the functional representatives can be recalled (Cole, 1920). The regional character of political decision-making will ensure sufficient proximity for the representatives to be held to account through the right of recall, which the likes of Cole (1920: 111) have depicted as the 'final safeguard' for making representation democratic. Finally, as just mentioned, some issues like economic redistribution, education, and climate change cannot be solved on a strictly local or regional basis. They require some degree of centralized governance. For this reason, the system of dialogical coordination, the commune and functional ministers make up a system characterized by what Martell (2023) calls the 'dual power' approach, which recognizes dialogical coordination and the commune's capacity to develop a collective will, while insisting on a circumscribed role for periodically elected functional ministers in either enacting this will or steering its development.

These features make it possible for the commune to assert and uphold the kind of relationality entailed by radical interdependence. Under the modern liberal-capitalist state, the political body controls 'who can relate and under what terms' (Gilmore in Melamed, 2015: 78). As 'producer of principles of classification' (Bourdieu, 2014: 165), it is in a position to turn the undifferentiated mass of occasional voters into distinct groups with different rights. Difference might co-exist with some sort of interconnectedness, but the latter exists in spite of the former and because the state chose to impose it 'in terms that feed capital' (Melamed, 2015: 78). Under this light, the right for same-sex couples to marry connects them to heterosexual couples and to heteronorms. The state therefore tends to connect through assimilation. It connects by suppressing difference. In contrast, relationality presupposes difference, upon which it thrives. The commune is a vehicle of relationality insofar as it channels associative life into the political body through functional representation and provides a basis for the represented to recall their representatives. Laws, and the rights they enshrine, are formulated by the functional representatives, who do not merely represent an association's interest and function, but also the public opinion formed within it. As intersectional socialism's political body, the commune is not an abstract community but a real one, that is, one through which 'the actual individual man [sic] [takes] the abstract citizen back into himself' (Marx, 2000e: 64) amid the re-organization of economic life into democratic associations functionally represented within the commune. The commune facilitates what Marx (2000e: 54) called 'real, practical emancipation' by channelling associative life into itself. But in doing so it also upholds what I chose to call pluriversal emancipation in this work, that is, the affirmation that one's self-actualization is realized through – and not despite of – the self-actualization of others. Put differently, the commune is a political body particularly appropriate for a relational politics of difference to the extent that the associations or groups do not 'lie outside one another' (Young, 1990: 171), but complement each other in the realization of the general social interest as different functions making up the production of life.

Finally, it is important I address the expected relationship between political life and the caring practices I discuss in Chapter 6. In that part of the book I explore how the kind of attentiveness and radical interdependence such practices entail could re-organize economic life, alter the relationship between production and reproduction, and change the way humans relate to other humas as well as non-humans. Under their guise, economic life would effectively accommodate what Val Plumwood called the 'intentional recognition stance', that is, 'practices of openness and recognition able to make us aware of agentic and dialogical potentialities of earth others' (2002: 177). This echoes the communicative theory of 'asymmetrical reciprocity' formulated by Iris Marion Young, according to which individuals acknowledge their difference before seeking to 'mutually recognize [and understand] one another' (1997: 53). It does not seek to eliminate difference but to affirm it and turn it into a basis for deliberation. Like the intentional recognition stance it is about 'being open to learning about the other person's perspective' (Young, 1997: 53). What nevertheless distinguishes Plumwood from Young is the former's insistence that nature ought to be treated 'as agent in our joint undertakings and as potentially communicative other' (Plumwood, 2002: 177). Young limits the scope of communicative action to human-to-human relations. A question therefore arises: what relationship does this communicative stance bear with political life in an intersectional socialist utopia? For Young, it is at the centre of political life, for such an 'asymmetrical positioning' is particularly suitable for 'discussing moral and political issues' (1997: 39). What I nevertheless proposed is to move beyond the 'lifeworld' (normative) and 'system' (technical) binary and entrench communicative channels firmly within economic life. This is not to say that intentional recognition or asymmetrical reciprocity ought to be lifted out of political life and confined to economic life. Rather, it entails envisioning a sphere of economic life and one of political life that share similar communicative credentials. By channelling the form of associative life depicted in Chapters 5 and 6 into itself, the commune also effectively channels intentional recognition/asymmetrical reciprocity into political life. It therefore accommodates communicative practices that, in virtue of the openness, attentiveness, and radical interdependence they cultivate, are particularly appropriate for the development of relations of care between humans, as well as between humanity and non-human nature.

Intersectional socialism goes global

The intersectional socialist utopia whose contours are drawn in this book is not only resolutely anti-capitalist but is also anti-racist and anti-imperialist. As such, it is inscribed in the tradition of internationalist socialists such as James Connolly and David Widgery, who were dismayed at the exclusionary and supremacist tendencies of some sections of the labour movement. To be sure, socialism has not always assumed an internationalist outlook. The working class might have been the social class least receptive to nationalist sentiments (Virdee, 2014), but it was not totally immune to them. The approach adopted here questions the organization of the world order into territorially defined nation-states, treating it as a core challenge for the realization of pluriversal emancipation globally. Consistent with postcolonial and decolonial perspectives, I regard the nation-state as a divisive political institution both domestically and internationally. Not only does it partition the world into tightly controlled national territories, it has also served to subjugate and divide people into colonialists and colonized, 'National-Natives (autochthons) and Migrants (allochthons)' (Sharma, 2020: 13). It is a 'means of separating people' (Sharma, 2020: 142) and, as such, is fundamentally opposed to the logic of pluriversal emancipation. What is offered next is an internationalist vision, stripped of the nation-state and organized, instead, around a form of international functionalism that directs our attention away from national territories and towards human need and open borders. Before I tackle this alternative head on, let me review some of the epistemological lessons to be learned from a critique of the separatist ontology of the nation-state system.

As a unit of analysis for the study of international relations, the nation-state forces us to locate agency in the hands of one or more states. Under its guise, action is bound to a national territory. This has a tendency to create an onto-epistemic state of affairs whereby history or a simple account of a world event, is circumscribed by the experiences and forms of representation found within a particular national territory, but ultimately treated as universalizable. Such a state of affairs, in fact, could be said to constitute 'metro-centrism' in social theorizing, that is 'the transposition of narratives, concepts, categories, or theories derived from the standpoint of one location onto the rest of the world, under the assumption that those narratives, concepts, and categories are universal' (Go, 2016: 94).

Take, for example, the Global North narratives of modernity or capitalism, such as those of Frankfurt School critical social theorists. Those accounts tend to assume a Eurocentric character, locating the origins of modernization and capitalist expansion in European thought and practice (Bhambra, 2007; Go, 2016; Mignolo and Walsh, 2018). What they overlook or under-appreciate are the ways in which modernity and 'capitalist development globally [were] fundamentally dependent upon colonial exploitation and appropriation' (Bhambra, 2021: 8). Indeed, as Patnaik and Patnaik (2021: 70) powerfully showed in their analysis of the relationship between capitalism and imperialism, 'there is a whole range of goods the metropolis cannot do without but whose supplies at the margin must come from the tropical and semi-tropical regions'. Particularly important here is not only the idea that histories of the Global North and the Global South are connected, but also that they are mutually constitutive (Go, 2016). Capitalism and modernization do not flow from a European centre to a periphery outside the Global North, as Eurocentric accounts would have it. They are as much constituted by the Global South as by the Global North. Thus, adopting this postcolonial approach entails doing more than simply recognizing the impact of the Global North on the Global South. It means appreciating 'how colonized peoples have helped constitute "the West"' (Go, 2016: 113). Under such a reading, the Haitian revolution is not said to result from France 'benevolently bestow[ing] rights upon its slaves' but from 'slaves seiz[ing] what is rightfully theirs, changing everything about the Revolution in the process' (Go, 2016: 131). Using the nation-state as a frame of reference, however, makes this exercise acutely difficult, for, as an organ of domination, it tends to favour a territorially defined narrative pervading knowledge like an imperial power colonizes territories. It also foregrounds divisions and obscures constitutive connections across national borders. In short, it diverts attention away from the kind of relationalism that is required to capture the complex radical interdependence of historical processes like the development of capitalism or modernity.

I would therefore argue that the central lesson to be learned from this critique of the nation-state system is that the latter has gone hand in hand with what Aníbal Quijano (2007) called the 'coloniality of power',[2] that is, a territorial occupation accompanied by a deeper but equally pervasive form of repression: the repression of modes of knowing that do not conform to those of the dominant nation-state(s). Paradoxically, while the nation-state system is underpinned by, or shot through with, difference, a nation-state cannot tolerate it and often seeks to either eliminate or subjugate the different 'other'. This is most visible in the national sentiments the nation-state has elicited over the years and the fact that nationalism turns difference into a barrier or wall, as opposed to turning it into a basis for radical interdependence. I would argue that in order to achieve the latter at an international scale, one must re-organize the international system around the classical functional idea that 'authority ought to be linked to a specific activity, instead of a territory, and should serve a human need' (Holthaus, 2018: 193).

Let me clarify this position, which is inspired by democratic pluralists like G.D.H. Cole and David Mitrany.[3] Instead of envisioning a world organized around the nation-state, and inter-governmental institutions like the WTO, UN, IMF, and World Bank, international functionalists envision an international system articulated around the functional principle (Holthaus, 2018: 141) and international functional associations. What this concretely means is that producer, consumer, and user group associations would be represented by functional representatives at the international level and that relations between individuals across the globe would be governed by need rather than nationality (Holthaus, 2018). As Cole himself put it: 'International functional association would undertake, in the wider sphere, the work undertaken in the narrower sphere by national functional organisation, and the central co-ordinating body would reproduce internationally the federal structure of the national co-ordinating bodies' (1920: 143).

Cole envisions an international system of coordination that, unlike an international organizations arranged around nation-states like the UN, would be articulated around functions. This coordinating body would in this sense act as the 'synthesis of the various essential forms of association' (Cole, 1920: 138) and be composed of international functional representatives. The latter would effectively be representatives of associations of producers, consumers, and user groups found at the societal level interacting within the confines of an international coordinating body. Here borders are not expected to delimit the scope of what one does or does not do or what one represents on a world stage. What defines individuals' interests, their actions and relations is not a national identity but a *vocational identity*. For example, relations between France and China would no longer be governed by each other's interests as nation-states but by the interests of international functional associations, representing, within the international coordinating body, the interests of (societal) associations of producers, consumers, and user groups making up, say, the international automobile association or international garment association. Put differently, international functional representatives would not so much seek to represent a national interest as the interest of an international functional association on the world stage.[4]

Under such a model, the needs and interests (the vocational identity) of democratically organized vocational associations making up societies across the world knows no territorial borders. As such, international functionalism provides an institutional framework for affirming both connections across the globe and their mutually constitutive character. For, after all, no international functional association could exist without the direct contribution of different functional representatives across different parts of the globe. International functionalism presupposes radical interdependence and facilitates the growth of what Cole (1920: 142) called a 'World Society'.

What is therefore being envisaged here is a relationship between international economic and political life akin to the relationship identified at the societal level. Like functional representation within the commune, international functional representation channels the radical interdependence of the dialogically coordinated production of life. Furthermore, like 'the internal ... means of coercion', their external counterpart 'must be in the hands of the body which represents the various social functions, and is entrusted with the task of co-ordination' (Cole, 1920: 142).[5] In addition to facilitating a self-regulating society on a global scale, international functionalism is expected to provide the basis for international solidarity.

I would in fact argue that such a re-organization of the political-economic world order provides a fruitful basis upon which to build the 'liberatory politics of "no borders"' defended by Nandita Sharma (2020: 276) and bring to life something akin to the 'plurinationality' and 'interculturality' envisioned by decolonial scholar Catherine Walsh (2018). For, international functionalism entails the demise of nation-states and, along with it, the end of categories like 'National-Natives' and 'Migrants' upon which past and present forms of class, patriarchal, racial, and colonial domination have depended (Sharma, 2020). By removing the borders and ensuring that need and vocational identity connects individuals across the world, international functionalism would effectively facilitate the creation of 'a space and place of dialoguing, thinking, analyzing, theorizing, and doing in community and in concert *with*, that encourage alliances, commitments, collaborations, and interculturalizations that cross disciplinary (de)formations, investigative interests, national borders, and racial, ethnic, sexual, and gendered identifications' (Walsh, 2018: 84–5).

As loci for the development of a (collective) vocational identity on a global scale, international associations would enable dialogue around a range of issues related to the vocation/function in question. Dialogue would not, however, be limited to economic and political issues. By acting as international public spheres, international associations would also create a space for engaging with lifestyle/cultural issues. For, to develop a conception of what exactly members of an association need, they have to engage with conceptions of how they want to live. Such conceptions, and the need developing therefrom, would not be circumscribed by national territorial borders but by the function/vocation of an association. Given participation in an association is voluntary and not limited to one association, international functionalism is expected to bring into 'existence ... multiple loyalties within a decentred social' (Walsh, 2018: 62). It would '*turn the Postcolonial New World Order upside down*' (Sharma, 2020: 281, emphasis in original), to create a world without borders in which individuals identify their obligations not with a nation-state but with members of multiple associations. International relations would thus shift from questions of territorial belonging and demands for 'choosing sides' (Sharma, 2020: 4) to questions of need and demands for how to live collectively.

So, consistent with pluriversal emancipation, international functionalism affirms difference while turning it into a basis for international solidarity. It can do so because difference is articulated around functions rather than nations. National difference essentializes, ethnicizes, and divides. In contrast, functional difference presupposes relations of complementarity. Take the example of an international transportation association and an international garment association. Each performs a different function and in virtue of doing so does not oppose but complement the other, for each makes a distinct and necessary contribution to the realization of the general social interest. Each might even directly depend on the other to the extent that, say, a garment association may have to rely on international transportation with specific functions and communicate those needs via one or more representatives in an association of transportation consumers. Shifting attention away from nationality and towards need helps make explicit relations of interdependence of this kind.

Finally, since relations of complementarity emanating from democratic decision-making processes are never fixed nor absolute, the vocational identity of an association is never fixed nor absolute either. Functionalism, including its international form, does not subvert identity but cultivates it. It nevertheless does so in such a way as to prevent the 'permanent reification of identities, which disallows the subject the fundamental freedom of diverse self-expression' (Asenbaum, 2021: 88). The dialogical coordination of the production of life and its functional representation at the local, regional, societal, and international levels, therefore, entail the kind of 'diversification of spaces' envisioned by Hans Asenbaum (2021: 101) for radicalizing democratic practice and combining self-expression while 'increas[ing] the freedom of the subject to change'. Vocational identities formed and represented within a (continuously evolving) dialogically coordinated general social interest are always provisionally cast. Identification, here, presupposes 'dis–identification' (Munoz, 1999) as hegemonic identities within associations are continuously contestable and contested through the labour of dialogue. International functionalism, then, does not merely accommodate radical interdependence, but also provides a fruitful institutional basis upon which (vocational) identities can be transformed in the light of new outcomes negotiated by members of functional associations.

Conclusion

The nation-state system emerged as the political framework around which modernity organizes international relations. Under its guise, democracy assumes a parliamentary form and relations between states are governed by national interests. As I sought to show in this chapter, however, the modern liberal-capitalist state is shot through with structures of domination. This socio-political institution has served the interests of those it has historically been under the control of Global North (white) bourgeois men. Despite attempts to remedy its institutional biases in the form of, for example, the recognition of Indigenous people's rights or redistributive mechanisms, the modern liberal-capitalist state has fallen short of creating the conditions for pluriversal emancipation. This is why it is more appropriate to think beyond the state or, at the very least, radically democratize it. An institution with severely limited functions like the commune was presented as a possible alternative. Here the political body would not play any role in economic relations but simply ensure that the dialogically coordinated production of life is adequately integrated and coordinated. An alternative to parliamentary representation was also offered in the form of functional representation. This, it was argued, would ensure that relations between associations in society and at the global level are governed by need and radical interdependence. It marks a shift away from national identity and towards what I chose to name vocational identity. With this functionalism – be it societal or global – one finds the institutional tools for affirming relations of complementarity between people and the associations they belong to. With it, one turns attention away from conflict and division, and towards solidarity and cooperation.

But of course, it is worth reminding the reader here that just like the insights provided in previous chapters, this institutional model is not so much a guide as a method for social transformation. It should therefore be treated as a means to think the world anew, not as a blueprint. For, after all, it is neither desirable nor possible to assume that an alternative can be known in advance. What can – and indeed must – be known is that the world can be otherwise. What we must know is that our relations to people across the globe need not be governed by national interests, conflicts, and divisions. They can, instead, be governed by need, function, and mutual reciprocity. Finally, since the latter can only exist outside the parameters of the nation-state system, what can also be known is that moving beyond national interests must entail moving beyond the modern liberal-capitalist state itself.

8

Conclusion

While the year 2022 might have marked a return to 'normal' following a global pandemic that pretty much closed down advanced capitalist economies, it also marked the return of high inflation rates and an acute cost of living crisis, particularly in the UK. Meanwhile energy companies are accumulating record profits. To be able to deal with such inflationary pressures partly caused by exorbitant energy prices, British workers in sectors like the railways, the National Health Service, and Royal Mail chose to strike to demand a pay rise decent enough to be able to cope with the rising cost of living. As I write the conclusion of this work, the strikes are ongoing and nobody can say whether workers will succeed. What can be said with confidence, however, is that the crisis has brought into sharp relief the follies of the capitalist market. Most notable of these is not so much the fact that capitalism creates winners and losers but that some (a few) effectively benefit from the destitution of others (many). It is under such circumstances that change comes to be desired;[1] that utopias provide us with the hope that things could be otherwise.

So how would the utopia offered in this book be expected to deal with such problems? Is a cost of living crisis even likely to exist under intersectional socialism? Before I answer those questions, let's look more closely at the underlying causes of the crisis in an advanced capitalist society like the UK. A very sharp rise in energy prices is certainly to blame for this. For, it does not only directly affect consumers of energy like the gas or electricity used to heat water, but also the businesses those consumers rely on for, say, their weekly food shopping. An increase in energy prices, therefore, leads to a more general rise in the cost of living. Individual consumers are pretty much powerless in the face of such developments. Only the energy companies and governments can choose to act to reduce the prices in question, but doing so would go against the capitalist logic of accumulation. The main role of a privatized energy company is to provide their shareholders with a return on their investment. Any measure that would likely decrease this return would be regarded as problematic. The role of the modern liberal-capitalist state is to create conditions favourable for capital accumulation, not to interfere with it. Under the capitalist logic of accumulation individuals *qua* producers and consumers are responsible for their own fate. The realization of the general social interest is left to the invisible hand of the market, that is, to producers risking it all while attempting to satisfy a need consumers might or might not want, whose price and supply consumers have little or no control over.

The intersectional socialist utopia formulated in this book provides an altogether different basis upon which to organize the allocation of resources and would deal with cost of living issues in a very different way. In fact, while it is not possible to say with certainty that no such crisis would exist under intersectional socialism, the role consumers are expected to play in allocating resources means that they would be in a position to exert a non-negligible degree of control over prices and potentially prevent sharp cost of living rises. Workers democratically organized in producer associations would, too, be in a position to set their own wages and choose to increase them along with the increase in the cost of living. Under such state of affairs, workers would not have to give up some of their pay to participate in strikes whose success is highly uncertain. Instead, they would decide what to do collectively and in dialogue with consumers and user groups. Consumers would be given a voice in their democratically organized associations in dialogue with producers. Responsibility would be collective. Interdependence would be radical to the extent that producers' would be conscious of the inextricable character of their decisions from those of consumers and user groups – and *vice versa*. The visible hand of democratically organized associations in dialogue with one another would effectively replace the invisible hand of the capitalist market.

But I would not want to conclude this work without engaging with a range of potential objections to the intersectional socialist utopia I formulate in it. Ideas and images, like reality, have their limitations. Much could indeed be said about the means proposed to achieve radical interdependence. In fact, one could even question the desirability of radical interdependence itself. After all, is dependence of any form not something likely to interfere with one's freedom? Is having to rely on others not indicative of a failure to be free? If one adopts a modernist or neoliberal understanding of freedom, then one is likely to answer those questions in the affirmative. Take, for example, the position of key Enlightenment figure Immanuel Kant. In his famous *What is Enlightenment?* essay, the German philosopher makes his position on the relationship between freedom and dependence very clear:

> Enlightenment is man's leaving his self-caused immaturity. Immaturity is the incapacity to use one's intelligence without the guidance of another. Such immaturity is self-caused if it is not caused by lack of intelligence, but by lack of determination and courage to use one's intelligence without being guided

by another. *Sapere Aude*! Have the courage to use your own intelligence! is therefore the motto of the enlightenment. (Kant, 1949: 132)

To know means to be free, but to know is equated with using of one's own reason. Knowledge and freedom are therefore construed as solitary exercises. In fact, they are best achieved individually. To know and to be free means to free oneself from one's dependence on another. It underpins a way of apprehending and being in the world that is distinctively modernist, to the extent that emancipation is construed as an act of self-mastery, and freedom and dependence are the constitutive elements of a binary. Such a position is reflected in the rugged individualism of proponents of capitalism, from Adam Smith to Friedrich Hayek. Under their reading, success and well-being are matters of individual self-interest. Dependence is a weakness or symptom of vulnerability. Responsibility is individual.

But as I hope to have made clear in this book, pluriversal intersectionality and the conception of emancipation informed by it, question the worldview underpinning the modern-capitalist freedom/dependence binary. For, a genuine counter-culture of capitalism must not only oppose the material injustices the latter engenders, it must also offer another way of being and apprehending the world, that is, offer an alternative onto-epistemic vision. It must contest the view that dependence is a barrier to freedom. To this end, I draw on decolonial thought, which is directly informed by worldviews embodied in the Latin American philosophy of *Buen Vivir* and Southern African principle of *Ubuntu*, whose relational understanding of the world offers a radical alternative to the outlined binary. According to the latter, 'there are no intrinsically existing objects, subjects, or actions' for 'what we call "experience" is always coemerging with the experiences of many other beings' (Escobar, 2020). At the core of this particular way of apprehending and being in the world, is the notion that collective well-being is aligned with individual well-being or that the well-being of one depends on the well-being of another. As Arturo Escobar (2020: 92) himself put it, '[e]verything exists because everything else exists'. What we therefore find is a reconciliation of freedom and dependence through a redefined relationship between the individual and the group. *Ubuntu* could in this sense be said to echo the *Asuwada* theory the Yoruba people of West Africa subscribe to, which 'emphasises the relevance of the individual within the group and the integral importance of association for social good' (Omobowale and Akanle, 2017: 45). To interpret the world through *Ubuntu* therefore means to treat radical interdependence not only as a defining feature of the world but also as basis upon which people are expected to thrive.

The social philosophy of *Buen Vivir*, which has informed the formulation of the Ecuadorian Constitution, also emphasizes the relational character of all living things and the collective character of well-being (Escobar, 2020). The term *Buen Vivir* is the Spanish translation of Quechua people of the Andes' notion of *Sumak Kawsay*, which broadly translates as 'good living' (Escobar, 2020). But 'good living', here, does not mean a life filled with material possessions or luxury, as the Global North tends to interpret it. It means a life marked by the harmony of all living things – between humans, as well as between them and non-humans. Central to it is the view that nature itself has rights. Accordingly, radical interdependence ought to be central not only to the way humans co-exist but also to the way humans co-exist with non-humans.

Under capitalism, the radical interdependence of all living things is not only concealed, it is also devalued, construed as the ultimate sign of weakness. But, along with the worldviews listed, *Intersectional Socialism* subscribes to the view that there is no better way to think about freedom than when we are in a position to realize our 'capacity to care and to make commitments to what we care about' (Tronto, 2013: 94). In other words, there is no better way to be free than when we choose to assert our radical interdependence: to care for others and be cared for.

What, then, can be said about the means for achieving radical interdependence? What objections could one level at, for example, the dialogical coordination of democratically organized associations of producers, consumers, and user groups? One thing is sure: it would constitute a radical alternative to the capitalist market. But to what extent would it solve some of the problems associated with economic planning of the form observed in countries like the USSR? Any form of planning requires a vast amount of information to be effective. Pat Devine (1988), for example, recognized that a system of allocation of resources like the one formulated here would entail planning too. Only this would not be state planning but negotiated planning. Instead of vast amounts of information having to be collected by a centralized state, information would circulate across different associations and communicated through dialogue. Furthermore, as mentioned in Chapter 5, digital technology could be deployed to facilitate the exchange of information and optimize the efficiency of dialogue. Much greater flexibility in the allocation of resources would therefore be expected with dialogical coordination than with centralized planning. In short, while there is a case for suggesting that dialogical coordination constitutes a form of planning, I would insist that it need not replicate the same pitfalls as centralized planning. It is indeed expected that the democratic character and institutionalized interdependence of the different associations involved in the process would act as barriers to the degeneration of dialogical coordination into centralized planning.

But could the associations themselves not degenerate into hierarchically managed organizations? Yes, they could. Like in any democratic organization, one cannot take for granted the processes that underpin it. Take, for example, worker cooperatives. While many do start with fully-fledged democratic mechanisms, some have a tendency to 'degenerate' into organizational forms akin to conventional businesses (Cornforth, 1995). Often, though, such developments result from external pressures, like those exerted by the invisible hand of the capitalist market. Since dialogical coordination presents democratic associations with an acutely different set of conditions, it is difficult to appreciate how those associations are likely to respond. What is sure, however, is that, as Chris Cornforth (1995) concluded with respects to worker cooperatives, to remain democratic associations will need to review their structures and procedures regularly.

Another objection could be levelled at the proposal to treat associations as both agents of the satisfaction of needs and spheres for the legitimation of norms. Because such a proposal appears to blur the lines between economic and political life it may seem to entail the kind of 're-feudalization' of the economy Jürgen Habermas (1989) warned against in his work on the public sphere. Such a development could indeed be regarded as a problem for democratic life in virtue of stifling the creation of deliberative spaces that could help question dominant norms and shape new ones. But to envision public spheres within economic life itself need not entail imagining the demise of the public sphere as a mediator of economic and political life. It does not necessarily mean that economic life is expected to be controlled by the political class like under the feudal age or state socialism. It simply entails envisioning an altogether different form of public sphere and different relationship between economic life, which Habermas (1984; 1987a) located within the 'system', and identity formation and norm-legitimation (the 'lifeworld'), which he located outside of economic life. When economic life is democratically organized around a dialogue between supply and demand, it necessarily brings within its scope questions regarding how individuals want to live and paves the way for a discussion of matters a capitalist economy typically excludes. For Habermas, including them within economic life is akin to halting the process of modernization and interfering with human emancipation. Technological and scientific progress, it is thought, is best achieved by freeing the 'system' from 'lifeworld' issues like norm-legitimation or questions about how individuals want to live. But, drawing inspiration from the work of ecofeminists like Val Plumwood (2002), I contended that a central barrier to emancipation across the human and non-human world is not so much the end of the separation of a sphere of strategic interests and one of norm-legitimation as the reduction of economic life to a narrow set of cognitive faculties, mainly guided by strategic interests. As I showed in Chapters 5 and 6, pluriversal emancipation is instead grounded in caring practices that call upon a broad range of bodily and cognitive faculties that are no longer guided by economic value creation or strategic (self-)interests, but by the creation of social value. Contrary to Habermas, then, I questioned the value of preserving the 'system'/'lifeworld' binary and, more fundamentally, questioned the capacity of modernist binaries to pave the way for pluriversal emancipation. Radical interdependence requires us to think beyond such binaries and make explicit the connections they tend to obscure. *Intersectional Socialism* is in this sense a counter-culture of both capitalism and modernism.

I also anticipate some readers to question the lack of in-depth engagement with the digital economy and the particular challenges it poses for socialism. For example, is the rise of the 'prosumer' (Ritzer and Jurgenson, 2010) not seriously undermining the dialogical model of coordination offered here? While the phenomenon of user-generated content does indeed change the way consumers relate to the goods they consume, with users contributing to the production of the goods themselves, they are not in control of the platform making those goods available. In the case of Facebook or YouTube users are still using a service provided to them by privately owned companies. They have to adapt to updates and various other changes imposed on them by the platforms in question. While their contributions could in some cases be monetized, they do not choose the terms of this monetization. Their control is therefore severely limited. Consequently, I would argue that the key issue is not having to deal with a new relationship between production and consumption but with the fact that digital platforms are, like many offline businesses, privately owned and hierarchically organized. The digital economy is one of many components of the capitalist economy. Like offline businesses, digital platforms could be organized into associations (Muldoon, 2022), each performing a particular function within the general social interest.

Some may also question the value or even desirability of formulating a utopia in purely theoretical terms. After all, is one not better off drawing on 'concrete utopias' (Dinerstein, 2015) or 'real utopias' (Wright, 2010), that is, already existing experiments and initiatives such as those found in Latin American resistance movements or on the margins of the capitalist economy in the form of, say, online peer-to-peer production? Do such concrete experiences not offer a much more fruitful basis upon which to envision a non-capitalist future? Such work is, of course, needed, if only to be reminded of the fact that capitalism's rule is not total and of the formidable creativity of various groups, organizations, and movements across the globe. In fact, I do draw on some of those real/concrete utopian practices in places. For example, I show how othermothering and Black ballroom 'houses' could inspire a reimagining of the relationship between productive and reproductive life. But the task set out in this work aims, first, to provide a holistic vision of a socialist counter-culture and to do so through the deployment of an intersectional lens. As such, it is not limited to an analysis of one or more initiatives shedding some light on one or more components of the economy but offers a holistic basis upon which to think the world anew. It asks: what could a world informed by radical interdependence look like? It also asks what form a counter-culture of capitalism at the intersection of diverse struggles against domination could take. In doing so, it engages with knowledge projects associated with particular resistance movement like Black feminist thought and critical disability studies. Despite its theoretical character, then, *Intersectional Socialism* partly results from concrete activist practices and resistance movements.

On a similar note, scholars like Chris Dixon (2014) and Marla Morris (2002) warned against the dangers of utopian thinking. To think the world anew, we are better off adopting what Chris Dixon (2014: 61) called a 'revelatory' approach, that is, an 'open-ended, synthetic approach based on the revelations ... that we experience together through the process of struggle'. Utopian thinking, we are told, '*prescribes* what we should think and do based on a predetermined "right" analysis' (Dixon, 2014: 61, emphasis in original). But I would suggest that the form of utopian thinking Dixon has in mind differs from the one adopted here. To treat utopia as a 'method' (Levitas, 2013) in fact means engaging with thought in a revelatory manner, akin to what Dixon himself envisaged. For, *Intersectional Socialism* does not aim to provide answers as such. Since it is imbued with necessary failure it is better understood as a basis for dialogue and asking what future individuals wish to shape if the future in question were non-capitalist. In this sense it is compatible with Dixon's own demand for 'an [revelatory] approach of collectively asking questions, of exploring and experimenting together' (2014: 61).

Accordingly, then, the answers I seem to offer in this book, either in the preceding chapters or as the earlier responses to possible criticisms, are not expected to serve a prescriptive purpose but simply to shed light on the kind of institutions that could frame another way for humans to relate to other humans and non-humans. The aim is not to impose a vision of the way things could become. It is to cultivate the desire for change by making explicit the virtues of a libertarian socialist alternative to capitalism informed by pluriversal intersectionality's principle of radical interdependence. It is to help re-energize utopianism and restore socialism's status as capitalism's ferocious opponent. It is to remind ourselves that we do not have to accept an existence defined/governed by greed, fear, subjugation, and self-interest. In short, it is to renew hope in the possibility for another, more equitable, more caring, and more fulfilling world whose construction *Intersectional Socialism* intends to contribute to.

Notes

Chapter 1

[1] It is worth noting that Mason does reference Gorz's work but what he does not do is name his ideas as socialist.

Chapter 2

[1] For example, it was under a coalition government led by Conservative (neoliberal) Prime Minister David Cameron that gay marriage was legalized in the UK.

[2] She identified a third, 'additive', version which other intersectionality theorists do not tend to regard as sufficiently intersectional to belong to the tradition of intersectionality (Bohrer, 2019). The reason for this is that additive approaches do not offer a sufficiently complex picture of the way different structures of power and domination interact. For example, they cannot tell us how such structures constitute one another in the production of inequality.

[3] New materialism is not a homogenous theoretical paradigm. There are different new materialisms, the breadth of which I do not have space to cover here. I am therefore mainly focusing on features most new materialist approaches are likely to share.

[4] In fact, it is around this time that du Bois joins the Communist Party (Kihss, 1961).

[5] Some of the scholars and activists labelled libertarian socialist here may not directly identify as such. Kropotkin, for example, identified as anarchist. However, I see more parallels than differences between anarchism and libertarian socialism, not least in the fact that many anarchists subscribe to the self-management of workers and to the goal of social empowerment that are core to libertarian socialism.

[6] It is worth noting here thar Paul Hirst was an advocate of associative democracy without subscribing to socialist politics. Much of what he had to say about associations is not, however, incompatible with libertarian socialism.

[7] Guild socialism was a short-lasting movement of the early twentieth century. It advocated workers' control of industry through its organization around democratically organized trade-related associations known as guilds.

Chapter 3

[1] By 'Indigenous thought', I refer to the worldviews of Indigenous peoples across the globe that have been subjected to colonial rule in one way or another. Like Salvatore Engel-Di Mauro (2013: 143) I recognize that the 'immense diversity of Indigenous worldviews is staggering' and choose focus on a 'unifying aspect', which is their 'inherent anti-capitalism'.

Chapter 4

[1] My use of Hardt and Negri's work here might appear misleading to anyone who read their work. For the quotation I chose to extract from their work was effectively assigned to the concept of liberation, which they explicitly contrasted with the concept of emancipation (2009: 331–2). My decision to use it to define emancipation is aimed at highlighting the difference between their definition of emancipation and my own (as well as Wright's own).

[2] In fact, one of queer scholarship's key debates is whether queer thought should be relational or anti-relational (Ruti, 2017).

[3] I wish to maintain here my commitment to the term intersectionality and reiterate its capacity to both grasp the complex interlocking of systems of oppression and accommodate a conception of self-hood that is dialogical and therefore attuned to instability of identities and structures shaping affecting those identities.

[4] I have chosen to use the term 'pluriversal emancipation' instead of 'pluriversal intersectional emancipation' because of the close affinity between pluriversality and intersectionality exposed in Chapter 2 – and because it is a less cumbersome term to use.

[5] All quotations extracted from this piece are my English translations of the original French text.

Chapter 5

[1] It must be noted that the contributions in question do not use the term 'dialogical coordination'. Devine, for example, speaks of 'negotiated coordination'. Albert and Hahnel speak of participatory economics. However, the system they have in mind involve an allocation of resources coordinated through a dialogue between the different bodies involved in the process of satisfaction of needs.

[2] In the middle of his career he did nevertheless come to accept forms of state planning as a necessity. This position is most developed in his work, *The Next Ten Years* (Cole, 2011).

[3] It must nevertheless be noted that Proudhon did vacillate between different positions throughout his career, sometimes contradicting himself. For example, as Daniel Guérin put it '[t]here is a decentralizing and federalist Proudhon, who mistrusts all planning for fear of reviving authority, and there is a Proudhon who does not hesitate to prescribe economic centralization and stresses the unitary character of production' (2017: 60).

[4] The website of this e-commerce business can be found here: Raízs – Organic products direct from the producer (raizs.com.br).

Chapter 6

[1] What it does not entail, however, is a complete elimination of the private sphere. It is important to note, here, that politicizing the personal is not equated with a total collapse of private life. For example, it does not mean forcing those involved in child rearing to 'eat shit collectively in the canteen' (Dalla Costa and James, 1975: 40). Collectivizing reproductive work means creating the conditions under which those with such caring responsibilities can choose to either undertake them themselves or by other members of a day-care association in a day-care centre or the home of the child being cared for. In both cases the associations in question are expected to support the carer. This is done financially for home care and in kind for day-care centres or home-care service.

Chapter 7

[1] It is pluralist to the extent that it channels rather than stifles difference in political life.

[2] See Chapter 3 for a discussion of this concept.

[3] Cole was in fact a major influence of Mitrany's intellectual development (Holthaus, 2018).

4   It is worth noting that the kind of democratic pluralism discussed here has informed the design and evaluation of actually existing international associations like the International Labour Organisation (Holthaus, 2018). Some of international functionalism's principles have in this sense already contributed to shaping reality.

5   It is nevertheless worth pointing that Cole (1920: 142) anticipated the disappearance of those coercive means 'before the growth of international cooperation'.

Chapter 8

1   For example, a YouGov poll shows fairly strong support for nationalizing energy companies: Support for bringing energy companies back into public ownership (yougov. co.uk).

References

Abberley, P. (1987) 'The Concept of Oppression and the Development of a Social Theory of Disability', *Disability, Handicap & Society*, 2(1): 5–19.

Abberley, P. (1996) 'Work, Utopia and Impairment', in L. Barton (ed) *Disability and Society: Emerging Issues and Insights*. London: Longman.

Abensour, M. (1999) 'William Morris: The Politics of Romance', in M. Blechman (ed) *Revolutionary Romanticism*. San Francisco: City Lights Books.

Abensour, M. (2008) 'Persistent Utopia', *Constellations*, 15(3): 406–21.

Acker, J. (2004) 'Gender, Capitalism and Globalisation', *Cultural Sociology*, 30(1): 17–41.

Adorno, T.W. (1991) 'Culture industry', in J.M. Bernstein (ed) *The Culture Industry*. London: Routledge.

Albert, M. (2003) *Parecon: Life After Capitalism*. London: Verso.

Alsultany, E. (2002) 'Los Intersticios: Recasting Moving Selves', in G. Anzaldúa and A. Keating (eds) *This Bridge We Call Home: Radical Visions for Transformation*. New York: Routledge.

Amsterdamska, O. (1990) 'Surely You Are Joking, Monsieur Latour! [Review of *Science in Action*, by B. Latour]', *Science, Technology, & Human Values*, 15(4): 495–504.

Anzaldúa, G. (1983) 'La Prieta', in C. Moraga, and G.E. Anzaldúa (eds) *This Bridge Called My Back: Writings by Radical Women of Color*. New York: Kitchen Table.

Anzaldùa, G. (1987) *Borderlands/LaFrontera: The New Mestiza*. San Francisco: Aunt Lute Books.

Anzaldùa, G. (2002) 'Preface: (Un)natural Bridges, (Un)safe Spaces', in G. Anzaldua and A. Keating (eds) *This Bridge We Call Home: Radical Visions for Transformation*. New York: Routledge.

Asenbaum, H. (2021) 'The Politics of Becoming: Disidentification as Radical Democratic Practice', *European Journal of Social Theory*, 24(1): 86–104.

Bailey, M.M. (2013) *Butch Queens Up in Pumps: Gender, Performance and Ballroom Culture in Detroit*. Ann Arbor: University of Michigan Press.

Bakunin, M. (1970) *God and the State*. New York: Dover Publications.

Bakunin, M. (2002) *Anarchism: A Collection of Revolutionary Writings*. New York: Dover Publications.

Barnes, C. (1996) 'Theories of Disability and the Origins of the Oppression of Disabled People in Western Society', in L. Berton (ed) *Disability and Society: Emerging Issues and Insights*. London: Longman.

Bastani, A. (2019) *Fully Automated Luxury Communism: A Manifesto*. London: Verso.

Bates, K., Goodley, D., and Runswick-Cole, K. (2017) 'Precarious Lives and Resistant Possibilities: The Labour of People with Learning Disabilities in Times of Austerity', *Disability & Society*, 32(2): 160–75.

Bauman, Z. (1976) *Socialism: An Active Utopia*. London: George Allen and Unwin Ltd.

Benanav, A. (2020) *Automation and the Future of Work*. London: Verso.

Benería, L. (1979). 'Reproduction, Production and the Sexual Division of Labour', *Cambridge Journal of Economics*, 3(3): 203–25.

Benería, L. (1999) 'Globalization, Gender and the Davos Man', *Feminist Economics*, 5(3): 61–83.

Berger, M.T. and Guidroz, K. (2009) *The Intersectional Approach: Transforming the Academy Through Race, Class, and Gender*. Chapel Hill: University of North Carolina Press.

Berlant, L. and Warner, M. (2002) 'Sex in Public', in M. Warner (ed), *Publics and Counterpublics*. New York: Zone Books.

Bhambra, G.K. (2007) *Rethinking Modernity: Postcolonialism and the Sociological Imagination*. Basingstoke: Palgrave Macmillan.

Bhambra, G.K. (2021) 'Colonial Global Economy: Towards a Theoretical Reorientation of Political Economy', *Review of International Political Economy*, 28(2): 307–22.

Blanco, H. (2013) 'Let's Save Humanity from Extinction', *Capitalism Nature Socialism*, 24(3): 151–9.

Bloch, E. (1986) *The Principle of Hope, Vol. 1*. Oxford: Basil Blackwell.

Bohrer, A. (2018) 'Intersectionality and Marxism: A Critical Historiography', *Historical Materialism*, 26(2): 46–74.

Bohrer, A.J. (2019) *Marxism and Intersectionality: Race, Gender, Class and Sexuality under Contemporary Capitalism*. Bielefeld: Transcript.

Bollier, D. and Helfrich, S. (2019) *Free, Fair and Alive: The Insurgent Power of the Commons*. Gabriola Island: New Society Publishers.

Bon, A., Dittoh, F., Lô, G., Pini, M., Bwana, R., WaiShiang, C. et al (2022) 'Decolonizing Technology and Society: A Perspective from the Global South', in H. Werthner, E. Prem, E.A. Lee and C. Ghezzi (eds) *Perspectives on Digital Humanism*. Springer, Cham. https://doi.org/10.1007/978–3–030–86144–5_9

Bookchin, M. (1999) 'Libertarian Municipalism', in J. Biehl (ed) *The Murray Bookchin Reader*. Montreal: Black Rose Books.

Bourdieu, P. (1986) *Distinction: A Social Critique of the Judgement of Taste*. London: Routledge.

Bourdieu, P. (2000) *Pascalian Meditations*. Cambridge: Polity.

Bourdieu, P. (2014) *On the State Lectures at the College de France, 1989–1992*. Cambridge: Polity.

Bracey, G.E. (2015) 'Toward a Critical Race Theory of State', *Critical Sociology*, 41(3): 553–72.

Braverman, H. (1974) *Labor and Monopoly Capital: The Degradation of Work in the Twentieth Century*. New York: Monthly Review Press.

Bremner, J. and Lu, F. (2006). 'Common Property among Indigenous Peoples of the Ecuadorian Amazon', *Conservation and Society*, 4(4): 499–521.

Brown, W. (1995) *Power and Freedom in Late Modernity*. Princeton: Princeton University Press.

Butler, J. (1990) *Gender Trouble: Feminism and the Subversion of Identity*. London: Routledge.

Butler, J. (1993) 'Imitation and Gender Insubordination', in H. Abelove, M.A. Barable and D.M. Halperin (eds) *The Lesbian and Gay Studies Reader*. New York: Routledge.

Butler, J. (1998) 'Merely Cultural', *New Left Review* 1/227, January/February.

Butler, J. and Athanasiou, A. (2013) *Dispossession: The Performative in the Political*. Cambridge: Polity Press.

Cabral, A. (1973) 'National liberation and culture', in Africa Information Service (ed) *Return to the Source: Selected Speeches by Amilcar Cabral*. London: Monthly Review Press.

Cabral, A. (2016) *Resistance and Decolonisation*. London: Rowman and Littlefield.

Calhoun, C. (1992) 'Introduction: Habermas and the Public Sphere', in C. Calhoun (ed) *Habermas and the Public Sphere*. Cambridge, MA: MIT Press.

Césaire, A. (2000) *Discourse on Colonialism*. New York: Monthly Review Press.

Césaire, A. (2003) 'Discours sur la Négritude', Available at: http://www.montraykreyol.org/article/negritude-ethnicity-et-cultures-afro-aux-ameriques [Accessed 28 March 2023].

Césaire, A. (2010) 'Letter to Maurice Thorez', *Social Text*, 28(2): 145–52.

Chandler, D. and Reid, J. (2018) '"Being in Being": Contesting the Ontopolitics of Indigeneity', *The European Legacy*, 23(3): 251–68.

Chandler, D. and Reid, J. (2020) 'Becoming Indigenous: The "Speculative Turn" in Anthropology and the (Re)colonisation of Indigeneity', *Postcolonial Studies*, 23(4): 485–504.

Charles, N. (2014) '"Animals Just Love You as You Are": Experiencing Kinship across the Species Barrier', *Sociology*, 48(4): 715–30.

Cho, S., Crenshaw, K.W. and McCall, L. (2013) 'Toward a Field of Intersectionality Studies: Theory, Applications and Praxis', *Signs*, 38(4): 785–810.

Chun, J., Lipsitz, G. and Shin, Y. (2013) 'Intersectionality: Theorizing Power, Empowering Theory', *Signs*, 38(4): 917–40.

Clark, B., Auerbach, D. and Xuan Zhang, K. (2018) 'The Du Bois Nexus: Intersectionality, Political Economy, and Environmental Injustice in the Peruvian Guano Trade in the 1800s', *Environmental Sociology*, 4(1): 54–66.

Cohen, C.J. (1997) 'Punks, Bulldaggers, and Welfare Queens', *GLQ: A Journal of Lesbian and Gay Studies*, 3: 437–65.

Cole, G.D.H. (1917) *Self-Government in Industry*. London: G. Bell and Sons, LTD.

Cole, G.D.H. (1920) *Social Theory*. London: Methuen & Co.

Cole, G.D.H. (1946) 'Cooperation, Labour and Socialism, Co-operative Partnership Propaganda Committee', Sixth Thomas Blandford Memorial Lecture.

Cole, G.D.H. (1950) *Essays in Social Theory*. London: Macmillan.

Cole, G.D.H. (1980) *Guild Socialism Restated*. London: Transaction Books.

Cole, G.D.H. (2011) *The Next Ten Years in British Social and Economic Policy*. London: Routledge.

Collins, P.H. (2000) *Black Feminist Thought: Knowledge, Consciousness, and the Politics of Empowerment*. 2nd edition. London: Routledge.

Collins, P.H. (2017) 'The Difference That Power Makes: Intersectionality and Participatory Democracy', *Investigaciones Feministas*, 8(1): 19–39.

Collins, P.H. (2019) *Intersectionality as Critical Theory*. London: Duke University Press.

Collins, P.H. and Bilge, S. (2016) *Intersectionality*. Cambridge: Polity.

Collins, P.H. and Bilge, S. (2020) *Intersectionality*. 2nd edition. Cambridge: Polity.

Combahee River Collective (2017) 'Combahee River Collective Statement', in K.-Y. Taylor (ed) (2017) *How We Get Free: Black Feminism and The Combahee River Collective*. Chicago: Haymarket Books.

Connell, R. (2007) *The Global Dynamics of Knowledge in Social Science*. Crows Nest: Allen and Unwin.

Convivialist International (2020) 'The Second Convivialist Manifesto: Towards a Post-Neoliberal World', *Civic Sociology*. Available at: https://doi.org/10.1525/001c.12721 [Accessed 11 August 2022].

Coole, D. (2015) 'Emancipation as a Three-dimensional Project', *Hypatia*, 30(3): 530–46.

Cornforth, C. (1995) 'Pattern of Cooperative Management: Beyond the Degeneration Thesis', *Industrial and Economic Democracy*, 16: 487–523.

Coulthard, G.S. (2014) *Red Skins, White Masks: Rejecting the Colonial Politics of Recognition*. Minneapolis: University of Minnesota Press.

Crenshaw, K. (1989) 'Demarginalizing the Intersection of Race and Sex: A Black Feminist Critique of Antidiscrimination Doctrine, Feminist Theory and Antiracist Politics', *University of Chicago Legal Forum*, 1989(1): Article 8.

Crenshaw, K. (1991) 'Mapping the Margins: Intersectionality, Identity Politics, and Violence against Women of Color', *Stanford Law Review*, 43(6): 1241–99.

Cronin, C. (1996) 'Bourdieu and Foucault on Power and Modernity', *Philosophy and Social Criticism*, 22(6): 55–85.

Dahl, R.A. (1985) *A Preface to Economic Democracy*. Berkeley, CA: University California Press.

Dalla Costa, M. and James, S. (1975) *The Power of Women and the Subversion of Community*. Bristol: Falling Wall Press.

Davis, A.Y. (1998) 'Women and Capitalism: Dialectics of Oppression and Liberation', in J. James (ed) *The Angela Y. Davis Reader*. Oxford: Blackwell.

Davis, A.Y. (2012) *The Meaning of Freedom and other Difficult Dialogues*. San Francisco: City Lights Books.

Davis, A.Y. (2013) 'Critical Refusals and Occupy', *Radical Philosophy Review*, 16(2): 425–39.

Dawson, M.C. (2013) *Blacks in and Out of the Left*. Cambridge, MA: Harvard University Press.

Dawson, M.C. (2016) 'Hidden in Plain Sight: A Note on Legitimation Crises and the Racial Order', *Critical Historical Studies*, 3(1): 143–61.

De Beauvoir, S. (1997) *The Second Sex*. London: Vintage Classics.

D'Emilio, J. (1993) 'Capitalism and Gay Identity', in H. Abelove, M.A. Barale and D.M. Halperin (eds) *The Lesbian and Gay Studies Reader*. London: Routledge.

De Sousa Santos, B. (2014) *Epistemologies of the South: Justice Against Epistemicide*. London: Routledge.

Delany, S.R. (1999) *Times Square Red, Times Square Blue*. New York: New York University Press.

Della Porta, D. (2015) *Social Movements in Times of Austerity*. Cambridge: Polity.

Deranty, J.-P. (2022) 'Post-work Society as an Oxymoron: Why We Cannot, and Should Not, Wish Work Away', *European Journal of Social Theory*, 25(3): 422–39. Available at: https://journals.sagepub.com/doi/10.1177/13684310211012169 [Accessed 28 March 2023].

Devine, P. (1988) *Democracy and Economic Planning: The Political Economy of a Self-Governing Society*. Cambridge: Polity Press.

Di Leonardo, M. (1987) 'The Female World of Cards and Holidays: Women, Families, and the Work of Kinship', *Signs*, 12(3): 440–53.

Dinerstein, A.C. (2015) *The Politics of Autonomy in Latin America: The Art of Organising Hope*. Basingstoke: Palgrave Macmillan.

Dixon, C. (2014) *Another Politics: Talking across Today's Transformative Movements*. Oakland, CA: University of California Press.

Dolphijn, R. and van der Tuin, I. (2012) *New Materialism: Interviews and Cartographies*. Ann Arbor: Open Humanities Press.

Du Bois, W.E.B. (1898) 'The Study of the Negro Problems', *The Annals of the American Academy of Political and Social Science*, 11: 1–23.

Du Bois, W.E.B. (1998) *Black Reconstruction in America: 1860–1880*. New York: Free Press.

Du Bois, W.E.B. (2008) *Souls of Black Folk*. Oxford: Oxford University Press.

Dufays, F., O'Shea, N., Huybrechts, B. and Nelson, T. (2020) 'Resisting Colonization: Worker Cooperatives' Conceptualization and Behaviour in a Habermasian Perspective', *Work, Employment and Society*, 34(6): 965–84.

Duggan, L. (2002) 'The New Homonormativity: The Sexual Politics of Neoliberalism', in R. Castronovo and D. Nelson (eds) *Materializing Democracy: Toward a Revitalized Cultural Politics*. Durham: Duke University Press.

Duggan, L. (2003) *The Twilight of Equality? Neoliberalism, Cultural Politics, and the Attack on Democracy*. Boston: Beacon Press.

Durkheim, E. (1984) *The Division of Labour in Society*. 2nd edition. Basingstoke: Palgrave Macmillan.

Eisenstein, Z.R. (1978) *Capitalist Patriarchy and the Case for Socialist Feminism*. New York: Monthly Review Press.

Engel-Di Mauro, S. (2013) 'Bridging Indigenous and Socialist Perspectives: An Introduction to the Special Issue', *Capitalism Nature Socialism*, 24(3): 141–6.

Engels, F. (2008) *Socialism: Utopia and Scientific*. New York: Cosimo.

Escobar, A. (2018) *Designs for the Pluriverse: Radical Interdependence, Autonomy, and the Remaking of Worlds*. London: Duke University Press.

Escobar, A. (2020) *Pluriversal Politics: The Real and the Possible*. Durham: Duke University Press.

Espinosa, P. and Bustamante-Kuschel, G. (2022) 'Indigenous Patrimonialization as an Operation of the Liberal State', *Philosophy & Social Criticism*, 48(6): 882–903.

Fanon, F. (2000) 'The Fact of Blackness', in L. Back and J. Solomos (eds) *Theories of Race and Racism: A Reader*. London: Routledge.

Farris, E.M. and Holman, M.R. (2015) 'Public Officials and a "Private" Matter: Attitudes and Policies in the County Sheriff Office Regarding Violence Against Women', *Social Science Quarterly*, 96(4): 1117–35.

Federici, S. (2004) *The Caliban and the Witch: Women, the Body and Primitive Accumulation*. New York: Automedia.

Federici, S. (2019) *Re-Enchanting the World: Feminism and the Politics of the Commons*. Oakland, CA: PM Press.

Ferdinand, M. (2022) *Decolonial Ecology: Thinking from the Caribbean World*. Cambridge: Polity.

Ferguson, R. (2004) *Aberrations in Black: Toward a Queer of Color Critique*. Minneapolis: University of Minnesota Press.

Flesher-Fominaya, C. (2014) *Social Movements and Globalization, How Protests, Occupations and Uprisings are Changing the World.* Basingstoke: Palgrave Macmillan.

Floyd, K. (2009) *The Reification of Desire: Toward a Queer Marxism.* Minneapolis: University of Minnesota Press.

Foster, J.B., Clark, B. and York, R. (2010) *Ecological Rift: Capitalism's War on the Earth.* New York: New York University Press.

Foucault, M. (1978) *The History of Sexuality, Volume 1: An Introduction.* New York: Pantheon Books.

Foucault, M. (1990) *The Care of the Self: The History of Sexuality.* Volume 3. London: Penguin Books.

Foucault, M. (1992) *The Use of Pleasure: The History of Sexuality* Volume 2. London: Penguin Books.

Foucault, M. (1997) 'The Ethics of Concern for Self as a Practice of Freedom', in P. Rabinow (ed) *Ethics, Subjectivity and Truth.* New York: New Press.

Foucault, M. (1998) *The Will to Knowledge: The History of Sexuality* Volume 1. London: Penguin Books.

Foucault, M. (2009) *Security, Territory, Population: Lectures at the Collège de France.* Basingstoke: Palgrave Macmillan.

Fraser, N. (1992) 'Rethinking the Public Sphere: A Contribution to the Critique of Actually Existing Democracy', in C. Calhoun (ed) *Habermas and the Public Sphere.* Cambridge, MA: MIT Press.

Fraser, N. (1994) 'After the Family Wage: Gender Equity and the Welfare State', *Political Theory*, 22(4): 591–618.

Fraser, N. (1995) 'From Redistribution to Recognition? Dilemmas of Justice in a "Post-socialist" age', *New Left Review*, 1/212, July–August: 68–93.

Fraser, N. (1998) 'Heterosexism, Misrecognition and Capitalism: A Response to Judith Butler', *New Left Review*, 1/228, March–April: 140–9.

Fraser, N. (2014) 'Behind Marx's Hidden Abode: For an Expanded Conception of Capitalism', *New Left Review*, 86, March–April: 55–72.

Fraser, N. (2016) 'Expropriation and Exploitation in Racialized Capitalism: A Reply to Michael Dawson', *Critical Historical Studies*, 3(1): 163–78.

Fraser, N. (2019) *The Old is Dying and the New Cannot Be Born: From Progressive Neoliberalism to Trump and Beyond.* London: Verso.

Fraser, N. (2020) 'What Should Socialism Mean in the Twenty-first Century?', *Socialist Register*, 56: 1–13.

Fraser, N. and Honneth, A. (2003) *Recognition or Redistribution? A Political-Philosophical Exchange.* London: Verso.

Frazier, D. (2017) 'Interview with Demit Frazier', in K.-Y. Taylor (ed) *How We Get Free: Black Feminism and The Combahee River Collective.* Chicago: Haymarket Books.

Freire, P. (2005) *Pedagogy of the Oppressed.* New York: Continuum.

Friedan, B. (2010) *The Feminine Mystique.* London: Penguin.

Fourier, C. (1967) *Le Nouveau Monde Amoureux*. Paris: Editions Anthropos.

Fourier, C. (1996) *The Theory of the Four Movements*. Cambridge: Cambridge University Press.

Fox, N.J. and Alldred, P. (2018) 'Social Structures, Power and Resistance in Monist Sociology: (New) Materialist Insights', *Journal of Sociology*, 54(3): 315–30.

Fukuyama, F. (1989) 'The End of History?', *The National Interest*, 16, 3–18.

Fulcher, G. (1996) 'Beyond Normalisation But Not Utopia', in L. Berton (ed) *Disability and Society: Emerging Issues and Insights*. London: Longman.

Gibson-Graham, J.K. (2006) *The End of Capitalism (as We Knew it): A Feminist Critique of Political Economy*. Minneapolis: University of Minnesota Press.

Giddens, A. (1991) *Modernity as Self-Identity: Self and Society in the Late Modern Age*. Cambridge: Polity.

Giddens, A. (1998) *The Third Way: The Renewal of Social Democracy*. Cambridge: Polity.

Go, J. (2016) *Postcolonial Thought and Social Theory*. Oxford: Oxford University Press.

Goldberg, D.T. (2002) *The Racial State*. Oxford: Blackwell.

Goldberg, D.T. (2009) *The Threat of Race: Reflections on Racial Neoliberalism*. Oxford: Blackwell.

Goodley, D. and Runswick-Cole, K. (2010) 'Len Barton, Inclusion and Critical Disability Studies: Theorising Disabled Childhoods', *International Studies in Sociology of Education*, 20(4): 273–90.

Gorz, A. (1989) *Critique of Economic Reason*. London: Verso.

Gorz, A. (1994) *Farewell to the Working Class: An Essay on Post-Industrial Socialism*. London: Pluto Press.

Gorz, A. (2012) *Capitalism, Socialism, Ecology*. London: Verso.

Graeber, D. (2018) *Bullshit Jobs: A Theory*. London: Penguin.

Greenfield, P. (2020) '"Sweet City": The Costa Rica Suburb That Gave Citizenship to Bees, Plants and Trees', *The Guardian*. Available at: https://www.theguardian.com/environment/2020/apr/29/sweet-city-the-costa-rica-suburb-that-gave-citizenship-to-bees-plants-and-trees-aoe [Accessed 3 August 2022].

Grosfoguel, R. (2007) 'The Epistemic Decolonial Turn', *Cultural Studies*, 21(2–3): 211–23.

Guérin, D. (2017) *For a Libertarian Communism*. Oakland, CA: PM Press.

Habermas, J. (1971) *Toward a Rational Society: Student Protest, Science and Politics*. London: Heinemann.

Habermas, J. (1984) *The Theory of Communicative Action*, Vol. I. London: Polity Press.

Habermas, J. (1986) 'The New Obscurity: The Crisis of the Welfare State and the Exhaustion of Utopian Energies', *Philosophy and Criticism*, 11(1): 1–18.

Habermas, J. (1987a) *The Theory of Communicative Action*, Vol. II. London: Polity Press.

Habermas, J. (1987b) *Knowledge and Human Interests*. Cambridge: Polity.

Habermas, J. (1989) *The Structural Transformation of the Public Sphere*. London: Polity.

Habermas, J. (1996) *Between Facts and Norms*. Cambridge: Polity.

Habermas, J. (1998) *The Inclusion of the Other*. Boston: MIT Press.

Hahnel, R. (2016) 'In defence of participatory economics', in R. Hahnel and E.O. Wright (eds) *Alternatives to Capitalism: Proposals for a Democratic Economy*. London: Verso.

Hall, S. (2017) *The Fateful Triangle: Race, Ethnicity, Nation*. Cambridge, MA: Harvard University Press.

Hall, S. (2018) 'Race, Articulation, and Societies Structured in Dominance', in D. Morley (ed) *Essential Essays, Volume 1: Foundations of Cultural Studies*. New York: Duke University Press.

Halperin, D.M. (1995) *Saint Foucault: Towards a Gay Hagiography*. Oxford: Oxford University Press.

Hancock, A.-M. (2016) *Intersectionality: An Intellectual History*. Oxford: Oxford University Press.

Haraway, D. (2018) *Second_Millennium. FemaleMan © Meets_ OncoMouse: Feminism and Technoscience*. London: Routledge.

Hardt, M. and Negri, A. (2004) *The Multitude: War and Democracy in the Age of Empire*. New York: The Penguin Press.

Hardt, M. and Negri, A. (2009) *Commonwealth*. Cambridge, MA: Belknap Press.

Harvey, D. (2003) *The New Imperialism*. Oxford: Oxford University Press.

Hawkeswood, W.G. (1996) *One of the Children: Gay Black Men in Harlem*. Berkeley: University of California Press.

Hennessy, R. (2000) *Profit and Pleasure: Sexual Identities in Late Capitalism*. London: Routledge.

Hirst, P. (ed) (1989) *The Pluralist Theory of the State: Selected Writings of G.D.H. Cole, J.N. Figgis and H.J. Laski*. London: Routledge.

Hirst, P. (1994) *Associative Democracy: New forms of Economic and Social Governance*. Cambridge: Polity Press.

Holthaus, L. (2014) 'G.D.H. Cole's International Thought: The Dilemmas of Justifying Socialism in the Twentieth Century', *The International History Review*, 36(5): 858–75.

Holthaus, L. (2018) *Pluralist Democracy in International Relations: L.T. Hobhouse, G.D.H. Cole, and David Mitrany*. London: Palgrave Macmillan.

Honneth, A. (2017) *The Idea of Socialism*. Cambridge: Polity.

hooks, b. (1984) *Feminist Theory: From Margin to Centre*. Boston, MA: South End Press.

hooks, b. (2015) *Talking Back: Thinking Feminist, Thinking Black*. London: Routledge.

Horvat, B. (1980) 'Ethical Foundations of Self-government', *Economic and Industrial Democracy*, 1(1): 19.

Horvat, B., Markovic, M. and Supek, R. (eds) (1975) *Self-Governing Socialism: Sociology, Economics and Politics*. New York: International Arts and Sciences Press.

Horwitz, S. (2015) *Hayek's Modern Family: Classical Liberalism and the Evolution of Social Institutions*. Basingstoke: Palgrave Macmillan.

Isoke, Z. (2013) *Urban Black Women and the Politics of Resistance*. Basingstoke: Palgrave Macmillan.

Jackson, T. (2021) *Post-Growth: Life After Capitalism*. Cambridge: Polity.

Jagose, A. (1996) *Queer Theory: An Introduction*. Melbourne: Melbourne University Press.

James, J. (1998) 'Introduction', in J. James (ed) *The Angela Y. Davis Reader*. Oxford: Blackwell.

Jessop, B. (2002) *The Future of the Capitalist State*, Cambridge: Polity Press.

Johnson, H. (2002) 'Bridging Different Views: Australian and Asia–Pacific Engagements with *This Bridge Called My Back*', in G.E. Anzaldúa and A. Keating (eds) *This Bridge we Call Home: Radical Visions for Transformation*. New York: Routledge.

Kallis, G., Paulson, S., D'Alisa, G. and Demaria, F. (2020) *The Case for Degrowth*. Cambridge: Polity.

Kant, I. (1949) "What Is Enlightenment?", in C.J. Friedrich (ed) *The Philosophy of Kant*, pp 132–39. New York: Random House.

Keating, A. (2002) 'Forging El Mundo Zurdo: Changing Ourselves, Changing the World', in G.E. Anzaldùa and A. Keating (eds) *This Bridge we Call Home: Radical Visions for Transformation*. New York: Routledge.

Keating, A. (2009) 'From Intersections to Interconnections: Lessons for Transformation from *This Bridge Called My Back*: Radical Writings by Women of Color', in M.T. Berger and K. Guidroz (eds) *The Intersectional Approach: Transforming the Academy Through Race, Class, and Gender*. Chapel Hill: University of North Carolina Press.

Kemple, T. M. and Mawani, R. (2009) 'The Sociological Imagination and its Imperial Shadows', *Theory, Culture & Society*, 26(7–8): 228–49.

Kihss (1961) 'Dr W.E.B. Du Bois Joins the Communist Party', *New York Times*, 23 November. Available at: https://credo.library.umass.edu/view/full/mums312-b154-i370 [Accessed 30 August 2022].

King, D. K. (1988) 'Multiple Jeopardy, Multiple Consciousness: The Context of a Black Feminist Ideology', *Signs*, 14(1): 42–72.

Kowalik, T. (1990) 'Central Planning', in J. Eatwell, M. Milgate and P. Newman (eds) *Problems of the Planned Economy*. Basingstoke: Palgrave.

Kropotkin, P. (2002) *Anarchism: A Collection of Revolutionary Writings*. New York: Dover Publications.

Kropotkin, P. (2012) *The Conquest of Bread and other Writings*. Cambridge: Cambridge University Press.

Labour Party, The (2017) *Alternative Models of Ownership*. Report to the Shadow Chancellor and Shadow Secretary of State for Business, Energy and Industrial Strategy. Available at: https://labour.org.uk/wp-content/uploads/2017/10/Alternative-Models-of-Ownership.pdf [Accessed 8 August 2022].

Laclau, E. and Mouffe, C. (2001) *Hegemony and Socialist Strategy: Towards a Radical Democratic Politics*. 2nd edition. London: Verso.

Lane, D.S. (1996) *The Rise and Fall of State Socialism: Industrial Society and the Socialist State*. Cambridge: Polity.

Lassale, F. (1884) *The Working Man's Programme: An Address*. London: Modern Press.

Latouche, S. (2009) *Farewell to Growth*. Cambridge: Polity.

Latour, B. (1990) 'Technology is Society Made Durable', *The Sociological Review*, 38: 103–31.

Latour, B. (1993) *We Have Never Been Modern*. Cambridge, MA: Harvard University Press.

Latour, B. (2004) 'Why Has Critique Run out of Steam? From Matters of Fact to Matters of Concern', *Critical Inquiry*, 30: 225–48.

Latour, B. (2005) *Reassembling the Social*. Oxford: Oxford University Press.

Lefèbvre, H. (1975) 'Elements for a Sociology of Self-management', in B. Horvat, M. Markovic and R. Supek (eds) *Self-Governing Socialism: Sociology, Economics and Politics*. New York: International Arts and Sciences Press.

Lentin, A. and Titley, G. (2011) *The Crises of Multiculturalism: Racism in a Neoliberal Age*. London: Zed Books.

Levitas, R. (2013) *Utopia as Method: The Imaginary Reconstitution of Society*. Basingstoke: Palgrave Macmillan.

Lilia, M. and Vinthagen, S. (2013) 'Sovereign Power, Disciplinary Power and Biopower: Resisting What Power with What Resistance?', *The Journal of Political Power*, 7(1): 107–26.

Linebaugh, P. (2008) *The Magna Carta Manifesto: Liberties and Commons for All*. Berkeley: University of California Press.

Lorde, A. (1984) *Sister Outsider: Essays & Speeches*. Trumansburg, NY: Crossing Press.

Lorde, A. (1993) *Zami, Sister Outsider, Undersong*. New York: Quality Paperback Book Club.

Lorde, A. (2018) *The Master's Tools Will Never Dismantle the Master's House*. London: Penguin.

Lutz, H., Vivar, M.T.H. and Supik, L. (2011) 'Framing Intersectionality: An Introduction', in H. Lutz, M.T.H. Vivar and L. Supik (eds) *Framing Intersectionality: Debates on a Multi-Faceted Concept in Gender Studies*. Farnham: Ashgate.

Lyotard, J.F. (1984) *The Postmodern Condition: A Report on Knowledge.* Minneapolis: University of Minnesota Press.

MacGregor, S. (2021) 'Making Matter Great Again? Ecofeminism, New Materialism and the Everyday Turn in Environmental Politics', *Environmental Politics*, 30(1–2): 41–60.

MacKinnon, C.A. (1989) *Toward a Feminist Theory of the State.* Cambridge, MA: Harvard University Press.

Marable, M. (1996) *Speaking Truth to Power: Essays on Race, Resistance and Radicalism.* Oxford: Westview Press.

Marable, M. (2001) 'Why Black Americans Are Not Socialists', in M.H. Howard (ed) *Socialism: Key Concepts in Critical Theory.* New York: Humanity Books.

Marcuse, H. (1969) *An Essay on Liberation.* Boston: Beacon Press.

Marcuse, H. (2002) *One Dimensional Man: Studies in the Ideology of Advanced Industrial Society.* London: Routledge.

Marinucci, M. (2010) *Feminism Is Queer: The Intimate Connection between Queer and Feminist Theory.* London: Zed Books.

Markovic, M. (1975) 'Philosophical Foundations of the Idea of Self-management', in B. Horvat, M. Markovic and R. Supek (eds) *Self-Governing Socialism: Historical development, Social and Political Philosophy.* New York: International Arts and Sciences Press.

Martell, L. (2023) *Alternative Societies: For a Pluralist Socialism.* Bristol: Bristol University Press.

Marx, K. (2000a) 'Economic and Philosophical Manuscripts', in D. McLellan (ed) *Karl Marx: Selected Writings.* Oxford: Oxford University Press.

Marx, K. (2000b) 'Critique of Hegel's *Philosophy of Right*', in D. McLellan (ed) *Karl Marx: Selected Writings.* Oxford: Oxford University Press.

Marx, K. (2000c) 'Grundrisse', in D. McLellan (ed) *Karl Marx: Selected Writings.* Oxford: Oxford University Press.

Marx, K. (2000d) 'The German Ideology', in D. McLellan (ed) *Karl Marx: Selected Writings.* Oxford: Oxford University Press.

Marx, K. (2000e) 'On the Jewish Question', in D. McLellan (ed) *Karl Marx: Selected Writings.* Oxford: Oxford University Press.

Mason, P. (2015) *Postcapitalism: A Guide to Our Future.* London: Penguin.

Masquelier, C. (2014) *Critical Theory and Libertarian Socialism: Realizing the Political Potential of Critical Social Theory.* New York: Bloomsbury.

Masquelier, C. (2017) *Critique and Resistance in a Neoliberal Age: Towards a Narrative of Emancipation.* London: Macmillan.

Matsuda, M.J. (1991) 'Beside My Sister, Facing the Enemy: Legal Theory out of Coalition', *Stanford Law Review*, 43(6): 1183–92.

May, V.M. (2015) *Pursuing Intersectionality, Unsettling Dominant Imaginaries.* New York: Routledge.

Mbembe, A. (2017) *Critique of Black Reason.* Durham: Duke University Press.

McCall, L. (2005) 'The Complexity of Intersectionality', *Signs*, 30(3): 1771–800.

McCarthy, T. (1992) 'Practical Discourse: On the Relation of Morality to Politics', in C. Calhoun (ed) *Habermas and the Public Sphere*. Cambridge, MA: MIT Press.

McClintock, A. (1995) *Imperial Leather: Race, Gender and Sexuality in the Colonial Context*. London: Routledge.

McDuffie, E.S. (2011) *Sojourning for Freedom: Black Women, American Communism and the Making of Black Left Feminism*. Durham: Duke University Press.

McKean, M. (2000) 'Common Property: What is it, What is it Good for, and What Makes it Work?', in C.C. Gibson, M.A. McKean and E. Ostrom (eds) *People and Forests: Communities, Institutions and Governance*. Cambridge, MA: MIT Press.

Melamed, J. (2011) *Represent and Destroy: Rationalizing Violence in the New Racial Capitalism*. Minneapolis: University of Minnesota Press.

Melamed, J. (2015) 'Racial Capitalism', *Critical Ethnic Studies*, 1(1): 76–85.

Mellor, M. (1992) 'Green Politics: Ecofeminist, Ecofeminine or Ocomasculine?', *Environmental Politics*, 1(2): 229–51.

Merchant, C. (1990) *The Death of Nature: Women, Ecology and the Scientific Revolution*. 2nd edition. San Francisco: Harper and Row.

Mies, M. (2014a) *Patriarchy and Capital Accumulation on a World Scale: Women in the International Division of Labour*. London: Zed Books.

Mies, M. (2014b) 'White Man's Dilemma: His Search for What He Has Destroyed', in M. Mies and V. Shiva (eds) *Ecofeminism*. 2nd edition. London: Zed Books.

Mies, M. and Shiva, V. (2014) *Ecofeminism*. 2nd edition. New York: Zed Books.

Mignolo, W.D. (2018) 'The Decolonial Option', in W.D. Mignolo and C.E. Walsh (eds) *On Decoloniality: Concepts, Analytics, Praxis*. Durham: Duke University Press.

Mignolo, W.D. (2000) *Local Histories/Global Designs: Coloniality, Subaltern Knowledges and Border Thinking*. Princeton: Princeton University Press.

Mignolo, W.D. and Walsh, C.E. (2018) *On Decoloniality: Concepts, Analytics, Praxis*. Durham: Duke University Press.

Miliband, R. (1969) *The State in Capitalist Society*. New York: Basic Books.

Miliband, R. (1983) 'State Power and Class Interests', *New Left Review*, 1/138. March/April: 57–68.

Moore, J.W. (2015) *Capitalism in the Web of Life*. London: Verso.

Moraga, C. and Anzaldúa, G. (eds) (1983) *This Bridge Called My Back: Writings by Radical Women of Color*. New York: Kitchen Table.

Morris, M. (2002) 'Young Man Popkin: A Queer Dystopia', in G. Analdua and A. Keating (eds) *This Bridge We Call Home: Radical Visions for Transformation*. London: Routledge.

Morris, W. (1995) *News From Nowhere*, Cambridge: Cambridge University Press.

Muldoon, J. (2022) *Platform Socialism: How to Reclaim our Digital Future from Big Tech*. London: Pluto.

Muñoz, J.E. (1999) *Disidentifications: Queers of Color and the Performance of Politics*. Minneapolis: University of Minnesota Press.

Muñoz, J.E. (2019) *Queer Utopia: The Then and There of Queer Futurity*. 10th anniversary edition. New York: New York University Press.

Neate, R. (2022) 'Supercar Sales Accelerate in the UK', *The Guardian*. Available at: https://www.theguardian.com/business/2022/jul/25/supercar-sales-accelerate-in-the-uk#:~:text=Wealthy%20people%20in%20the%20UK,a%2019%25%20increase%20on%202020. [Accessed 11 August 2022].

Nichols, R. (2020) *Theft is Property! Dispossession and Critical Theory*. Durham: Duke University Press.

Nyman, P. (2014) 'Toward a Theory of Emancipation: Feminist Critiques of Postmodernism', *International Journal of Humanities and Social Science*, 4(6): 203–8.

Oliver, M. (1990) *The Politics of Disablement*. Basingstoke: Macmillan.

Olstrom, E. (1990) *Governing the Commons: The Evolution of Institutions for Collective Action*. Cambridge: Cambridge University Press.

Omi, M. and Winant, H. (2014) *Racial Formation in the United States*. 3rd edition. London: Routledge.

Omobowale, A.O. and Akanle, O. (2017) '*Asuwada* Epistemology and Globalised Sociology: Challenges of the South', *Sociology*, 51(1): 43–59.

Pasic, N. (1975) 'The Idea of Direct Self-managing Democracy and Socialization of Policy-making', in B. Horvat, M. Markovic and R. Supek (eds) *Self-Governing Socialism: Sociology, Economics and Politics*. New York: International Arts and Sciences Press.

Patel, R. (2010) *The Value of Nothing: How to Reshape market Society and Redefine Democracy*. London: Picador.

Pateman, C. (1988) *The Sexual Contract*. Stanford: Stanford University Press.

Patnaik, U. and Patnaik, P. (2021) *Capital and Imperialism: Theory, History and Present*. New York: Monthly Review Press.

Piketty, T. (2020) *Capital and Ideology*. Cambridge, MA: Harvard University Press.

Piore, M.J. and Sabel, C.F. (1984) *The Second Industrial Divide: Possibilities for Prosperity*, New York: Basic Books.

Pleyers, G. (2010) *Alter-Globalization: Becoming Actors in the Global Age*. Cambridge: Polity.

Plumwood, V. (2002) *Environmental Culture: The Ecological Crisis of Reason*. London: Routledge.

Postone, M. (1992) 'Political Theory and Historical Analysis', in C. Calhoun (ed) *Habermas and the Public Sphere*. Cambridge, MA: MIT Press.

Poulantzas, N. (1969) 'The Problem of the Capitalist State', *New Left Review*, 1/58, November/December: 67–78.

Poulantzas, N. (1978) *Political Power and Social Classes*. London: Verso.

Proudhon, P.J. (1993) *What is Property?* Cambridge: Cambridge University Press.

Puar, J.K. (2007) *Terrorist Assemblages: Homonationalism in Queer times*. Durham: Duke University Press.

Quijano, A. (2007) 'Coloniality and Modernity/Rationality', *Cultural Studies*, 21(2–3): 168–78.

Quijano, A. and Ennis, M. (2000) 'Coloniality of Power, Eurocentrism, and Latin America', *Nepantla: Views from South*, 1(3): 533–80.

Rabaka, R. (2009) *Africana Critical Theory: Reconstructing the Black Radical Tradition, from W.E.B. Du Bois and C.L.R. James to Frantz Fanon and Amilcar Cabral*. New York: Lexington Books.

Ransby, B. (2017) 'Comments by Barbara Ransby', in K.-Y. Taylor (ed) *How We Get Free: Black Feminism and The Combahee River Collective*. Chicago: Haymarket Books.

Rich, A. (1993) 'Compulsory Heterosexuality and Lesbian Existence', in H. Abelove, M.A. Barable, and D.M. Halperin (eds) *The Lesbian and Gay Studies Reader*. New York: Routledge.

Richards, M. (1997) 'Common Property Resource Institutions and Forest Management in Latin America', *Development and Change*, 28(1): 95–117.

Ritzer, G. and Jurgenson, N. (2010) 'Production, Consumption, Prosumption: The Nature of Capitalism in the Age of the Digital Prosumer', *Journal of Consumer Culture*, 10(1): 13–36.

Ritzer, G. and Stepnisky, J. (2019) *Contemporary Sociological Theory: Its Classical Roots*. London: Sage.

Robinson, C.J. (1983) *Black Marxism: The Making of the Black Radical Tradition*. London: University of North Carolina Press.

Rousseau, J.J. (1993) *The Social Contract and Discourses*. London: Everyman.

Ruti, M. (2017) *The Ethics of Opting Out: Queer Theory's Defiant Subjects*. New York: Columbia University Press.

Salhins, M. (2008) *The Western Illusion of Human Nature: With Reflections on the Long History of Hierarchy, Equality, and the Sublimation of Anarchy in the West, and Comparative Notes on Other Conceptions of the Human Condition*. Chicago: Prickly Paradigm Press.

Sayer, A. (2011) *Why Things Matter to People: Social Science, Values and Ethical Life*. Cambridge: Cambridge University Press.

Severs, E., Celis, K. and Erzeel, S. (2016) 'Power, Privilege, and Disadvantage: Intersectionality Theory and Political Representation', *Politics*, 36(4): 346–54.

Shah, P. (2002) 'Redefining the Home', in N. Holmstrom (ed) *The Socialist Feminist Project: A Contemporary Reader in Theory and Politics*. New York: Monthly Review Press.

Sharma, N. (2020) *Home Rule: National Sovereignty and the Separation of Natives and Migrants*. Durham: Duke University Press.

Shawki, A. (2006) *Black Liberation and Socialism*. Chicago: Haymarket Books.

Shiva, V. (2014) 'Preface to the Critique, Influence, Change Edition', in M. Mies and S. Shiva, *Ecofeminism*. 2nd edition. New York: Zed Books.

Simpson, L. (2011) *Dancing on our Turtle's Back: Stories of Nishnaabeg, Recreation, Resurgence and a New Emergence*. Winnipeg: Arbeiter Ring Publishing.

Smith, A. (2010) 'Queer Theory and Native Studies: The Heteronormativity of Settler Colonialism', *GLQ: A Journal of Lesbian and Gay Studies*, 16(1): 42–68.

Smith, B. (2017) 'Interview with Barbara Smith', in K.-Y. Taylor (ed) *How We Get Free: Black Feminism and The Combahee River Collective*. Chicago: Haymarket Books.

Smooth, W.G. (2013) 'Intersectionality from Theoretical Framework to Policy Intervention', in A.R. Wilson (ed) *Situating Intersectionality: Politics, Policy, and Power*. Basingstoke: Palgrave Macmillan.

Sommo, A. and Chaskes, A. (2013) 'Intersectionality and the Disability: Some Conceptual and Methodological Challenges', *Disability and Intersecting Statuses*, 7: 47–59.

Sörbom, A.E.P. and Wennerhag, M. (2011) 'Individualization, Life Politics and the Reformulation of Social Critique: An Analysis of the Global Justice Movement', *Critical Sociology*, 39(3): 453–78.

Spivak, G.C.S. (2010) 'Can the Subaltern Speak?', in R.C. Morris (ed) *Can the Subaltern Speak? Reflections on the History of an Idea*. New York: Columbia University Press.

Srniceck, N. and Williams, A. (2015) *Inventing the Future: Post-Capitalism and a World Without Work*. London: Verso.

Standing, G. (2019) *Plunder of the Commons: A Manifesto for Sharing Public Wealth*. London: Pelican Books.

Streeck, W. (2016) *How Will Capitalism End?* London: Verso.

Sunkara, B. (2019) *The Socialist Manifesto: The Case for Radical Politics in an Era of Extreme Inequality*. New York: Basic Books.

Super, R. (1975) 'The sociology of workers' self-management', in B. Horvat, M. Markovic and R. Supek (eds) *Self-Governing Socialism: Sociology, Economics and Politics*. New York: International Arts and Sciences Press.

Taylor, C. (1989) *Sources of the Self: The Making of the Modern Identity*. Cambridge, MA: Harvard University Press.

Taylor, K.-Y. (2017) (ed) *How We Get Free: Black Feminism and The Combahee River Collective*. Chicago: Haymarket Books.

Taylor, Y., Hines, S. and Casey, M.E. (2010) *Theorizing Intersectionality and Sexuality*. Basingstoke: Palgrave Macmillan.

Tronto, J.C. (2013) *Caring Democracy: Markets, Equality and Justice*. New York: New York University Press.

Vaid, U. (1998) 'A Shared Politics of Social Justice', in W. Laduke (ed) 'Power is in the Earth', in M. Albert, N. Chomsky, B. Ehrenreich, b. hooks, P. Kwong, W. LaDuke, Manning Marable, U. Vaid, H. Zinn (eds), *Talking About a Revolution*. Cambridge, MA: South End Press Collective.

Vilaça, A. (2002) 'Making Kin Out of Others in Amazonia', *The Journal of the Royal Anthropological Institute*, 8(2), 347–65.

Violet, I. (2002) 'Linkages: A Personal-Political Journey with Feminist-of-Color Politics', in G. Anzaldúa and A. Keating (eds) *This Bridge We Call Home: Radical Visions for Transformation*. New York: Routledge.

Virdee, S. (2014) *Racism, Class and the Racialized Other*. Basingstoke: Palgrave.

Viveiros de Castro, E. (2012) *Cosmological Perspectivism in Amazonia and Elsewhere*. Masterclass Series 1. Manchester: HAU Network of Ethnographic Theory.

Viveiros de Castro, E. (2014) *Cannibal Metaphysics: For a Post-Structural Anthropology*. Minneapolis: Univocal.

Walker, H. (2020) 'Equality Without Equivalence: An Anthropology of the Common', *Journal of the Royal Anthropological Institute*, 26(1): 146–66.

Walsh, C.E. (2018) 'Decoloniality in/as Praxis', in W.D. Mignolo and C.E. Walsh (eds) *On Decoloniality: Concepts, Analytics, Praxis*. Durham: Duke University Press.

Warner, M. (1999) *The Trouble with Normal: Sex, Politics and the Ethics of Queer Life*. Cambridge, MA: Harvard University Press.

Warner, M. (2002) *Publics and Counterpublics*. New York: Zone Books.

Warren, K.J. (2000) *Ecofeminism: A Western Perspective on What It Is and Why It Matters*. Oxford: Rowan and Littlefields.

Warren, M.E. (2001) *Association and Democracy*. Princeton: Princeton University Press.

Washington, J. (2020) *The Dispossessed: A Story of Asylum at the US-Mexican Border and Beyond*. London: Verso.

Weeks, J. (2003) *Sexuality*. 3rd edition. London: Routledge.

Weston, K. (1997) *Families We Choose: Lesbians, Gays, Kinship*. New York: Columbia University Press.

Whittle, A. and Spicer, A. (2008) 'Is Actor Network Theory Critique?' *Organization Studies*, 29(4): 611–29.

Wright, E. (1993) 'Explanation and Emancipation in Marxism and Feminism', *Sociological Theory*, 11(1): 39–54.

Wright, E.O. (2010) *Envisioning Real Utopias*. London: Verso.

Wright, E.O. (2016a) 'Participatory Economics: A Sympathetic Critique', in R. Hahnel and E.O. Wright, *Alternatives to Capitalism: Proposals for a Democratic Economy*. London: Verso.

Wright, E.O. (2016b) 'Final Thoughts', in R. Hahnel and E.O. Wright, *Alternatives to Capitalism: Proposals for a Democratic Economy*. London: Verso.

Young, I.M. (1990) *Justice and the Politics of Difference*. Princeton: Princeton University Press.

Young, I.M. (1997) *Intersecting Voices: Dilemmas of Gender, Political Theory, and Policy*. Princeton: Princeton University Press.

Yuval-Davis, N. (2009) 'Intersectionality and Feminist Politics', in M.T. Berger and K. Guidroz (eds) *The Intersectional Approach: Transforming the Academy Through Race, Class, and Gender*. Chapel Hill: University of North Carolina Press.

Yuval-Davis, N. (2011) 'Beyond the Recognition and Re-distribution Dichotomy: Intersectionality and Stratification', in H. Lutz, M.T.H. Vivar, and L. Supik (eds) *Framing Intersectionality: Debates on a Multi-Faceted Concept in Gender Studies*. Farnham: Ashgate.

Index